KNOW MY NAME

KNOW MY NAME

A MEMOIR

———◆———

CHANEL MILLER

VIKING
an imprint of
PENGUIN BOOKS

VIKING

UK | USA | Canada | Ireland | Australia
India | New Zealand | South Africa

Viking is part of the Penguin Random House group of companies
whose addresses can be found at global.penguinrandomhouse.com.

First published in the United States of America by Viking 2019
First published in Great Britain by Viking 2019
001

The Victim Impact Statement on pages 333–357 was originally
published by BuzzFeed News on 3 June 2016

The poem "And then, all the *and thens* ceased"
excerpted from *A Year with Hafiz* by Hafiz,
translated by Daniel Ladinsky (Penguin Books, 2011),
used with permission from Daniel Ladinsky

Printed and bound in Great Britain by Clays Ltd, Elcograf S.p.A.

A CIP catalogue record for this book is available from the British Library

HARDBACK ISBN: 978–0–241–42827–6
TRADE PAPERBACK ISBN: 978–0–241–42828–3

www.greenpenguin.co.uk

MIX
Paper from
responsible sources
FSC
www.fsc.org FSC® C018179

Penguin Random House is committed to a
sustainable future for our business, our readers
and our planet. This book is made from Forest
Stewardship Council® certified paper.

mom dad tiffy

INTRODUCTION

The fact that I spelled subpoena, *suhpeena*, may suggest I am not qualified to tell this story. But all court transcripts are at the world's disposal, all news articles online. This is not the ultimate truth, but it is mine, told to the best of my ability. If you want it through my eyes and ears, to know what it felt like inside my chest, what it's like to hide in the bathroom during trial, this is what I provide. I give what I can, you take what you need.

In January 2015, I was twenty-two, living and working in my hometown of Palo Alto, California. I attended a party at Stanford. I was sexually assaulted outside on the ground. Two bystanders saw it, stopped him, saved me. My old life left me, and a new one began. I was given a new name to protect my identity: I became Emily Doe.

In this story, I will be calling the defense attorney, *the defense*. The judge, *the judge*. They are here to demonstrate the roles they played. This is not a personal indictment, not a clapback, a blacklist, a rehashing. I believe we are all multidimensional beings, and in court, it felt harmful being flattened, characterized, mislabeled, and vilified, so I will not do the same to them. I will use Brock's name, but the truth is he could be Brad or Brody or Benson, and it doesn't matter. The point is not their individual significance, but their commonality, all the people enabling a broken system. This is an attempt to transform the hurt inside myself, to confront a past, and find a way to live with and incorporate these memories. I want to leave them behind so I can move forward. In not naming them, I finally name myself.

My name is Chanel.

I am a victim, I have no qualms with this word, only with the idea that it is all that I am. However, I am not *Brock Turner's victim*. I am not his anything. I don't belong to him. I am also half Chinese. My Chinese name is Zhang Xiao Xia, which translates to *Little Summer*. I was named summer because:

I was born in June.

Xia is also China's first dynasty.

I am the first child.

"Xia" sounds like "sha."

Chanel.

The FBI defines rape as any kind of penetration. But in California, rape is narrowly defined as the act of sexual intercourse. For a long time I refrained from calling him a rapist, afraid of being corrected. Legal definitions are important. So is mine. He filled a cavity in my body with his hands. I believe he is not absolved of the title simply because he ran out of time.

The saddest things about these cases, beyond the crimes themselves, are the degrading things the victim begins to believe about her being. My hope is to undo these beliefs. I say *her*, but whether you are a man, transgender, gender-nonconforming, however you choose to identify and exist in this world, if your life has been touched by sexual violence, I seek to protect you. And to the ones who lifted me, day by day, out of darkness, I hope to say thank you.

When you know your name, you should hang on to it,

for unless it is noted down and remembered,

it will die when you do.

—Toni Morrison

In the beginning I was so young and such a stranger to

myself I hardly existed. I had to go out into the world and

see it and hear it and react to it, before I knew at all

who I was, what I was, what I wanted to be.

—Mary Oliver, *Upstream*

. . . it is our duty, to matter.

—Alexander Chee

1.

I AM SHY. In elementary school for a play about a safari, everyone else was an animal. I was grass. I've never asked a question in a large lecture hall. You can find me hidden in the corner of any exercise class. I'll apologize if you bump into me. I'll accept every pamphlet you hand out on the street. I've always rolled my shopping cart back to its place of origin. If there's no more half-and-half on the counter at the coffee shop, I'll drink my coffee black. If I sleep over, the blankets will look like they've never been touched.

I've never thrown my own birthday party. I'll put on three sweaters before I ask you to turn on the heat. I'm okay with losing board games. I stuff my coins haphazardly into my purse to avoid holding up the checkout line. When I was little I wanted to grow up and become a mascot, so I'd have the freedom to dance without being seen.

I was the only elementary school student to be elected as a conflict manager two years in a row; my job was to wear a green vest every recess, patrolling the playground. If anyone had an unsolvable dispute, they'd find me and I'd teach them about I-Messages such as *I feel* ___ *when you* ___. Once a kindergartner approached me, said everyone got ten seconds on the tire swing, but when she swung, kids counted *one cat, two cat, three cat*, and when the boys swung, they counted *one hippopota-mus, two hippopotamus*, longer turns. I declared from that day forward everyone would count *one tiger, two tiger*. My whole life I've counted in tigers.

I introduce myself here, because in the story I'm about to tell, I begin with no name or identity. No character traits or behaviors assigned to me. I was found as a half-naked body, alone and unconscious. No wallet, no ID. Policemen were summoned, a Stanford dean was awakened to come see if he could recognize me, witnesses asked around; nobody knew who I belonged to, where I'd come from, who I was.

My memory tells me this: On Saturday, January 17, 2015, I was living at my parents' house in Palo Alto. My younger sister, Tiffany, a junior at Cal Poly, had driven three hours up the coast for the long weekend. She usually spent her time at home with friends, but occasionally she'd give some of that time to me. In the late afternoon, the two of us picked up her friend Julia, a Stanford student, and drove to the Arastradero Pre-serve to watch the sun spill its yolk over the hills. The sky darkened, we stopped at a taqueria. We had a heated debate about where pigeons sleep, argued about whether more people fold toilet paper into squares (me) or simply crumple it (Tiffany). Tiffany and Julia mentioned a party they were going to that evening at Kappa Alpha on the Stanford campus. I paid little attention, ladling green salsa into a teeny plastic cup.

Later that night, my dad cooked broccoli and quinoa, and we reeled when he presented it as *qwee-noah*. *It's keen-wah, Dad, how do you not know that!!* We ate on paper plates to avoid washing dishes. Two more of Tiffany's friends, Colleen and Trea, arrived with a bottle of cham-pagne. The plan was for the three of them to meet Julia at Stanford. They said, *You should come.* I said, *Should I go, would it be funny if I went.* I'd be the oldest one there. I rinsed in the shower, singing. Sifted through wads of socks looking for undies, found a worn polka-dotted triangle of fabric in the corner. I pulled on a tight, charcoal-gray dress. A heavy silver necklace with tiny red stones. An oatmeal cardigan with large brown buttons. I sat on my brown carpet, lacing up my coffee-colored combat boots, my hair still wet in a bun.

Our kitchen wallpaper is striped blue and yellow. An old clock and wooden cabinets line the walls, the doorframe marked with our heights over the years (a small shoe symbol drawn if we were measured while wearing them). Opening and closing cabinet doors, we found nothing but whiskey; in the refrigerator the only mixers were soy milk and lime juice. The only shot glasses we had were from family trips, *Las Vegas, Maui*, back when Tiffany and I collected them as little cups for our stuffed animals. I drank the whiskey straight, unapologetically, freely, the same way you might say, *Sure I'll attend your cousin's bar mitzvah, on the one condition that I'm hammered.*

We asked our mom to take the four of us to Stanford, a seven-minute drive down Foothill Expressway. Stanford was my backyard, my community, a breeding ground for cheap tutors my parents hired over the years. I grew up on that campus, attended summer camps in tents on the lawns, snuck out of dining halls with chicken nuggets bulging from my pockets, had dinner with professors who were parents of good friends. My mom dropped us off near the Stanford bookstore, where on rainy days she had brought us for hot cocoa and madeleines.

We walked five minutes, descended the slope of pavement to a large house tucked beneath pine trees. A guy with tiny tally marks of hair on his upper lip let us in. I found a soda and juice dispenser in the fraternity kitchen, began slapping the buttons, concocting a nonalcoholic beverage I advertised as dingleberry juice. *Now serving le dinglebooboo drank for the lady! KA, KA all day.* People started pouring in. The lights went off.

We stood behind a table by the front door like a welcoming committee, spread our arms and sang, *Welcome welcome welcome!!!* I watched the way girls entered, heads tucked halfway into their shoulders, smiling timidly, scanning the room for a familiar face to latch on to. I knew that look because I'd felt it. In college, a fraternity was an exclusive kingdom, throbbing with noise and energy, where the young ones heiled and the large males ruled. After college, a fraternity was a sour, yeasty atmosphere, a scattering of flimsy cups, where you could hear the soles of your shoes unpeeling from sticky floors, and punch tasted like paint thinner, and curls of black hair were pasted to toilet rims. We discovered a plastic handle of vodka on the table. I cradled it like I'd discovered water in the desert. Bless me. I poured it into a cup and threw it back straight. Everyone was mashed up against each other on tables, swaying like little penguins. I stood alone on a chair, arms in the air, a drunk piece of seaweed, until my sister escorted me down. We went outside to pee in the bushes. Julia and I began freestyle rapping. I rapped about dry skin, got stuck when I couldn't think of anything that rhymed with *Cetaphil*.

The basement was full, people spilling out onto the orb of light on the concrete patio. We stood around a few short Caucasian guys who wore their caps backward, careful not to get their necks sunburned, indoors, at night. I sipped a lukewarm beer, said it tasted like pee, and handed it to my sister. I was bored, at ease, drunk, and extremely tired, less than ten minutes away from home. I had outgrown everything around me. And that is where my memory goes black, where the reel cuts off.

I, to this day, believe none of what I did that evening is important, a handful of disposable memories. But these events will be relentlessly raked over, again and again and again. What I did, what I said, will all be sliced, measured, calculated, presented to the public for evaluation. All because, somewhere at this party, is him.

It was too bright. Blinking, I saw crusty patches of brown blood on the backs of my hands. The bandage on my right hand was already flapping loose, the adhesive worn. I wondered how long I'd been there. I was lying in a narrow bed with plastic guardrails on each side, an adult crib. The wall was white, the floor polished. Something cut deep into my elbow, white tape wrapped too tightly, the flesh of my arm bulging around it. I tried to wedge my finger beneath it, but my finger was too thick. I looked to my left. Two men were staring at me. An older African American man in a red Stanford windbreaker, a Caucasian man in a black police uniform. I blurred my eyes, they became a red square, black square, leaning against the wall, arms behind their backs, as if they'd been there awhile. I brought them into focus again. They made the face I make when watching an old person descend a set of stairs: tense, anticipating a tumble at any moment.

The deputy asked if I was feeling okay. As he leaned over me his eyes did not waver, did not wrinkle into a smile, just stayed perfectly round and still, two small ponds. I thought, *Yeah, should I not be?* I was turning my head around looking for my sister. The man in the red windbreaker introduced himself to me as a Stanford dean. *What's your name?* Their focus was unnerving. I wondered why they didn't ask my sister, she must be here somewhere. *I'm not a student, just visiting*, I said, *I'm Chanel.*

How long had I napped? I must've gotten too drunk, fumbled to the nearest building on campus to sleep it off. Did I crawl? How'd I scrape my hands? Who patched me up with this rinky-dink first-aid kit? Maybe they were a little miffed, another drunk kid they had to look after. Embarrassing really, I was too old for this. Anyway, I'd relieve them of me, thank them for the cot. I scanned the hallway wondering which door was the exit.

They asked if there was anyone they could call, to tell them I was here. Here where? I gave them my sister's number, and I watched the man in the windbreaker walk away out of earshot, taking my sister's voice into another room. Where was my phone? I began patting around, hoping to hit a hard rectangle. Nothing. I berated myself for losing it, I'd have to circle back.

The deputy turned to me. *You are in the hospital, and there is reason to believe you have been sexually assaulted,* he said. I slowly nodded. What a serious man! He must be confused, I hadn't talked to anyone at the party. Did I need to get cleared? Wasn't I old enough to sign myself out? I figured someone would come in and say, *Officer, she's good to go,* and I'd give a salute and head off. I wanted bread and cheese.

I felt a sharp pressure in my gut, needed to pee. I asked to use the restroom and he requested I wait because they may have to take a urine sample. *Why?* I thought. I lay there quietly clenching my bladder. Finally I was given the clear. As I sat up I noticed my gray dress was bunched up around my waist. I was wearing mint-green pants. I wondered where I'd gotten the pants, who had tied the drawstring into a bow. I sheepishly walked to the restroom, relieved to be out of their gaze. I closed the door.

I pulled down my new pants, eyes half closed, went to pull down my underwear. My thumbs grazed the sides of my thighs, touching skin, catching nothing. Odd. I repeated the motion. I flattened my hands to my hips, rubbed my palms along my thighs, as if they'd materialize, rubbing and rubbing, until heat was created, and then my hands stopped. I did not look down, just stood there frozen in my half squat. I crossed my hands over my stomach, half bent over in complete stillness like that, unable to sit, unable to stand, pants around my ankles.

I always wondered why survivors understood other survivors so well. Why, even if the details of our attacks vary, survivors can lock eyes and get it without having to explain. Perhaps it is not the particulars of the assault itself that we have in common, but the moment after; the first time you are left alone. Something slipping out of you. Where did I go. What was taken. It is terror swallowed inside silence. An unclipping from the world where up was up and down was down. This moment is not pain, not hysteria, not crying. It is your insides turning to cold stones. It is utter confusion paired with knowing. Gone is the luxury of growing up slowly. So begins the brutal awakening.

I lowered down onto the seat. Something was poking my neck. I touched the back of my head, felt rough textures inside knotted hair. I had gone outside briefly, had trees shed from above? Everything felt wrong, but inside my gut I felt a deadened calm. A still, dark ocean, flat and vast. Horror was present, I could feel it moving, shifting my insides, wet and murky and weighted, but on the surface, I saw only a ripple. Panic would arrive like a fish, briefly breaking the surface, flicking into the air, then slipping back in, returning everything to stillness. I could not fathom how I'd found myself in a sterile room, one toilet, no underwear, alone. I would not ask the deputy if he happened to know where my underwear was, because a part of me understood I was not ready to hear the answer.

A word came to me: *scissors*. The deputy used scissors to clip off my underwear, because underwear has vaginal, has vaginal germs they need for testing, just in case. I'd seen this on TV, paramedics slicing through clothes. I stood up, noticed dirt on the floor. I smoothed out my pants, tying my drawstring into two bunny ears. I hesitated at the faucet, unsure if I was allowed to wash the blood away. So I dipped the tips of my fingers in the narrow stream, touching water into my palms, leaving the dark stains preserved on the backs of my hands.

I returned as calm as I had been before, smiling politely, and hoisted myself back into my crib. The dean said my sister had been informed of my whereabouts, handed me his business card, *Let me know if you ever need anything.* He left. I held on to this little card. The deputy informed me that the SART building would not be open until morning. I didn't know what that building was, only understood I was supposed to go back to sleep. I lay flat on my back, but it felt cold and strange, the two of us in the stark lighting. I was grateful I wasn't alone, but wished he would read a book or go to the vending machine. I couldn't sleep while being watched.

A nurse appeared, glanced at me, and immediately turned to the deputy. *Why doesn't she have a blanket?!* The deputy said he had given me pants. *Well, get her a blanket! Why hasn't someone given her a blanket? She's lying there with no blanket!* I watched her wildly gesture, demanding more, so adamant about my warmth, unafraid to ask for it. I let it repeat in my head, *Somebody get her a blanket.*

I closed my eyes again, this time settling into warmth. I was ready to leave this messy dream, to wake up in my own bed, beneath my floral comforter and rice-paper lantern, my sister asleep in the room next to mine.

I was gently jostled, opened my eyes into the same brightness, same blankets. A golden-haired lady stood in a white coat, with two other women behind her. They were beaming at me like I was a newborn. One of the nurses' names was Joy and I took this to be a good sign from the universe. I followed them out the door into a small parking lot. I felt like a frumpy queen, the blanket dragging behind me like a velvet cape, flanked by my attendants. I squinted up at the sky to figure out the time. Was it dawn already? We entered a one-story building, empty. They guided me into an office. I sat in my pile of blankets on a couch, noticed the spines of binders on a shelf labeled SART. In black Sharpie, below it, *Sexual Assault Response Team.*

So this was who they were. I was nothing more than an observer, two eyes planted inside a beige cadaver with a nest of ratty brown hair. That morning, I would watch silver needles puncture my skin, bloody Q-tips emerge from between my legs, yet nothing would elicit a flinch or wince or intake of breath. My senses had shut off, my body a nerveless mannequin. All I understood was the ladies in the white coats were the ones to be trusted, so I obeyed every command, smiled when they smiled at me.

A stack of papers were set in front of me. My arm snaked out of the blankets to sign. If they explained what I was consenting to, it was lost on me. Papers and papers, all different colors, light purple, yellow, tangerine. No one explained why my underwear was gone, why my hands were bleeding, why my hair was dirty, why I was dressed in funny pants, but things seemed to be moving right along, and I figured if I kept signing and nodding, I would come out of this place cleaned up and set right again. I put my name at the bottom, a big loopy *C* and two lumps for the *M*. I stopped when I saw the words **Rape Victim** in bold at the top of one sheet. A fish leapt out of the water. I paused. No, I do not consent to being a rape victim. If I signed on the line, would I become one? If I refused to sign, could I remain my regular self?

The nurses left to prep the examination room. A girl introduced herself as April, a SART advocate. She wore a sweatshirt and leggings, had hair that looked fun to draw, a volume of scribbly ringlets in a ponytail. I loved her name like I loved Joy's; April was a month of light rain, the time when calla lilies bloomed. She gave me a lump of brown-sugar oatmeal in a plastic cup, I ate it with a flimsy white spoon. She appeared younger than me, but cared for me like a mother, kept encouraging me to drink water. I wondered how she'd awoken so early on a Sunday. I wondered if this was a normal day for her.

She handed me an orange folder. *This is for you.* Inside were black-and-white xeroxed packets about PTSD, crooked staples, convoluted lists of phone numbers. A pamphlet picturing a girl with an eyebrow piercing, so angsty, so peeved. In purple block letters it said, YOU ARE NOT ALONE. IT'S NOT YOUR FAULT! What's not my fault? What didn't I do? I unfolded a paper brochure, "Reactions in the Aftermath." The first category read, *0 to 24 hours: numbness, light-headedness, unidentified fear, shock.* I nodded, the similarity striking. The next category read, *2 weeks to 6 months: forgetfulness, exhaustion, guilt, nightmares.* The final category read, *6 months to 3 or more years: isolation, memory triggers, suicidal thoughts, inability to work, substance abuse, relationship difficulties, loneliness.* Who had written this? Who had mapped out an ominous future on this crappy piece of paper? What was I supposed to do with this timeline of some broken stranger?

Would you like to use my phone to call your sister? You can tell her you'll be ready to be picked up in a few hours. April held out her phone. I was hoping Tiffany would still be sleeping, but she picked up immediately. I know her cries; know when she's dented the car or can't find something to wear or if a dog has died on television. This crying sounded different, like birds beating their wings inside a glass box, chaos. The sound made my whole body stiffen. My voice became level and light. I could feel myself smiling.

Tiffy! I said. I could not make out what she was saying. This only made my voice calmer, smoothing hers over. *Dude, I'm getting free breakfast! Yes, I'm okay! Don't cry! They think something happened, no, they don't even know if it's true yet, it's all just a precaution, but it's better if I stay here a little while, okay? Would you be able to pick me up in a couple of hours? I'm at the Stanford hospital.* The intern gently tapped me on my shoulder, whispering, *San Jose. You're at Santa Clara Valley Medical Center.* I stared at her in misunderstanding. *Oh, sorry, I'm at a hospital in San Jose!* I said, thinking, I'm a forty-minute drive from home in a different city? *Don't worry!* I said. *I'll call you again when I'm ready!*

I asked April if she knew how I got here. *Ambulance.* I was suddenly worried, I couldn't afford this. How much would the exam cost? The pine needles kept itching my neck like little claws. I pulled out a spiky, auburn fern. A passing nurse gently instructed me to leave it alone, because they still needed to photograph my head. I put it back as if inserting a bobby pin. The examination room was ready.

I stood up, noticed tiny pine cones and pine needles scattered across the cushions. Where the hell was this coming from? As I bent to pick them up, my hair unraveled over my shoulder, releasing more onto the clean tiles. I got on my knees, beneath my blankets, started pushing the dead pieces into a neat pile. *Do you want these?* I asked, holding them out in my palm. *Can I throw them away?* They said not to worry about it, just leave them. I set them down again on the couch, embarrassed by the mess I was making, careless trails over the spotless floors and furniture. The nurse comforted me in a singsong voice, *It's just the flora and the fauna, flora and the fauna.*

Two nurses led me into a cold, gray room with a big mirror, morning light. They asked me to undress. It seemed excessive. I did not understand why I needed to reveal my skin, but my hands began removing my clothes before my mind approved the request. *Listen to them.* They held open a white paper lunch bag and I placed my beige padded bra with the worn straps inside. My gray dress went into another bag, never to be seen again. Something about checking for semen. When everything was gone, I stood naked, nipples staring back at me, unsure where to put my arms, wanting to cross them over my chest. They told me to hold still while they photographed my head from different angles. For portraits I was accustomed to smoothing my hair down, parting it on the side, but I was afraid to touch the lopsided mass. I wondered if I was supposed to smile with teeth, where I should be looking. I wanted to close my eyes, as if this could conceal me.

One nurse slid a blue plastic ruler from her pocket. The other held a heavy black camera. *To measure and document the abrasions,* she said. I felt latex fingertips crawling over my skin, the crisp edge of the ruler pressed against the side of my neck, my stomach, my butt cheeks, my thighs. I heard each click, the black lens of a camera hovering over every hair, goose bump, vein, pore. Skin had always been my deepest source of self-consciousness, since I began suffering from eruptions of eczema as a child. Even when my skin healed, I always imagined it blotted and discolored. I froze, magnified beneath the lens. But as they bent and circled around me, their gentle voices lifted me out of my head. They tended to me like the birds in *Cinderella*, the tape measures and ribbons in their beaks, flitting around taking measurements for her gown.

I twisted around to see what they were photographing and glimpsed a red crosshatch on my rear. Fear closed my eyes and turned my head to face forward again. Usually, I am my body's worst bully: *Your boobs are too far apart. Two sad tea bags. Your nipples are looking in different directions like iguana eyes. Your knees are discolored, almost purple. Your stomach is doughy. Your waist is too wide and rectangular. What's the point of long legs if they're not slender.* But as I stood stark naked beneath the light, that voice evaporated.

I locked eyes with myself as they continued up, down, around. I lifted the crown of my head, elongated my neck, pulled my shoulders back, let my arms go slack. The morning light melted onto my neckline, the curves of my ears, along my collarbone, my hips, my calves. *Look at that body, the nice slope of your breasts, the shape of your belly button, the long, beautiful legs.* I was a palette of warm, sandy tones, a glowing vessel in this room of bleached coats and teal gloves.

At last we were free to begin cleaning my hair. The three of us slid the pine needles out one by one, placing them into a white bag. I felt the snags of pieces getting caught, a sharp twinge when threads were plucked off my scalp. Pulling and pulling until the bag was stuffed to the brim with sticks and hair. *That should be enough,* she said. It was quiet as we pulled out the rest, discarding it onto the floor to be swept away. I blew softly on my shoulders, dispersing the dirt. I worked to untangle a dead needle shaped like a fishbone, while the nurses raked through the back of my clotted head. It felt endless. If they had told me to bow my head to shave it, I would've bent my neck with no questions.

I was given a limp hospital gown and escorted into another room with what looked like a dentist's chair. I laid back with my legs spread apart, feet perched on stirrups. Above me was a picture of a sailboat, thumbtacked to the ceiling. It seemed to have been ripped out of a calendar. Meanwhile the nurses brought in a tray; I'd never seen so many metal tools. Between the peaks of my knees I saw the three of them, a small mountain range, one sitting on a stool with two standing behind her, all staring into me.

You're so calm, they said. I didn't know who I was calm relative to. I stared at that little sailboat above me, thinking about it floating somewhere outside this small room in a place so sunny and so far away from here. I thought, *This little sailboat has a big job, trying to distract me.* Two long, wooden Q-tips were stuck inside my anus. The sailboat was doing its best.

Hours passed. I didn't like the chilled metal, the stiff heads of cotton, the pills, syringes, my thighs laid open. But their voices soothed me, as if we were here to catch up on life, handing me a cup of neon-pink pills like it was a mimosa. They kept making eye contact, every act preceded by explanation, before insertion. *How are you doing, are we doing all right. Here's a little blue paintbrush, just gonna glaze over the labia. It'll be a tad bit cold. Did you grow up around here? Any plans for Valentine's Day?* I knew the questions they'd asked me were for distraction. I knew the small talk was a game we were both playing, an act they were cuing me into. Beneath the conversation their hands were moving with urgency, the circular rim of the lens peering into the cave between my legs. Another microscopic camera snaked up inside of me, the internal walls of my vagina displayed on a screen.

I understood their gloved hands were keeping me from falling into an abyss. Whatever was crawling into the corridors of my insides would be dragged out by the ankles. They were a force, barricading me, even making me laugh. They could not undo what was done, but they could record it, photograph every millimeter of it, seal it into bags, force someone to look. Not once did they sigh or pity or *poor thing* me. They did not mistake my submission for weakness, so I did not feel a need to prove myself, to show them I was more than this. They knew. Shame could not breathe here, would be shooed away. So I made my body soft and gave it over to them, while my mind bobbed in the light stream of conversation. Which is why, thinking back on this memory with them, the discomfort and fear are secondary. The primary feeling was warmth.

Hours later they finished. April guided me to a large plastic garden shed against a wall. Every inch of it was stuffed with sweaters and sweatpants, smashed against each other in stacks, ready and waiting for new owners. *Who are they for,* I wondered. How many of us have come in and gotten our new clothes along with our folder full of brochures. A whole system had been set up, knowing there would be countless others like me: *Welcome to the club, here's your new uniform. In your folder you'll find guidelines that will lay out the steps of trauma and recovery which may take your entire lifetime.* The intern smiled and said, *You can choose whichever color you like!* Like choosing toppings on frozen yogurt. I chose an eggshell white sweatshirt and blue sweatpants.

All that was left was for me to get cleaned up. The detective was on his way. I was taken back to the cold, gray room where I now noticed the metal showerhead in the corner. I thanked them, closed the door. Hung up my hospital gown. Sifted through a haphazard basket of donated hotel shampoos, green tea, coastal breeze, spa sandalwood. I turned the handle. For the first time I stood fully naked and alone, no more cooing sounds or tender hands. It was quiet but for the water hitting the floor.

Nobody had said *rape* except for that piece of paper. I closed my eyes. All I could see was my sister under a circle of light before my memory flickered out. What was missing? I looked down, stretched out my labia, saw that it was dark from the paint, felt sick from its merlot eggplant color. Tell me what happened. I'd heard the nurses say *syphilis, gonorrhea, pregnancy, HIV,* I'd been given the morning after pill. I watched the clear water stream over my skin, useless; everything I needed to clean was internal. I looked down at my body, a thick, discolored bag, and thought, *Somebody take this away too, I can't be left alone with this.*

I wanted to beat my head against the wall, to knock the memory loose. I began twisting off the caps, pouring the glossy shampoos over my chest. I let my hair drop over my face, scorched my skin, standing among a scattering of empty bottles. I wanted the water to seep through my pores, to burn every cell and regenerate. I wanted to inhale all the steam, to suffocate, go blind, evaporate. The milky water swirled around my feet, streaming into a metal grate as I scrubbed my scalp. I felt guilty; California was parched, stuck in an unrelenting drought. I thought of my home, where my dad kept red buckets beneath every sink, carrying our leftover soapy water to the plants. Water was a luxury, but I stood unmoving, watching gallon after gallon flow into the drain. *I'm sorry, I have to take a long one today.* Forty minutes must have gone by, but nobody rushed me.

I turned off the faucet. I stood in the fog and silence. My fingertips had withered into pruney, pale rivulets. I smudged the mirror, clearing the condensation. My cheeks were pink. I combed my wet hair, slid my limbs through the cotton sweatshirt, draped my necklace back over my neck, centering it on my chest. I laced up my boots, the only other item I'd been allowed to keep. I stuffed my blue sweatpants inside them, on second thought, untucked them, pulling them over the outside, better. As I shaped my hair into a bun, I noticed a tag dangling from my sleeve. On it a tiny drawing of a clothesline, *Grateful Garments.*

Every year Grandma Ann (not blood related but our grandmother all the same) made extravagant paper hats out of recycled material; the mesh netting of pears, colored comics, indigo feathers, origami flowers. She sold them at street fairs and donated the proceeds to local organizations, including Grateful Garments, which provided clothes for survivors of sexual violence. Had this organization not existed, I would have left the hospital wearing nothing but a flimsy gown and boots. Which meant all the hours spent cutting and taping hats at the dinner table, selling them at a little booth in the sun, had gifted me a gentle suit of armor. Grandma Ann wrapped herself around me, told me I was ready.

I walked back into the office and sat with hands clasped between my knees, waiting. The detective appeared in the doorframe, neatly cut hair, rectangular glasses, a black coat, wide shoulders, and a nametag that said KIM, he must be Korean American. He stood at the door apologetically, as if this were my home and he was about to enter with muddy boots. I stood up to greet him. I trusted him because he looked sad, so sad that I smiled to assure him I was all right.

He laid down a legal pad, a black rectangular audio recorder, notified me that everything I said would be on record. *Of course,* I said. He sat with his pen hovering over the page, the little wheels of the cassette rolling. I did not feel threatened; his expression told me he was here to listen.

He had me walk through what type of food my dad served, how much I ate, how many shots, how far apart, brand of whiskey, why I went to this party, time of arrival, number of people at the party, what alcohol was consumed, was it a sealed container, where and when I peed outside, what time I went back inside. I kept looking up at the ceiling as if this could somehow make me think better. I was not used to recalling mundane things so precisely. All the while he was scribbling, giving small nods, working his way down the legal pad, flip, flip, flip. When I arrived at the part about standing on the patio, I watched him write *LAST SHE REMEMBERS.* His pen clicked off. He looked at me, he was still searching for something. We were going somewhere and then the road cut off. I didn't have what he needed.

According to the transcripts, all he said that morning was that a couple people saw me passed out, deputies arrived, but I remained unresponsive. He said, *Because of the nature of, where you were, and your condition, we always, we have to consider that there was a possibility of some type of sexual assault.* The nature, your condition. He said when the investigation was done, the man's name and information would become public record. *We don't know exactly what happened yet either,* he said. *Hopefully nothing. But, worst-case scenario, we have to work off of that.* All I heard was, *Hopefully nothing.*

CHANEL: Um, do you know where it was exactly that they found me?

OFFICER: Okay. In between there and the house, there's a little area, um, I believe it's a dumpster. Not in the dumpster.

CHANEL: Yeah, no.

OFFICER: No, but the area behind.

He said, *Some people passing by saw you were there, and they're like, "Wait, that doesn't look right." And then they stopped, um, they saw someone . . . and then another person came by, saw you. And called, called us . . . Um, naturally in the beginning, um, we assume a possible rape.*

I didn't understand. How'd I get outside? What didn't look right? The detective shifted in his seat, and I caught a slight wince as he said, *Did you hook up with anyone?* This struck me as a weird question. I said no. *So no one had permission to touch you anywhere.* The way he looked sorrowful, like he already knew the answer. I felt my body stiffen. I said, *They caught him like, like last night right? Were they trying to escape?*

He said, *So now we just have to make sure that this is the right person, so was this the person that was doing something to you, or trying to do something to you? Um, but someone was acting really hinky around you.* Hinky. *I'm trying to be cautious to say that this person is the person. According to the penal code, we can arrest someone based on probable cause, since rape is a felony, we can arrest someone based on probable cause to believe that a felony occurred. Even if it didn't occur.*

There was subtext that something grave had happened, but every sentence was capped off with an alternate scenario where I was left untouched. *Even if it didn't occur. Doing or trying. Hopefully nothing. Hinky.* I had a foothold in two different worlds; one where nothing happened, one where I may have been raped. I understood he was withholding information because the investigation was still pending. Maybe he also saw that my hair was dripping and I was wearing the wrong clothing. Maybe he was thinking about my sister, who was about to arrive.

Detective Kim said tomorrow I might remember more, he'd give me his card. I nodded, but knew I'd given him all I had. He said I'd be able to pick up my phone at the police station later that evening. Behind him, my sister appeared, hunched up, face drained. The victim in me vanished as I became the older sister. On the tape at the end of my interview you can hear her arrive:

I said, *Hey.*

Oh my god.

Hey.

Oh my god.

I'm so sorry.

Oh.

I made you worry.

No, it's okay.

Oh, sorry.

She said, *Don't apologize.*

I was upright, unshakable, I was the adult showing her that the other strangers in this room were kind, you could talk to them. April was pouring her water, pulling up a chair. Tiffany could not stop crying. As the detective began questioning, my eyes stayed on her. She was talking through the same drinks, names of friends, atmosphere of party. She mentioned there'd been a blond guy that kept putting his face in hers, touching her hips, following her around. All her friends started avoiding him. She said she thought it was weird the guy never said anything, just stared with large eyes as he leaned in. She said she started laughing from discomfort and as a result their teeth hit.

She said she'd left me briefly to take care of a sick friend, thinking I'd be fine on my own. When she returned police were clearing out the party. She asked two students who'd been manning the door, *What's going on*, and they told her the party had been shut down due to a noise complaint. She asked a policeman in the parking lot and he said he couldn't say. She assumed I'd left to meet up with friends in downtown Palo Alto. Still she wandered around asking, *Have you seen a girl who looks like me?* She and Colleen swung open every door of the fraternity, mad and then worried when I never picked up my phone. They yelled my name into the trees, while I was being carted out the side on a gurney, disappearing into the boxy white vehicle.

Students stopped him, I said. *Cool, right.* That morning, I understood bystanders had seen a man acting peculiar, had pursued him in a chase. I was unaware any physical contact had been made. I did not know this man had touched me beneath my clothes, had no idea that any of my body parts had been exposed. I told myself the crisis had been averted, the bad guy had been arrested, and now we were free to leave. The detective thanked us. We would go to the Stanford police station in the evening to pick up my phone. The white-coated ladies surrounded me in a hug, a tight hold, then release.

The sun was out now, harshly reflecting off sparse cars in the lot. What a surreal Sunday morning. *How nuts was that? That was like the nuts-est thing to have ever happened. They stuck so much stuff into my hoo hoo. I can't even—like look at what I'm wearing. How sick is this outfit?* I was modeling my slicked-back hair, my oversized sweat suit, strutting a walk, a little spin. Tiffany was still teary-eyed, her breathing uneven, hiccuping her laughs.

We sat in the car, stared at a chain-link fence, she was waiting for me to tell her where to go. She was still visibly shaken. I wasn't thinking about who he was, or how I felt, or where the photographs would end up. All my thoughts wrapped around her, my baby sister, for whom I'm supposed to have the answers.

Holding it together for her was what I'd been trained for. One time she became ill on a plane, lurching forward, and I held out my hands to catch her vomit before it could hit her lap. When my grandma crumbled blue cheese over our salads, Tiffany pinched her nose, and I'd wait for my grandma to turn around before shoveling her cheesy leaves into my mouth. After we watched *E.T.* she slept in my bed every night for the next seven years, terrified of that dehydrated alien and his wrinkly finger. When people kissed in movies I held a pillow in front of her face, *Inappropriate, you're too young.* I wrote and redrafted persuasive essays that convinced my parents to get us Nokia cell phones. At every class party, I'd wrap half of my donut or snickerdoodle in a napkin so I could deliver it to her at recess. When I loved horses, I tied her to a chair with a dog leash, called her Trinity, put a bath mat on her back like a saddle, brushed her hair, and made her eat Cheerios out of my hand. I still remember when my parents found her in her "stable." *If you want to play, you have to be the horse,* my parents said. You sacrifice for her, you protect her from aliens, you eat the blue cheese. I understood that was the first and most important job I had.

But I was not ready to go home to my parents. I needed time to think. Tiffany and I were old enough to have the freedom to come and go; not coming home meant we'd stayed at a friend's house, no reason to worry, our neighborhood safe. I understood I couldn't tell them I woke up in a hospital, covered in vegetation, because someone was acting hinky, and have them accept that information. *But it's okay,* I would say. *It's not okay,* they would say. My dad would say *who and where and why and how.* My mom would make me lie in bed and drink a heated concoction with ginger. When you tell your parents, there is fuss. I did not want fuss. I wanted everything to go away.

I was convinced the police would tell me a man tried to do something but did not succeed, we apologize for the inconvenience. In fact, I was so sure that this was all an error, that when my sister asked if I was going to tell our parents, I said, *Maybe in a few years.* I imagined one day dropping it casually into a conversation at dinner. *Did you know one time I was almost assaulted?* They'd say, *Oh, I'm so sorry, I never knew that happened to you. Why didn't you tell us?* I'd say, *Well, it was a long time ago, it turned out to be nothing really,* and I'd wave my hand and ask them to pass the string beans.

Sitting in that parking lot, the only place I could think to go was In-N-Out. It was ten in the morning, early for burgers, but In-N-Out was different. We'd treated the white-tiled interior like a church growing up. It was where we gravitated when one of us was upset or celebrating or heartbroken. All that salt and sauce always made me feel better. But by the time we arrived, I felt embarrassed in my clothes and requested that we do drive-through. We ordered our burgers and pulled over to eat. I took one bite but didn't taste the sauce. I slipped the burger under its wrapper and set it down by my feet. I had killed enough time. By now we knew the house would be empty, Dad out running errands, Mom with friends, off on their regular Sunday routines.

My dad is a retired therapist, who had worked six days a week, twelve hours a day, listening to people. All the money that has housed and fed us comes from guiding people through stories we will never hear. My mom is a writer who has authored four books in Chinese, which means her books are ones I cannot yet read. As open as my parents are, much of their lives are unknowable to me.

After two decades of private practice, my dad said he has heard every scenario you could imagine. Having grown up during the Cultural Revolution in rural China, my mom has seen every atrocity you could see. They both understand that life is large and messy, that nothing is black and white, there is no such thing as a linear trajectory, and at the end of the day it is a miracle just to wake up in the morning. They were married at the only Chinese cultural center in Kentucky, an attractive, unlikely pairing.

None of our furniture matches. Our towels are not plush and white, but worn, featuring Scooby-Doo. When we have guests over for dinner parties, Tiffany and I hide all the books and deflated basketballs and lotion samples until everything is spotless. We aim to emulate the polished sheen of our friends' houses. But afterward, it's as if the house can unbutton its pants, release its gut, all of our items pouring out again.

My home is a place where everything grows and all spills are forgiven, where anyone is welcome at any time of day. My family is four planets orbiting in the same small universe. If we had a slogan it'd be, *Feel free to do your own thing.* Home is unconventional. Home is warmth. Home is closeness while maintaining independence. Home is where darkness could not get in. I was determined not to let it.

As we pulled into the driveway, my sister's phone rang with a call from the detective. She passed it over. *Would you like to press charges?* he said. *What does that mean?* I asked. He said he wouldn't be able to tell me much about the process, that it was more in the district attorney's department. He said that the department was already legally inclined to press charges, but it was up to me whether I wanted to participate. He said it would make things easier for them if I did, but that I did not have to. I asked if I could have a minute to decide, that I would call him back.

I hung up and turned to my sister. I had nobody to ask, and Tiffany had no idea. *Should I? Yeah, right? Maybe I shouldn't. But they are anyway, so I might as well, I mean, what is? How can?* I sat and looked around, stumped. *I'm probably supposed to, right? If they are.* At the time I figured it was equivalent to signing a petition, a little stamp of affirmation, saying I endorsed the police's decision to pursue this case. I was afraid that if I said no, it would mean I was on the stranger's side. Court hadn't even crossed my mind, was nothing more than an obscure, dramatic showdown that happened on television. Plus, the guy was already in jail. If it turned out he did nothing, he'd be let go, otherwise he'd stay and serve time. They had all the evidence needed to make the conviction. This was just a formality. I called him back. *Uh, yes. Yes, I will. Thanks.*

I didn't know that money could make the cell doors swing open. I didn't know that if a woman was drunk when the violence occurred, she wouldn't be taken seriously. I didn't know that if he was drunk when the violence occurred, people would offer him sympathy. I didn't know that my loss of memory would become his opportunity. I didn't know that being a victim was synonymous with not being believed.

Sitting in the driveway, I didn't know this little *yes* would reopen my body, would rub the cuts raw, would pry my legs open for the public. I had no idea what a preliminary hearing was or what a trial actually meant, no idea my sister and I would be instructed to stop speaking to each other because the defense would accuse us of conspiring. My three-letter word that morning unlocked a future, one in which I would become twenty-three and twenty-four and twenty-five and twenty-six before the case would be closed.

I walked down the hall to my room, told my sister I'd be out soon. I locked the door and took another shower, washing the hospital off me. She set up the pullout couch in the living room, turned on the TV. I laid down next to her. As I did, her arm rested on me like a paperweight, as if she was worried I'd blow away. The TV droned on, the afternoon sun dissolving through the living-room windows, our parents walked up and down the hall, as we drifted in and out of sleep. We'd gone to the party together and we'd been separated, and now we were together again, but not the same.

When night fell, we emerged, told our parents we were going to get ice cream. I regret this, because when I get ice cream now, my mom eyes me, and I have to say, *I promise, real ice cream.*

First we picked up Julia, who was studying in the library on campus. She and Tiffany had been friends since their little teeth had been notched up with braces. Julia was always lively, but when I pulled up, she looked shaken.

As I looked at the two of them in my car, it weighed on me that my secrecy had become theirs. I understood this was not how we were supposed to be handling things. If Tiffany was ever in a hospital, I would want my parents to know. But I was in a strange position. When asked, *Why didn't you tell your parents?* I ask, *Why didn't anyone tell me?* I needed to keep the story in my control until I knew more.

The parking lot was quiet, dark. I'd passed this building many times before. It was small, surrounded by a moat of tanbark and stocky shrubs, moths ricocheting off the outdoor lights, lines of white illuminated thread. The door buzzed and we were let into dingy halls covered in corkboard bulletins and fliers. Detective Kim was not there. Instead I was introduced to a deputy wearing a windbreaker; she had olive skin, and thin black hair nearly down to her waist. I followed her into a small room, where a notepad and audio recorder sat on the table, while Tiffany and Julia waited in a room down the hall. I thought she'd tell me what happened with the man, hand me my phone, and wish me well. But the door was closed, blinds pulled down. The questions began again, asking me to recall every trifling detail from the previous night, even more precise this time. The transcript of our conversation would come out to seventy-nine pages. It felt tedious and redundant and I could not understand the significance of what I was saying or how it would come into play.

A knock, another deputy, tall in an acorn-colored uniform, thick mustache, black belt full of black shapes. He looked stern and weary, said he was glad to see that I was okay. The way he said it made it sound like a miracle, like I had died and come to life. He told me that one of the guys who had found me had paused while speaking to cry and catch his breath. The sergeant said he almost choked up too. *Grown men are crying*, I thought. *What the hell happened.*

The female deputy pulled my phone out of a large envelope. The blue case was covered in dirt, a crisp, brown border caked along the edges, as if my phone had been buried and then unearthed. I had dozens of missed calls and texts from Tiffany and Julia, *Where are you, I'm scared.* The deputy asked me to email her all the photos I'd taken that night. There was one of me holding a red cup, eyes deliberately crossed. Why couldn't I have smiled normally, just this once. I sent her photos and screenshots of everything, unaware they'd all be filed as evidence. She gave me the opportunity to ask questions. According to transcripts I said, *Um, they said that something had happened to me. I didn't really understand what that meant. I still real—, don't really understand what it means.*

She said she hadn't been fully briefed yet. She said I'd been *found by two Stanford students,* said no more. So I asked her why the man ran. She told me because *something didn't look right.* I was trying to get closer to the crime scene, edging toward the commotion of parked police cars and yellow tape. But every time I stepped closer, she stepped in front of me. When I stepped to my right, she sidestepped. I craned my neck to try to see what they were hiding, but it was no use, the area off-limits. I was to remain behind some unspoken line.

Here's what I did understand. The rooms I walked into, the air changed. People's expressions darkened, they used indoor voices. They approached me with hesitancy, like an animal they didn't want to spook. They scanned my face for something, and I'd look blankly back in return. And all of them said they were impressed to see how well I was doing. She said, *I have to say, you are very calm, you've very . . . Are you usually that way?* I nodded, said that when my younger sister was present, I downplayed my emotions. Still they seemed perplexed by my composure; it seemed, given the circumstances, I should be reacting some other way entirely, and this unnerved me.

I explained that I hadn't told my parents. *That's understandable,* she said. *You know, you're trying, I think you're trying to save your parents emotionally . . . until you can . . . kinda get a better grip of what happened and occurred.* She was very kind, validating my feelings, but she redirected all my questions.

Before the interview ended I made two things clear:

1. No one was to contact my parents until I understood what happened.
2. I never wanted to see or be in contact with whoever this man was again.

I was led into a waiting room with dusty trophies while Tiffany went in for her interview. The deputy typed up the following notes:

One of the other guys was a quiet guy, who did not speak. Colleen and Tiffany thought he was weird because he was aggressive. Tiffany described him to be about 5'11 to 6'0 tall. He had blond curly hair, and blue eyes. He appeared clean shaven. He wore a baseball cap backwards. He had on pants, not shorts. She could not remember what kind of shirt he wore. She thought he looked like one of her friends from college. The aggressive guy was giving out beers. And one point, he came up to Tiffany and started making out on her cheek. Then he went in for her lips. She laughed in shock. Colleen, and Julia saw it happen, and also laughed. The guy left. Then a short time later, while Tiffany was talking face to face to Colleen, the aggressive guy came back. He stepped between her and Colleen, and tried to make out with Tiffany again. He grabbed her from in front, at her lower waist, and kissed her on the lips. She told him she had to go, and wiggled out from his hold.

When we got home, Tiffany went inside while I sat in the car. I realized my boyfriend, Lucas, would be wondering why I'd been mute all day. He lived in Philadelphia and we'd been dating for a few months.

He picked up after the first ring. *I was worried about you last night,* he said. *Did you make it home okay?*

I was unaware I'd even called him. I scrolled through my phone log, found his name buried in my missed calls. I had phoned him around midnight, woken him up at 3:00 A.M. his time. *Did you find Tiffany?* He asked. *I was worried you'd wake up in a bush or something.* My stomach hardened. He knew? How could he know? *What do you mean?* I said. He said by the end of our conversation I wasn't speaking English, that I kept rambling gibberish. Every time there was a pause in my speech, he would yell into the phone to go find Tiffany, but I never responded. He knew I'd been alone, incapacitated. I felt myself sinking. *You left me a voice mail,* he said. *You sound obliterated.* I said, *Don't delete it. Promise me you won't delete it?*

Is everything okay? You sound sad, he said. I nodded, as if he could hear this. *Just sleepy,* I said. I went inside, stripped my iPhone of its dirty case, but didn't wash it. I folded my sweat suit, tucked it into the back of my drawers. I slid my orange folder onto my shelf, my hospital bracelet clipped off and tucked inside it. I had a strange desire to preserve everything, artifacts that proved the existence of this alternate reality.

The next day was Martin Luther King Day, the last day of the long weekend. Before Tiffany drove back to school, I wanted to show her this was not a time to disengage or distance ourselves, we had to stay close to Mom and Dad. I proposed we go out for dinner. We stood waiting to be seated, next to red paper decorations, a bowl of melon candies, a tank full of frowning fish. We ordered an entire Peking duck. As always, my mom prepped us with a demonstration; lay out the circular bun, spread a dollop of plum sauce, add a crispy morsel of crimson duck meat, a few sprigs of green onion and cucumber stalks, wrapping it all up. *Mom is rolling duck blunts. Mom, Mom look, Quack Kush.* After dinner, my sister drove the two hundred miles back to school, through stretches of flatland,

Gilroy, Salinas, King City, back to San Luis Obispo. She said she was scared to leave me alone. *Why?* I said. *That's ridiculous, I'll be fine.*

At the time it was very simple; I put the memory of that morning inside a large jar. I took this jar and carried it down, down, down, flights and flights of stairs, placing it inside a cabinet, locking it away, and walking briskly back up the stairs to continue with the life I had built, the one that had nothing to do with him, or what he could ever do to me. The jar was gone.

I did not know that at 11:00 P.M. the previous night, he had been released on $150,000 bail. Less than twenty-four hours after being arrested, he was already free.

2.

PALO ALTO IS lined with magnolia trees full of creamy blossoms, blue mailboxes, oranges like round dots on trees. Temperatures average in the seventies, you can smell the sun baking fallen shards of eucalyptus bark. There's mottled shade in spotless parks, pink-tongued dogs. Cul-de-sacs with Eichler houses, wooden garage doors, Japanese maples. Sidewalks are smoothly paved, kids bicycle to school and adults bicycle to work; everybody has degrees and everybody recycles.

I was working at a start-up creating educational apps for kids, in a one-room office with eleven other people, our desks clustered close, a few glass-walled meeting rooms to the side. I had been there about six months, my first job out of school. I'd created a semblance of an adult life, waking earlier, going out less. I entered meetings and office birthdays into my Google calendar, stacked with lavender- and tangerine-highlighted tabs. I ordered print cartridges, purchased a sleek white road bike with my first paycheck, named it Tofu. Tried to minimize the number of exclamation points I used in formal emails.

I had no room for words such as *rape, victim, trauma, abrasions, attorneys* in the world I was trying to build. I had my own word bank; *Prius, spreadsheets, Fage yogurt, building credit, trips to Napa, improving posture.* My semblance of an adult life may have been a toothpick-and-marshmallow replica, but it was significant to me, no matter how fragile the framework.

How was your weekend? my coworker said. *Did your sister have a good visit?* Saturday, I'd gone to the party. Sunday, the hospital and police station. Monday, Peking duck. *Yes, so fun.*

I stood under the fluorescent light of the office kitchen. My strudel spun in the microwave. I crossed my arms, noticed strange shadows on my hand, upon examination, bruises. They had blossomed beneath my skin, the color of morning glories. I pulled up my sleeves and found more purple stains on the insides of my elbows. I pressed the spots, bleached white beneath my thumb. I was mesmerized, as if watching myself transform into another creature. In first grade, I'd discovered the sides of my hands had turned a shimmering silver. *I am a mermaid,* I whispered to a friend. She explained it was lead, pencil smears from my paper. A simple, boring explanation; I'm sure these bruises had one too. I took pictures of each spot, to verify they weren't imagined. I pulled my sleeves back down. Why look, when everything was taken care of. My strudel was burning, microwave exhaling, I was dish towel flapping, before smoke could drift into the office.

When I came home that evening, the jar I had carried down into the depths of my mental cellar was sitting in the center of the room, waiting for me. That's funny, how did you get here? Again I picked it up, opened the door, and walked down, down, down the stairs to lock it away.

I woke up into pure quiet at four in the morning. It was still dark out. I clicked on my helmet, a shell of dried Styrofoam, and rolled Tofu into the street. I biked down long gravel paths, beneath sprawling oak trees, small wooden bridges. When I returned through the courtyard, I could see my dad through the kitchen window, hair tufty, making coffee, barefoot in his worn blue bathrobe. He was stunned. *You're awake?* he said. *I was trying out my new bike,* I said. *I love it.*

Applying lotion after showering, my skin prickled and stung. I imagined bees with little teeth, chewing my raw flesh. I ignored the aches and reminded myself nothing was broken. Whenever my mind began drifting off into disturbing scenarios, I said, *Stop. It's over. I'm home, Tiffy's home.* Still I wondered why my arms were littered with lavender blotches. I told myself, *Hope.* I told myself, *Hinky.* Meanwhile unease churned deep in my gut.

Bike, sunrise, work, sunset. Days passed. My phone remained void of messages. I felt restless, began biking at night, long roads, along highways. This worried my dad, who added an extra headlight. My handlebars strobed, light shooting out in every direction, preventing me from dissolving into the darkness.

We used to have a white cat named Dream. We loved him for twelve years. Two weeks before Christmas, Dream went missing. Tiffany and I ventured out, calling his name, flashlight beams swinging across fields. When Christmas passed, my parents informed us that Dream had been hit by a car, found by the side of the road a few weeks prior. They handed us his ashes in a box, with a certificate from the crematorium that said *Dream Miller,* beneath a rainbow. They had waited to tell us because they did not want to ruin Christmas. I found it strange they had let us wander out into the fields while the cat was dead in a box in the closet. What I had now was another dead cat. I could hide it in my closet and maintain the illusion that I was fine. Or I could say, *I might have been raped, right near our home,* and show them a box full of ashes. I decided there was no rush, I did not want to ruin Christmas.

It was never in my nature to lean on others. Growing up, when my mom tried to carry me I'd thrash my legs and say, *Wo ziji zou!* (I walk alone!). My sister would stand glued to the ground with her arms lifted until she was picked up. I was older, had seen my mom weep when one of our dog's new puppies had suffocated, had seen my father wearing a turquoise dress in the hospital when he had a pulmonary embolism. It had dawned on me that they were not invincible, that if anything happened I would need to be able to take care of us both.

Thursday my sister was summoned to her local police station in San Luis Obispo. The officers wanted to walk her through a lineup of photos that had been sent to them by the Stanford police department. Her job was to identify the aggressive male subject she'd told them about. The police had clicked through pictures of white guys with unkempt hair and acne, and when his face came onscreen, she locked up. The police report stated, *Without hesitation, Tiffany identified photo #4*. When asked how positive she was percentagewise, she said, *One hundred percent*. She called me, *I saw him*.

What do you mean? I was confused, how did the police figure out which guy had tried to kiss her? Did they take mug shots of every guy at the party? Was this a process of elimination? Why were they spending time pursuing him instead of focusing on the assailant?

No, she said. *He must be the one.*

That can't be, I said.

The guy who tried to kiss me went after you. I'm fucked up, she said, *that fucked me up.*

That night he had stared into her face. *I can't get his image out of my head*. But still he had no name. Still nobody called me.

Every time I thought of that morning, another jar was born. Now jars filled every inch of my mind. I had nowhere to put them. They cluttered the stairwells, could not be contained in cabinets. I was full of these sealed jars, no room to sit or walk or breathe.

Ten days of emptiness passed. I woke up to a text. My sister had sent me a screenshot of the *Stanford Daily* Police Blotter. One bullet point read: *A victim's reportedly U-locked bike was stolen from in front of Roble Hall sometime between 3 p.m. on Friday and 10 a.m. on Sunday.* Another read: *Sunday, Jan. 18. An individual was arrested and transported to the San Jose Main Jail for attempted rape at 1 a.m. near Lomita Court.* The first acknowledgment this was real. I didn't even exist in this sentence. I absorbed the word *attempted*. The lurking man must not have succeeded. He must have seen me passed out, eyed me suspiciously, and some guys swatted him away. A part of me was grateful, but a part of me was sad. That's it? A little phrase, easy to miss, hidden among reports of petty thefts. If this was how actual assaults were reported, how many had I missed? That morning, I believed this was all the press my case would receive, a single sentence that could fit on a fortune-cookie paper.

Later I was at my desk sipping a mug of coffee, scrolling through a sandwich menu for lunch. I clicked back to the news on my homepage, saw *Stanford athlete*, saw *raping*, saw *unconscious woman*. I clicked again, my screen filled with two blue eyes and a neat row of teeth, freckles, red tie, black suit. I had never seen this man before. *Brock Turner*. I read he had been charged with five felony counts: *rape of an intoxicated person, rape of an unconscious person, sexual penetration by a foreign object of an intoxicated woman, sexual penetration by a foreign object of an unconscious woman, assault with intent to commit rape.* Too many words, jumbled together. Read it again, slower. I typed into Google, *what is a foreign object*. The panic was quiet and slow. It was defined as an *object that intrudes where it should not be, as into a living body or machinery. Examples include: a speck of dust in the eye, splinter, wood chip, fishhook, glass.* What intruded into me.

The article mentioned the victim had been digitally penetrated. My mind went to digital cameras. I Googled that too. *Digital,* Latin *root digitalis, from* digitus *"finger, toe."* He must have fingered her, me. Google finally sat me down and broke the news. I slouched in my rolling chair, listening to the clacking keyboards, someone refilling their water. I stared at this man while he smiled back at me. I had been told I was found passed out with a man around me. No one had ever said, *The man was found inside you.*

My phone was ringing. I closed the tab and stepped off into the kid-testing room with the glass walls, yellow beanbag in the corner, humpback whale wallpaper, a jar of crayons on the table. A woman said hello, introduced herself as my Deputy District Attorney, *Alaleh*, she said. Pronounced *Ah-lah-lei*. I said it once and then again. Three syllables, like a petal falling, left right left. *Ah-lah-lei*. I picked up a green crayon, a scrap of paper.

She said something like, Are you doing okay I wish we could've met under different circumstances we won't be able to confirm it was rape until the DNA results come back they've been sent to the lab but rape kits take months to process yours may be expedited due to media pressure but for now we'll assume penile penetration and move forward with five felonies it's easier to charge now than add them later but if semen is not found the two rape charges will be dropped and we'll go down to three felonies for assault and attempted rape just be aware his team may be trying to contact you and your family disguising themselves as supporters so tell family members not to talk to anyone who hasn't been approved by *Ah-lah-lei* and if the press tries to contact you don't respond they're not allowed to contact you there's going to be a press conference if they ask about the victim I'll tell them to mind their own business you'll be assigned an advocate who can answer any legal questions does that sound good nice to meet you I'm sure we'll meet soon take care.

I stepped out to get a pen, stopped short, stepped in again as my phone began ringing. A call from Stanford, a woman, she was head of the something, we just wanted to let you know he's not allowed on campus anymore, okay? I thought this was good, but I was not on campus either. Where was he? This handful of minutes would be the first and last time I'd hear from Stanford for almost two years.

Detective Kim called, explained that when the report was filed it became available to the public, which was how the media found it. He was surprised by how quickly it'd been swept up by the press. He said Brock had hired private investigators, so for now it was better not to tell any friends. In those words my whole world fell away. *Investigators? What are they looking for?* I asked. He said, *There is no way of knowing, for now it is better to lay low, we'll be in touch.*

Another unfamiliar number, my advocate, her name was Bree, from the YWCA, and I thanked her because her voice was kind and I didn't know what else to say, I was still holding a crayon. My phone would not stop ringing.

Everyone in the office was sitting quietly, as I closed and opened the door to the glass room, phone glued to my face. The calls were quick and they all ended with, *Let me know if you have any questions.* I had thousands of questions. But, *Got it, got it,* I said. *Thank you, thank you,* I said. I had wanted to say, *Who are you? Where are you calling me from? What is an advocate? Was she my therapist? Where's the YWCA? Apply to the Victim Assistance what? Do they pay for therapy? What kind of name is Brock? He lives in Ohio? When did he leave jail? Will I get to stay anonymous? He'll be back for arraignment, arraignment is Monday, what is arraignment?* Emails appeared in my in-box, contacts I'd need, follow-up information. I labeled the new numbers in my phone, placing a red dot emoji next to each name.

Tiffany was calling me. She said her full name along with Julia's had been leaked in some of the articles. Julia had been outed, talk was swelling on campus and her mother, Anne, had already received emails from concerned Stanford parents. Anne told us to stay calm, passed on legal advice: *People will approach you and say they are an "investigator for the court"—which sounds very official, but they probably work for the defense or press. These folks could show up at your dorm or house. Be prepared to say "no comment." Hang in there, girls.*

We were being hunted. I called my DA again. Alaleh said my sister's name was not legally protected, only you, only the victim, there is nothing we can do. I refused this. I'd create an email under a pseudonym, email the media outlets myself. But how would they know it wasn't a random person? How could I make them listen to me? I was on fire, told Tiffany I was figuring it out, I just needed a minute. I told her I talked to the DA, she's really nice, her name is, I looked at my paper, scrawled in green waxy letters, AYLEELEE. I returned to the article.

Alleged victim said she "blacked out" after drinking two whiskey shots, two vodka shots, and stepping outside the frat house with her sister. How'd they know exactly what I'd had to drink? I'd never spoken to any reporters. Then I remembered myself at the hospital, sitting in that plastic chair, wet hair soaking my cotton neckline, chest caved to conceal that I wasn't wearing a bra, my insides still tender from the exam. Everything I had recollected, details I'd fumbled to provide into that little black recorder, had been typed into transcripts. Reporters must have sifted through them, using my words to construct their own narrative for the public to pore over. I felt the walls of my life being torn down, the whole world crawling in. If words spoken softly at a rape clinic were projected over a megaphone, where was it safe for me to speak?

I scrolled to the end of an article and saw, *the woman is recovering at a hospital. Turner, a freshman, was a three-time All-American high school swimmer and state record-holder in two freestyle events . . .* I saw hospital run seamlessly into record-holder. The final line: *If convicted Turner, who raced in the London 2012 U.S. Olympic trials, could face up to 10 years in prison.* If my name came out, what would they even say? *Chanel, who works a nine-to-five entry-level job, has never been to London.* This had never occurred to me as something to worry about. *Jervis said Turner was an excellent student and an excellent athlete. It's very tragic and he's a wonderful, wonderful . . .* I stopped reading. Why was he *excellent, excellent, wonderful, wonderful?* My coworker was asking me a question. Something about Twitter. Twitter, a teacher tweeted, what did the teacher tweet? *I'll get to it,* I said to her. Get to what, I don't know. She thanked me, for what I don't know.

The news linked to a police report, I clicked, scrolling, looking for victim, victim, victim. I found the deputy's carefully written notes. I found *the female subject, later identified as VICTIM*. I found her *on the ground behind the dumpster*. I found her *wearing a black, skin tight dress*. I found *her dress had been pulled up about her hips, and was gathered near her waist. Her entire buttocks were uncovered, and she was not wearing any underwear*. I found *her lower abdomen and pubic area was visible*. I found *her vagina and butt*. I found *her long hair was disheveled, knotted, and completely covered in pine needles all throughout*. I found her *lying in a position with her feet and legs bent in a 45–90 degree angle (fetal position) and her arms were in front of her chest with her hands on the ground near her face*. I found *her dress stretched down over both shoulders, bra pulled out*. I found *it was only covering her right breast*. I found the *necklace wrapped all the way around her neck so that the pendant portion was now centered on her back*. I found *a pair of white with black polka-dot panties lying bunched up on the ground about 6 inches in front of VICTIM's stomach*. I found her *silver iPhone on the ground behind her buttocks. There was a blue cell phone case that was approximately 4 inches away, separated from the iPhone*. I found *she was wearing brown boots that were still laced, with the laces tied in a bow*.

I found the first comment at the end of the article: *What was a college grad doing at a frat?* I didn't understand. Did we just read the same article? I closed the report. I decided right then it was not true, none of it was real, because I, Chanel, was sitting at the office, and the body being publicly taken apart did not belong to me. I suppose this was when Emily Doe was born, me but not me at all, and suddenly I hated her, I did not want this, her nakedness, her pain. It was Emily, all of this was Emily.

There is a layer that exists beneath Palo Alto's groomed lawns, gentle breeze, Teslas freshly painted. Scrape a layer below the sun and smiles, and there was pressure, not in a kettle-screaming sort of way, more like a simmering.

At Gunn High, the only sport we dominated in was badminton. No one could tell you the score from the football game, but winners of national math competitions were posted on windows. Our school was known for incubating gentle, humble geniuses. But the messiness was always missing. No one aspired to become a painter or sailor or literary recluse. You had to make sense, to stay aligned with the mass that progressed so smoothly upward. Struggling only slowed you down, and there was so much to do, so much to be, mental health came last on our list. To be unstable meant to fall behind.

In the spring of 2009, my junior year at Gunn, all teachers were summoned into the gym at lunch. Soon they trickled back out, walking so slowly. I noticed the way their shoulders curved, their faces paled, none of them speaking. The lunch bell rang, and we went to class, where the teacher read us a letter to inform us of the news: a classmate had stepped in front of the Caltrain and killed himself.

The shock was palpable, students calling out to each other in frantic tones. One month later, the exact same letter was read again, *Sorry to inform you, the loss of, if you need help please don't hesitate to,* except this time, the name was a girl's. She had been in my French class, a red rose placed on her empty desk. We sat in one hour of silence, sniffling, heads down. My friend began crying loudly and my teacher asked me to walk her to the counselor's office. After I dropped her off, I stood alone on the pavement, unsure what to do with myself. I wanted to run away.

She was buried in the cemetery across the street from school. I arrived late, everyone gone, wandering through the green grass and half-circle stones. I watched the curved arm of a bulldozer pat down the dirt on her grave, a dull, constant thudding. The pounding metal made my teeth ache. I wanted to tell them, *Be gentle, she's in there.*

Not long after, we were read the same exact letter, a new name.

Again another name. Four suicides by train in six months. At night we'd turn on the news to see a rickety gurney carting a covered cylindrical shape away. Other schools had snow days, we had days for students who died, tests got canceled, kids sliding down the walls in grief. If you had trouble, you'd simply whisper to your teacher and you'd get sent home or to the counselor's office.

After the first death, everyone showed up to school wearing black, but by the fourth, we were warned not to *glorify*, to *trigger*. The roses and letters were taken down, chalk messages hosed off, candles blown out, stuffed animals placed in bags. There was a sudden disjunction between what was felt and what was seen; all appeared normal. I learned celebrating a life could ignite a death.

Friends who vocalized their depression were immediately medicated, pills doled out, backpacks rattling like maracas. Some were hospitalized, put on suicide watch, gone for a few weeks, the rest of us courteous enough not to ask questions when they returned from "vacation." You were either treated as an extreme case on the verge of death, or you were expected to carry on; nothing in between. So we settled for perpetual numbness.

The bushes around the tracks were cleared out, the large hedges disappeared. A man was hired to watch the intersection, wearing a beanie, puffy black jacket, neon-orange vest, seated in a foldout chair. When it rained, a tiny clear tent was placed over him. He sat there, guarding the tracks, for over twelve hours a day, day after day, for years. In economics we learned how jobs were created to accommodate demand. What job was that? What did it mean that someone was hired to keep us from killing ourselves?

So many nights were lost to panic. If your friend wasn't doing well, you weren't sure if they'd be dead in the morning. Search parties broke out, racing to the tracks to catch one another. A dark, twisted game. One evening I walked to the tracks to lay down some daisies. I arrived to see squad cars parked at odd angles. I stood paralyzed. A student had just attempted but was thwarted. He was sitting alone in the back of a cop car, head down, blinking back tears, hands latched behind his back, mucus dangling from the tip of his nose. I never told anyone I saw him, and when he returned to school I pretended nothing had happened. I wondered if this was what I was supposed to be doing, if these were the new rules of the world we were living in.

I put a little pink slip in the guidance counselor's office, requesting a session, but they were backlogged. I attended a mental health session; we were instructed to lean back in our chairs, place a tangerine on our navels, monitoring our breathing by watching the rise and fall of the citrus sphere. I felt vacant, staring at the tangerine on my belly button.

Three more Gunn student suicides occurred while I was away in college. After graduation, when I moved back to Palo Alto, three more would happen within three months, two by train. When I'd learned of the most recent suicide in November 2014, I'd pulled my boss aside, wept, was released home.

Ten suicides, the name replaced ten times. These were not pill-swallowing, bridge-jumping, arm-slicing suicides, for those at least carried a sliver of a chance you'd survive. These were certain deaths. No one survived being hit by a wall of steel going eighty miles per hour. What struck me was how quickly the blood and remains on the metal were cleaned, the train restored to its hourly schedule, rushing to deliver commuters to work on time. How unsettling it was to watch cars glide so casually and continually over the intersection where they'd died, the tires bumping over the tracks.

So on that January morning in 2015, reading the story of the Stanford assault on the news was like being read a letter, *Sorry to inform you*, impersonal and flat, but it was not about a death on the tracks, it was about a sad and strange rape on a local campus, a body found stripped and disheveled. This time, it was my name.

I looked outside and saw the sun shining, ducks paddling through the pond, everyone working. I sat still at my desk, the same way I'd sat still in the classroom all those years before. I knew I would show up again at work the next morning, the same way tires bumped over the tracks, the same way that after learning about a death, you'd take out your textbook and carry on with the lesson. Whatever alarms arose in my body were silenced, the horror made distant. My eyes became wet, I would cry in private, but I knew I would do what I had always done: detach, keep going.

When I arrived home that night, I parked outside my small pink house. I admired the little pebbles out front, the twinkling lights, the waxy leaves of jade. I thought of the two people inside, my mom and dad, unaware the victim lived under their roof. I imagined them mulling about their evening routines; my dad emptying his coins out of his pockets, my mom chopping green onion into ringlets, and wanted to preserve their peace.

My parents are protectors. If anything was wrong growing up, they did a good job of shielding us from it. My sister and I picked up early on that they had serious discussions while walking our dogs. They'd head out in the evening, walking with arms linked, crinkly bags stuffed in their pockets. Tiffany and I would stalk them, ducking behind parked cars to listen. *Dad's worried your reading efficiency is behind!* As I stared at my house, I realized it was too small, I could not hide a secret that big, could not drag it down the hallway and muffle it inside my room. The thought of breaking the news made my stomach ache. Every time it rained, my dad said, *The plants must be so happy!* How would it feel when he'd learn his daughter had been raped? How to tell them? I would've wanted someone to have looked me in the eye, lowered their voice, gently laid their hand on mine. Perhaps I could do this for them.

And what if they were disappointed, what if I'd lost their trust. You've kept this from us the whole time? You snuck home from the hospital? If you're this good at putting on an act, what else are you hiding?

Mostly I feared what would happen when I experienced the assault through their eyes; their sadness would scare me. If I broke the news calmly, it was a hint they needed to respond calmly, no mouths agape, no crying. If your friend gets a horrendous haircut, there's a tacit agreement to say it looks fine. If you say, *GOOD GOD*, she will cry with her face in her hands saying, *What do I do now? I can't go out like this!* And you'll realize you should have given her hair a chance to grow back a little. Only then can you say, *Yes, that haircut was heinous.*

I thought if I executed my delivery correctly we could avoid suffering entirely. I would not say, *disheveled, bent, bloody, naked.* I sat on the corner of my bed, practiced whispering fragments of it under my breath. I would highlight the most important fact, that I had been saved. On the news, I had learned two Swedish graduate students on bicycles had come to the rescue. I said it aloud, *Two cyclists. Two cyclists intervened. Luckily, two cyclists chased him down, held him down! And then, two cyclists tackled him, they intercepted, pushed him to the ground! They ran after him, that's the good thing, two cyclists intervened.*

When I was ready I walked down the hallway, peeked my head into my dad's room, where he was sitting in his recliner wearing his Warriors sweatshirt watching the Warriors basketball game. *Whenever you're free I have something to tell you!* I said. *Not urgent!* My mom was sitting in the corner of the living room at the other end of the house on her computer, cracking sunflower seeds in her teeth, their pointed remnants scattering onto the floor. *Are you busy? When dad comes out I want to tell you guys something!*

They made their way to the dinner table while I stood at the head of it, as if conducting a small board meeting. I said, *There's news, don't look at the news, have you seen the news? That Stanford assault guy?* They shook their heads; my dad said, *Vaguely,* a word he often used. *Remember the party we went to, Tiffany and I, that guy tried to, he was caught. I'm not sure, but I think it was just his fingers, so that's good.* I shrugged. *I don't remember, so. But it's awful when you read it, so you don't need to, please don't, actually.* I couldn't say any more, stood smiling like an insane person. They stared at me, waiting for me to finish whatever it was I was trying to tell them, and I waited for them to say, *All righty! Glad you're okay!* But they remained still, as if a single movement would cause something to detonate.

My dad said something about, *honey,* something about, *I'm so sorry, do you remember if, can you tell us what . . .* But it was my mom's motionless face I watched, her expression growing dark. Her eyes became two black holes, her voice emerged low and level. *Who is he?* I shook my head to show her I didn't really know. *Which night was this? Was this when you were drinking in the kitchen? The night I drove you? Where is he?* I could not look at her anymore, just down at the table, shaking my head, half shrugging. The intensity silenced me, I could not bear what the room had become.

I saw the pool. I was six, my sister four, we were swimming in our backyard. My mom sat beneath an umbrella in a sun hat and floor-length orange dress, reading a magazine. I had a towel draped around my shoulders, had a funny idea to swim while wearing it. But I hadn't realized that my sister had seen me enter the water with the towel, had grabbed her own, and followed me in. She had sunk, letting it anchor her to the bottom. I heard my mom scream, watched her leap, orange smearing through the air. Beneath the water she became a wild flame with long black hair, scooping my sister up from the bottom. She emerged with her sunglasses askew, dress plastered to her skin, my sister wrapped around her body, sun hat floating like a lily pad nearby. My sister's eyes were scrunched tightly, mouth open like a little fish, gasping and wailing. And there was my mom, smoothing my sister's wet hair out of her eyes, carrying her to shallow waters.

As I stood at the head of the table, unable to fill the silence, I broke. Bent over, my mouth opened in cries of pain, wet gasps. I heard the chair scrape the wood as my mom pushed away from the table, springing up, immediate, the same way she had when my sister was drowning. She held on to me tightly, one arm locked firmly around my side, the other hand stroking my hair, whispering *Mommy's not mad, mommy's just scared*. She would be there until I found my breathing, until I felt the reassurance of ground beneath me.

That night my body could finally soften, exhale. I imagined as I slept they would discuss it out of earshot, the way they always did. I told my sister, *Mom and Dad know*, glad to give her this relief. I had survived the telling, the hardest parts were over. In Fearrington, North Carolina, my grandparents had lived by a pond, where geese plodded around with those curved black necks, squeaky honking. My Grandpa Miller explained that during migration, birds flew in V formation. The bird at the front, the tip of the V, had the hardest job facing the greatest amount of wind resistance. The air coming off the leader's flapping wings lifted the birds flying behind it. Being the leader was grueling, so the birds took turns. When a bird exhausted itself, it trailed to the back, where it wouldn't have to flap as hard, riding waves of wind that have been broken down by others. It saved its energy so that it could lead again. This was the only way to make the journey, to escape winter and make it to warmer places. I had spent two weeks pumping my wings, keeping a calm face, to protect my flock from brutal conditions. But resilience required rest. For the next eight months I was going to fall back. The most important thing to remember was that to be at the rear, to be slower, did not mean you were not a leader.

The next day, a lemon pie sat on the counter next to a note. In the hushed hours of morning while I'd been sleeping, my dad had picked lemons from the backyard, boiled sugar and eggs over the stove, pressed fingertips into crust along the edge, sprinkled powdered sugar on top. I brought it into work to share. I sat at my desk with my yellow slice and opened my browser.

Stanford swimmer denies alleged rape. I almost choked, felt I'd been slapped hard in the chest. This article had a trigger warning, this version more graphic, I brushed it aside, clicked the police report, eyes sliding back and forth. *Throughout the night, TURNER hooked up with a few girls.* In the report, all the people he'd kissed were named *girls,* but because he'd assaulted me, I was never called *girl,* only *victim. He stated that he kissed VICTIM while on the ground. He took off the VICTIM's underwear and fingered her vagina. He also touched the VICTIM's breasts.* I could not eat the mushy pie, my forehead hot, thighs pressed tightly together, clenching my fork. When arrested, the police had noted *a bulge* in Brock's *crotch area.*

TURNER does not know the identity of VICTIM. He never got her name and was not able to really describe her. He stated that he probably would not be able to recognize victim if he saw her again. In his mind, I didn't have a face or a name. But the article stated we had *met at a party,* as if the attraction had been mutual, involved cordial chatting.

He was having a good time with VICTIM and stated that she also seemed to enjoy the activity. Enjoy. I stared at this word, a little thing I did not recognize. I wanted to lunge at him, one arm snaking down his throat, grabbing his esophagus like a rope, yanking it clean.

TURNER started to not feel well and decided that it was getting late. He said that he stood up to leave and was suddenly tackled by a group of guys. When asked why he ran, he stated that he doesn't think that he ran. It's "getting late" is what you say when you take your napkin off your lap, place it on your crumb-covered plate, and say you should head home because you have work in the morning. "Getting late" isn't sliding your slick hand out of a woman, standing up with a full erection, brushing yourself off, trotting away, leaving a body behind. This should have been enough. This single line should have clogged the gears, kept them from spinning.

I called my DA, *Hey! Did you see this? He said I liked it! How is that even possible? I can't believe this, can you believe this? What is this?* I was half laughing, incredulous. But she did not match my tone. *I know,* she said, *I know.* She sighed the way you do before you begin a sentence with *unfortunately* or *regrettably.* She explained that pleading not guilty was a predicted formality. This was to be expected. *But I'm telling you now,* I said, *I didn't enjoy it. I don't know who he is. He doesn't even know what I look like.*

There was nothing in my mind up for debate. But as she spoke, her reasoning hit me with horrifying clarity: his only way out is through you. It was like watching wolves being clipped off their leashes while someone whispered in your ear that meat has been sewn into your pockets. The only chance he had of being acquitted was to prove that to his knowledge, the sexual act had been consensual. He'd force moans in my mouth, assign lecherous behavior, to shift the blame onto me.

When I'd been assigned a DA, I thought the letters stood for defense attorney. *District Attorney,* Alaleh corrected. *Brock has a defense attorney.* I thought, *But I need the defense, self-defense, to protect me from him.* He'd hired one of the most prestigious lawyers in the Bay Area. As she talked I realized surviving the assault had only been the first challenge. If I ever wanted to confront him, contest his side of the story, it'd have to be in court. Now, we had to assume his innocence. In the court system, the assault hadn't even happened yet. He'd seen me as a body, but would attempt to destroy me as a person.

Up until then I'd envisioned a limitless future. Now the lights went out, and two narrow corridors lit up. You can walk down the one where you attempt to forget and move on. Or you walk down the corridor that leads back to him. There is no right choice; both are long and difficult and take indefinite amounts of time. I was still running my hands along the walls looking for a third door, to a corridor where this never happened, where I could continue the life I had planned.

The dictionary definition of deny is to *refuse to admit the truth or existence of.* This refusal is another harm in itself. I deny your truth, it is not real, it does not exist. This will tinker with your sanity. The truth I had known would be complicated beyond understanding. It would be drowned in legal jargon, in personal attacks and manipulation, until it became so murky I would no longer be able to see it myself.

When I got home, I reopened the articles, squares stacking across my screen, all his neat rows of teeth. I was ready to see raised pitchforks, everyone in line with my disbelief. As I began reading, my scrolling slowed.

He was only nineteen! She hooked up with a freshman? Doesn't that make her the predator? Haven't you ever heard of gang rape in India. There are women out there suffering real abuse and you want to call this assault. Bored suburban kids can't keep it in their pants. Lame. It's not like he dragged her. If she had a boyfriend why wasn't he there? Mother of the year award. What kind of mom dumps her two daughters at a frat party? Not trying to blame the victim but something is wrong if you drink yourself to unconsciousness . . . She didn't even go to Stanford. Did she pass out with her underwear off while peeing? Whatever happened to the buddy system? I, for one, am not convinced there was a crime of the felony magnitudes charged here, and possibly no crime at all aside from consensual lewd behavior. Did he give her a roofie? If not, why would any woman get so drunk? I have never allowed myself to get so drunk that I don't know what I am doing.

They seemed angry that I'd made myself vulnerable, more than the fact that he'd acted on my vulnerability. Drinking is not inherently immoral: a night of heavy drinking calls for Advil and water. But being drunk and raped seemed to call for condemnation. People were confounded that I had failed to protect myself.

This is the real mystery: This was a top athlete, a highly intelligent, good-looking boy! One might think he'd find lots of girls who wanted to hook up with him! Instead, he ruins his life by doing this? It's hard to credit.

The indignation I imagined mirrored was absent. Some people wrote nasty things about him, *Pretty boy won't stand a chance in prison.* Some wrote kind comments, *Please, Emily, do not let this define you. Take back your identity and have an awesome life!!! If Brock Turner is innocent, I'm an extinct flying Juju bird. This is baloney.* These words temporarily lifted me, but their warmth faded quickly. I found people unmoved, mildly disgusted by the whole thing, hoping their kids would never suffer similar fates.

That night I understood a few things to be true: I knew he led the Oakwood team to state championship two years in a row. I knew he was a *heavily recruited athlete,* a *dominant swimmer,* who finished second in the 200-yard backstroke. I knew there were multiple jokes made about *breaststroke.* I knew they called me *finger lickin' good.* I knew I did not deserve help, because this was not real trauma. He was a kid, not a criminal. Accomplished, not dangerous. He was the one who lost everything. I was just the nobody it happened to.

The rage that had crackled and roared in my chest all morning had been reduced to a few dying embers in my throat. I closed my computer, laid back. I wondered how in an instant my identity had been reduced to the blacked-out and raped woman. This person who could never be a role model, at best a cautionary tale. If anyone ever found out, I understood I'd be publicly disgraced, permanently branded. This part of me had to be severed. I passed all of this mess, these new obstacles, uncertain future, soiled identity, to Emily. My ribs shook as I breathed out water, as I let go of the kind voices that'd said, *Juju bird, baloney.*

The next day, I stood in a coffee shop. I saw a stack of newspapers, a bright blue rectangle on the front page. It was pool water. I saw the pale slivers of Brock's arms, dark goggled eyes, capped head. There were blue rectangles littered on the tables around me, Brock swimming across the café. One man in a polo with a wide neck sat and spread the paper open in his hands. I looked around wondering if these people were the ones commenting, if I should resent them, fear them, question them.

I told my sister not to read the comments. I told her most people spent less than two minutes reading the articles, many of their facts blatantly incorrect. This was just a wee sample of the population; if you were to actually survey every person, you'd find responses that were much more reasonable, sympathetic. So don't read them, okay? Who cares?

What I really meant was that I was investigating each comment so she didn't have to. I thought, *Of course I get to read them, they're my messages.* I treated the comment sections like Emily's personal victim inbox. I refreshed them every night, digested every damaging note. When they said, *Why was she outside in a dress in the winter?* I said, *Winter in California you dunce, we hike in shorts on Christmas.* I wanted to fix everything, straighten it out one by one. Explain explain explain. But this defensiveness would carry over into my regular life. When my parents asked simple questions unrelated to the case, *Have you gotten a chance to mail in the, have you folded the clothes on your, can you take out the recycling,* I grew tense, a childish hostility. No I haven't, I'm busy. Stop blaming me, stop attacking me, you're saying this is all my fault. I dreaded more confirmation that I was not good.

I knew I shouldn't have been reading the comments, but I wanted to understand. Some supported me, but others had gifted themselves with the task of constructing every possible explanation and excuse to put me in the wrong. Was I crazy? Was I exaggerating? Was this even sad?

What was unique about this crime, was that the perpetrator could suggest the victim experienced pleasure and people wouldn't bat an eye. There's no such thing as a good stabbing or bad stabbing, consensual murder or nonconsensual murder. In this crime, pain could be disguised and confused as pleasure. I had been to the hospital, a place where people go when their bodies are sick or wounded. But I pulled my sleeves over my bruises, afraid I would not receive the same comforts as an injured person.

In rape cases it's strange to me when people say, *Well why didn't you fight him?* If you woke up to a robber in your home, saw him taking your stuff, people wouldn't ask, *Well why didn't you fight him? Why didn't you tell him no?* He's already violating an unspoken rule, why would he suddenly decide to adhere to reason? What would give you reason to think he'd stop if you told him to? And in this case, with my being unconscious, why were there still so many questions?

There was another line of argument that nagged at me: the suggestion that boys simply could not help themselves. As if he never had a choice. *I have told each of my girls heading off to college: If you walk in front of a semi truck expect to get hit. Don't walk in front of a semi. If you go to a frat party expect to get drunk, drugged and raped. Don't go to a frat party.* You went to a frat and got assaulted? What did you expect? I'd heard this in college, freshman girls in frats compared to sheep in a slaughterhouse. I understand you are not supposed to walk into a lion's den because you could be mauled. But lions are wild animals. And boys are people, they have minds, live in a society with laws. Groping others was not a natural reflex, biologically built in. It was a cognitive action they were capable of controlling.

It seemed once you submitted to walking through fraternity doors, all laws and regulation ceased. They were not asked to adhere to the same rules, yet there were countless guidelines women had to follow: cover your drink, stick close to others, don't wear short skirts. Their behavior was the constant, while we were the variable expected to change. When did it become our job to do all the preventing and managing? And if houses existed where many young girls were getting hurt, shouldn't we hold the guys in these houses to a higher standard, instead of reprimanding the girls? Why was passing out considered more reprehensible than fingering the passed-out person?

I also understood the way the environment of this case did not work in my favor. Does real crime even happen at schools? Crazy things happen on campuses all the time. If someone took a shit in a kiddie pool on a residential street, people would say, *That's filthy, unacceptable, absolutely not*. If someone took a shit in a kiddie pool on a fraternity lawn, people would say, *Well, that's college, ha ha!* You ran around with your shlong covered in a sock? College. Drunk on a Wednesday afternoon passed out in a giraffe suit? College. Situations are softened, stripped of severity and any kind of seriousness, any real punishment. People read this story, heard *frat, athlete, hookup, enjoy*. That word bank was all they needed for the whole scene to come to life. We get it, they said, they were hooking up, things got out of hand, haven't I done this, haven't you. Even the fact that it was on the ground didn't seem to raise eyebrows; in college didn't people screw beneath statues, in stairwells, in the bell tower, in the library? The media was no help. They counted my drinks and counted the seconds Brock could swim two hundred yards, topped the article with a picture of Brock wearing a tie; it could've doubled as his LinkedIn profile.

I wanted to trim all the fat, all these distractions, to show you the meat of the story. I saw: man goes to a party, kisses three women, finds one alone who cannot speak, takes her into the trees, strips her, sticks his hand up her, is tackled by two men who notice she isn't moving. He then denies running, can say nothing about the victim except that she *enjoyed it*. So take out the whiskey at 10:15, the urination, the younger sister's name, the Olympic freestyle, at the heart that's your whole damn story.

One Friday evening, I steered onto the highway. I turned my music loud, the windows vibrating, the knobs trembling, drowning myself in sound, began screaming. *I hate you, I hate you, leave me alone.* I pounded the wheel, choking on everything I was trying to get out. I swung off the highway, exited toward Ikea, slowed into a crowded parking lot flooded with light, pulling into the very center, locking myself in this grid of parked cars. I shut off the music. I couldn't get ahold of my breathing, my hands were violently shaking, the tears were more than wet, it felt like my insides were leaking out of me, thick, painful. *Help me help me.* I felt like no oxygen was getting to my brain, I was going to die if I couldn't breathe. Vision muddied, I sifted through the papers in my purse, pulled out the pamphlet I kept folded inside, scanned through the hotline numbers, so many numbers, calling the one that said *Stanford* in its description. I didn't want to alarm the woman with the sounds I was making, *I'm safe, I just need somebody. Stay with me I need somebody.* I could hardly get the sounds to shape into words. *The swimmer, the swimmer, I'm the person.* I let my head back, let my shoulders shake, hand plastered to my forehead, my face wet, my chin wet, my neck wet. I could feel the sides of my throat shredded, and let everything out, knowing this person would never see me and I would never see her, but at least someone was listening.

When she spoke, she sounded concerned. And I heard those words again, *It's not your fault.* She kept repeating it, like a mantra. I found irritation wedging its way in. His fault, her fault. How quickly victims must begin fighting, converting feelings into logic, navigating the legal system, the intrusion of strangers, the relentless judgment. How do I protect my life? From the investigators? The reporters? I was being equipped with a prosecutor, going into battle, but no one could tell me how to hold all this hostility, this wrecking sadness. I was alone, my story now sealed inside me, a faceless lady feeding me platitudes through the phone.

3.

EMILY AND I lived separate lives. My days were wonderfully ordinary, full of movement and texture; fresh salmon dinners with crispy skin, long talks on the phone with Lucas, bike rides through the Baylands with my dad across crunchy salt and pickleweed. I cut out heart-shaped valentines with handwritten couplets for everyone in the office. I filed invoices, licked envelopes, sniffed the half-and-half to make sure it was still okay. I made drawings of telephone poles and funny looking birds and sipped coffee with cross-legged friends. On the outside, life had seamlessly carried on. Emily lived inside a tiny world, narrow and confined. She didn't have any friends, appeared only occasionally to go to the courthouse, police station, or make calls in the stairwell. I did not like her fragility, how quietly she spoke and seemed to know nothing. I knew she was hungry for nourishment, to be acknowledged and cared for, but I refused to recognize her needs. I did not want to learn more about the court system, refused therapy. *You don't need it*, I told her.

In the beginning I was good at keeping the selves separate. You would never be able to detect that I was suffering. But if you looked closely enough, cracks appeared. Many nights I went to sleep with my eyes leaking, arriving at work the next morning with eyelids swollen and taut. I began keeping one spoon in the freezer, pressing the cold metal shell to each eye as I brushed my teeth. I sealed blocks of ice into a ziplock bag, one hand pressing it to my face, the other on the wheel as I drove to work, listening to KQED. In the evenings, I'd come back to my sealed bag of lukewarm water in my cup holder, emptying it into the grass.

One day, I told my boss I'd be gone briefly in the afternoon for a doctor's appointment. *Is everything okay?* I waved my hand, said it was just a checkup. When it was time, I drove down to the courthouse. During the car ride I transformed into Emily, letting the warmth of the day drain away.

As I pulled into the parking lot, the squat building looked impenetrable, unsympathetic, cold. The courthouse resembled an abandoned medical clinic, untouched since the sixties. Satellites and metal rods jutted off the roof. Two birch trees emerged from the dirt like bones, black branches dangling thin as hairs. I walked through glass doors to the security check, wiped my feet on a tattered mat. I noticed tangled cords on the ground, a Lysol spray can, two oranges, a metal thermos, a checkered grid of screens. Six deputies in beige uniforms, leaning back on stained rolling chairs behind a desk. I placed my purse in a Tupperware container and stepped through the janky security frame. I watched one's hand sift through my bag. I stared down the white hallway, the harshly reflected fluorescent light that was trapped in textured plastic covers above. He pushed the bin back to me and I stood blankly on the other side of the frame. *Do you know where to go?* he asked. I shook my head. He pointed me to a directory on the wall. Fourth floor.

The elevator doors opened to more emptiness. At the end of the hallway were two wooden doors. The door on the right led to a small waiting room I would later call the victim closet. I would spend many hours inside it. The door on the left opened into a room of gray cubicles and bulky printers, behind which was Alaleh's office. To the right of both doors was a long, narrow walkway that led to the courtroom.

I was going to meet Alaleh and my advocate, Bree, for the first time. My parents were on their way. I'd asked my parents if I should bring flowers to say thank you. They said flowers were something I could give them when this was over. But I thought this would be the first and last time we'd be meeting; I needed a prosecutor to negotiate the terms of the settlement and close the case. We did not know the end would be almost four years from now.

Bree was in her midtwenties. She had long auburn hair and freckles, her presence approachable and warm. Alaleh had dark hair, hazelnut skin, and a wide smile. She was wearing a fitted blazer, pointed heels green as spinach leaves. She seemed to be in her early thirties, with a kind vibrancy and natural fortitude. Each time I'd see her again, I'd notice dandelion yellow earrings, fuchsia fingernails, little flecks of color in this land of smoky grays. She'd been born to Iranian immigrants, a fact I'd learn later; her parents had opened an Irish pub, where she worked while attending law school.

I sat center, my mom on my left, my dad on my right. Alaleh sat behind a large desk, her window framing the tops of trees, her shelves clogged with manila files. I could see the leaves of trees outside shivering in the wind, but in here there was only stillness. Down below I saw Mollie Stone's Market, remembering the display inside where mechanical corn husks and blinking cows sang while Tiffany and I clapped. It was surreal, seeing my hometown from the fourth-floor window, while I was sealed off from it. My mom had taken my hand into the soft envelope of her own hands, massaging the pressure points. I wondered if I looked like a child, holding her hand, but my mom's primary forms of communication have always been touch and food. I'd noticed in American culture, some girls talked to their moms on the phone every day, sharing soup recipes, boy issues, the way to wash a piece of laundry. I was always fascinated by this kind of conversation. All my life I heard my mom typing English phrases into a small silver electronic dictionary that would speak aloud whatever word she was learning: *Spaghetti. Irony. Pernicious. Massachusetts.* This was the fifth voice in our house. She called toiletries, *toilet treats.* When she exclaimed, *Jesus Mary and Joseph,* I thought for so long she'd said, *Jesus Marion Joseph,* believing it to be his full name. I knew her accented English could be perceived as broken and simple, but it concealed genius. We were always getting boxes on the doorstep, and I'd watch her unwrap Chinese writing awards from packing peanuts, casually, as if unpacking pears from the grocery store. I could talk to her about death, love, foreign films, universal themes that transcended culture. But mostly, if she was worried about me, she'd make me a bowl of noodles larger than my head, or place her fingers on my temples, my stress slipping away beneath her fingertips.

Alaleh wanted to get a sense of my background. Did I live in Palo Alto, was I working, what was my experience with drinking? I said I had gone to University of California, Santa Barbara. I heard myself growing defensive, knowing UCSB was known for its heavy partying. I stated that I drank in college, mostly gatherings with the literature kids, people reading poems at the top of a ladder, Bowie-themed living-room parties. I was dating a guy named Lucas, yes, I'd blacked out before. I found myself rambling, unsure of what I was trying to explain. I wanted her to see that I was normal; that I drink, sure, but I didn't like being penetrated while unconscious. She said she went to college too, she understood.

My dad began asking questions, I could hear his frustration slipping through. He gets this pinched, exasperated look on his face, the same one I've seen when our flights have been delayed. *I mean what kind of guy, how could he, I just don't understand, wouldn't it be a little ridiculous if, you can't really tell me this is going anywhere.* Alaleh confirmed his incredulousness, *no doubt, it's unfortunate the way these things, I know it's hard to, luckily we have many, best to wait and see,* but she also hinted that this was only the beginning, that nothing was predictable. I would later learn she'd already run into Brock's defense attorney, who assured her his client would be receiving a misdemeanor for disturbing the peace. War had already been declared, but I did not know this.

It was dawning on me how little I knew about this process, how blindly I'd agreed. I thought I'd spend the hour hiding behind my parents as they protected me in this harsh territory. Instead I felt myself shifting from their hands to hers. If we proceeded, I'd be alone under the microscope, on the witness stand, my mom wouldn't be holding my hand.

My character was now an asset my DA would need. Investigators may be watching me. I had an image to uphold, could not be reckless. *Be on your best behavior.* I turned this comment over in my head. If I kept drinking, would the defense argue I was never affected? If I uploaded photos of myself smiling at a party, would the defense say I never suffered? And worst of all, if somehow I was assaulted again, would they say, well then clearly there's something wrong with her, not Brock, to get assaulted twice?

After the meeting I sat in my car, couldn't get myself to go back to work. I had not gotten the confirmation I wanted that it would go away. *Sit tight,* she'd said. *This is a long, slow process. For now just go back to your lives.* I'd told my boss I was at a doctor's appointment, but it ended up feeling like a job interview. They were deciding whether I'd make a good victim: is her character upstanding, does she seem durable, will the jury find her likable, will she stay with us moving forward. I walked out feeling like, *You got the job!* I did not want this job. I wanted my old life. But let him walk away? I could not let it happen. Pressing charges was my choice, they'd say, but sometimes you feel you don't have one.

Alaleh had requested the voice mail on Lucas's phone, but I had asked if she could wait; he was visiting in a week and I wanted to tell him in person. They were intent on collecting evidence, while I was trying to keep my life intact.

I drove to the airport to greet him, a spark in my chest when I saw his head in the crowd. We drove off to buy snacks for the evening. When we parked and stepped out of the car, I just held him, my face turned so he couldn't see. He thought it was a welcome home hug, began ruminating over which snacks we should get, while tears escaped from the corners of my eyes, funneling neatly into the corners of my lips; a water system I'd perfected. I'd been living with two teacups filled to the brim behind each eye, gotten used to a little spilling over every now and then. I wiped my face, then cast a vote for gummy worms.

I didn't realize how much I'd craved being wrapped in the arms of another person. When we think of people fitting together, we may think of a man inserting himself into a woman, but there are many ways we overlook. The way ears are thin as construction paper, allowing me to press the side of my face against his chest. Fingers can be interlaced without getting tangled. One hand can create a tiny chair for one chin. We are designed to bend and fold, to comfort ourselves and each other. We have so many small parts that need tending to. After the assault, I felt this need to be touched, but wanted nothing to do with *invade, inject, insert, inside,* only wanted the intimacy of being wrapped up safely in something.

That night, as we lay on our sides, his knees bent perfectly into mine, I decided it was very possible I could lose him. We'd only been dating a few months, and I remembered my dad saying that in every relationship there's a point of disillusion; the introduction of the first obstacle, where you decide to surmount it or part ways. Now I had this ugly, public mess latched on to me. I would leave the door open if he wanted to opt out of this nightmare.

I was still navigating how to love and be loved. If you ask me what experience I had with boys in high school, I'd tell you that one time I asked a guy to a dance by creating a trail of toilet paper through the school that led to me holding an index card that said, *If you gotta go, go with me!*

Before meeting Lucas, I had been in one long and serious relationship: senior year of high school there'd been a guy, half Japanese, kind eyed, intelligent, broad shouldered. All I understood was that at track meets, watching him arch his back over the high jump made me lightheaded. Before graduation, all seniors cut class and hiked down a steep cliff into a sandy alcove, to a pop-up village of multicolored tents, everyone drinking, bonfires, falling asleep by midnight. At seventeen I'd never tasted alcohol, smoked, or kissed anyone. This guy and I were sober, sitting on a log in front of the dark water, as the world slept behind us. We talked until the sun rose. When my sleepy friends emerged from their tent flaps, they whispered, *What happened? What'd you guys do?* I shrugged and said, *Nothing.* They were disappointed. *Nothing?* But it felt like everything. We shared my/his/our first kiss in my driveway on my eighteenth birthday. I made these elaborate life maps, tracing back all that had to happen for us to be at the same school at the same time, trying to understand how the universe had crafted a perfect human and then given him to me.

He and I departed to college on opposite coasts, my school at the beach, his school in the snow. I wrote notes to my professor saying my "cousin" was getting "married," then took off on planes to see him. I called them honeymoons with homework. He had a pet fish, and when its jaw could hardly open, he used his thumbnail to cut each pellet into bite-sized pieces. This was his level of attention, care. For the next three and a half years, I grew up protected, safe, and confident, sleeping in his room, where the pipes clanged with heat. At the end of college, something gave way. Our relationship became a Jenga tower, and one by one we began pulling out the pieces, the structure increasingly fragile. Right before my graduation, there was a school shooting, pools of red blood, the same weekend he was on a boat, a shimmering blue lake. I learned the divide between unthinkable violence and ordinary life was paper thin. We were cast into different universes; my side suddenly dark, his light. We fought, or rather, I screamed into the phone while he became increasingly mute. When we arrived home in Palo Alto after graduation, the tower tumbled, blocks spilling everywhere.

I'd heard about heartbreak in songs, sure, but holy shit, damn. There should be a name for that feeling. It really winds you. How to exist without this person? In his shelter, I was brave, loved. I emerged single, twenty-two, naive, and starving. The space that remained was cavernous and I vowed to fill it.

I remember people always telling me *there are other fish in the sea*, and I said, *Yes, that's where they fucking live.* But he had been a rare species of lionfish, and I'd lost him. What do you do when you lose someone, or when they choose to lose you? I went through anchovies, stodgy bass, pompous angelfish, to replace him. Sex had always been a tender, sacred, monogamous thing. But that summer I learned it could be a slippery thing, a floppy thing. A wrinkly thing. A feel-nothing thing. A quick-as-a-blink thing. A terribly boring thing. An *I-only-wanted-your-thing* thing. As a young woman freshly out in the world, I realized I possessed a power. Or at least I thought it was power, as I let myself be consumed, swallowed whole, by fish.

That summer, I never talked about the shooting, never talked about losing him. I got a job at a Chinese restaurant, trained to pack rice into take-out boxes for ten dollars an hour. My drink of choice was the bright blue AMF, short for *Adios Mother Fucker.* I said *adios* and the next morning my friend would tell me I'd cried uncontrollably in a way that scared her, said I'd been sitting on the edge of the bathtub, rocking back and forth, talking to myself, *You're okay, Chanel, you're okay, it's going to be okay*. But I never remembered this. Drinking was disguised as partying, when I know now it had been a sad kind of surrendering. I could not process the new realities I'd been given, could no longer tolerate the feelings inside of me, and believed myself to be worth very little. I drank to turn off the light, a pocket of death, a toe dip in and out again, with the promise of awakening.

But I grew tired. I'd had enough of the self-loathing that came from tossing myself into this churning sea. When I finally landed a new job, I was introduced to stability. I loved my new office, the natural lighting, planes gliding by my window. I was given a work laptop thin as a piece of paper, so sophisticated, it meant I was worth something. I began staying in. I went on dates with myself, driving to Bernal Hill, lying on the curve of grass to read for hours, drawing gorillas at the zoo, going to movies alone. By the time the sullen, alcohol-sunken summer came to a close, I was beginning to believe that being an adult on my own was going to be okay, maybe.

Late one Friday night, I woke up to my friend calling. She was at a bar, a guy was bothering her, could I come be with her. I arrived, swatted the guy away. All of a sudden this wedding party poured in, grooms-men in gray suits and striped socks following a dancing bride. One came up to me. His name was Lucas.

He had grown up near Palo Alto, was now living in Philadelphia to begin his first year at Wharton business school. He was tall, lean, laughed easily, and was a few years older than me. He knew things I did not: Spanish, rugby, math, confidence. He had gone to middle school in Japan, knew the texture of alpacas in Peru, dipped his toe in every corner of this little blue earth. Palo Alto was just a speck! I learned he'd won a belly flop contest in high school, had frosted tips in fifth grade. He asked me out to dinner the night before his flight back to Philly.

A few months after we started dating, I'd just woken from a nap when he said, *I love you*, out of the blue, as naturally as if he were to tell me, *It's raining outside.* It had been an uneventful afternoon, we'd gotten milk tea and egg custard tarts in Chinatown, he bought me a turquoise ring from a sidewalk vendor, and I wondered when, on this ordinary day, he had realized it. I smiled, but told him he was nuts. He said *love* like it was an exciting thing, when I knew it could be terribly painful. But Lucas did not seem to mind, he was coolheaded, patient, and I realized he was not just another fish.

In December 2014, he'd asked me to come visit him in Philadelphia. When I arrived, there were large white poster boards he'd bought me for drawing, a freezer stocked with ice cream. I still didn't know what to call our relationship, only knew that when I met him, the background of his phone had been Machu Picchu, and now it was a photo of me, smiling while wearing his bulky brown ski jacket, a happy potato mesmerized by the snow.

In January 2015, my sister would come home. We would go out to a party, where I would be found on the ground unconscious. Fast forward a few weeks and here he was in Palo Alto, sitting at my desk working, the sun streaming through my blinds, while I lay in bed. Maybe the universe had loaned me his presence to show me love was possible again, and would now take him back, leaving me to deal with this new eruption. At twenty-two I was beginning to wonder if adulthood was just a series of endless losses. What benefits were there to growing up? How do you feel all these heavy things for the rest of your life? Looking at the beautiful day outside, listening to him typing, I did not want to tell him. I wanted to sit in my room, with the light pouring in, and enjoy the afternoon with the man at my desk. I wanted this moment, to take it and eat it and live in it for eternity. Yet I was about to ruin it.

Do you still have that voice mail? He stopped typing and looked at me. *Why?* he asked. *I just wanted to hear it,* I said. He continued looking at me. His phone plopped into my blankets. I wrapped myself up, covering my face as I listened to it for the first time. The transcripts record it as follows:

VOICEMAIL LEFT FROM CHANEL TO HER BOYFRIEND ON 1-18-15 @ 3:39:34AM [ET]: Hi. Mm, (inaudible) fucking (inaudible). Hi, (inaudible) your phone. But all m-males present (inaudible) or whatever, and I like you the m-most. (Inaudible.) So I (inaudible), uh-huh. Uh. (Laughs.) You're, you're a dingus, and you know that. Even though you work so hard, I'll reward you in the summertime. If you work 24 hours a day, 24 hours a day out of 30, uh, how many hours a day, but however many hours you don't work, or work you by, you know what. But I'm making funny stuff. I, I like you, I like so m-much, and I want to, I want to tell you that. (Laughs.) Okay, byeeee. I, I like you so much, more than you think of me. Okay, uh, bye, (inaudible).

The words were indistinguishable, my voice sliding like butter in a hot pan, dragging from one to the next. Anyone who spoke to me would immediately have known I was incapacitated. Plus the message held my truest truth; even when my mind was muddled I had wanted Lucas, had called to deliver a sloppy valentine. I thanked blackout Chanel. Then I felt the eyes: starting a message with *fucking* would be a mark on my character. The defense could use this to prove I was vulgar, profane. If I wanted to be a good victim, I'd have to clean up my language. So many new standards I'd need to uphold.

I looked up to Lucas observing me. *What's going on?* he asked. I shrugged. *Nothing,* I said. It scared me the way he looked at me so intensely. I watched him adding it up in his head, clicking his laptop shut, climbing onto the bed. We sat inside a mass of silence. *Were you raped?* The way he said it out loud, the bluntness of it, shocked me, the words too strong. I shook my head. *I don't remember.*

He laid back in the pillows, staring straight ahead, somewhere distant. *What happened,* he asked. *Nothing,* I said. *That's not nothing,* he said. *Well, two guys stopped it,* I said. *They think it was only fingering. I don't remember, but the guy ran away. They caught him.* I still didn't know how to tell my story. I smiled. How creepy it must have looked, how badly I wanted to appear unfazed.

I knew it, he said, *I knew it, I had a bad feeling, I should have stayed on the phone with you. You were alone, I should've stayed on the phone with you, I didn't know what to do.* I shook my head to say no, this was not the reason it happened. I wanted to dissolve, watching the news sink into him. He was quiet for a long time. *I'm not going to let anything bad happen to you,* he said. It was impossible, but right then I let myself believe it. I put my head on his chest, and he continued looking straight ahead. Hours and hours we spent like this, folded over each other in the quiet afternoon, the sun burning outside without us, the whole day taken.

He could have left, decided it was too much. But he crawled right next to the pain, planted himself. *No matter what happens, I'm here.* Later he'd tell me he read the police reports on the plane ride back to Philadelphia, had become nauseous, unclasping his seat belt, sidestepping down the aisle, to vomit into the tiny sink basin. I thought of him in that little bathroom, its folding accordion door, the line of people waiting outside while he heaved the images of my body out of him. Loving someone is a painful thing.

I recently asked him about all of this, after writing out the chaotic timeline of how we met, all that followed. I said, *How were you willing to date me, when all that stuff was going on?* He said, *Because, you.* I pushed back, *Yeah, but what about the assault, my drinking, all of it.* He said, *What about you as you?*

In late February, I was called into the police station before work. Detective Kim said the purpose was to *dig into the relationship.* I pulled into the parking lot, fog still hanging in the eucalyptus trees, and was led into the same small room with cream of mushroom–colored walls, the black recorder on the table. I had learned to be skeptical of this little thing. I was asked for Lucas's full name, how long we'd been together, at what point it got more serious than just talking, FaceTiming, email, and texting, if we had an intimate relationship, if we were exclusive, where he was from, how we met, how often we communicated, when I had last seen him before the assault, if I'd seen him since. I was then asked what my feelings were for him.

My answer to all of these questions was *Brock Turner fingered me while I was unconscious.* But I thought hard, trying to specify our exact timeline; the frequency of visits, the exchange of *I love you*s, the meeting of my parents. We'd gone ice-skating in Union Square, did that prove we were a couple? I didn't know. I was self-conscious that somehow some of these answers could be wrong or insufficient. What was important, what was not, whose job was it to judge? Until then I'd never contemplated how to present love as evidence. I'd never documented the precise pacing and development of our relationship. I had just been living it as it was unfolding. Living, as people do.

I asked how this information would come up in a trial, would I be quizzed on it? If Lucas would have to testify, would our answers be cross-referenced? I asked if there would even be a trial. He said it was *way beyond him,* that it was *still too early to even seriously talk about any of that.* But he predicted that with all our new evidence, Brock would want to start backing out of the spotlight to begin rebuilding his life in private. *That's what I would do if I were him.* I was comforted by this.

He walked me back to my car, said it was good to see I was doing better. I thought back to the morning he met me and nodded. The fog had burned off, it was bright, I was late for work. I liked Detective Kim, around him I felt safe, and he always seemed sincerely apologetic for collecting fragments of my life. I also enjoyed talking about Lucas, could go on as long as he needed.

But as I sat in my car, keys in my hand, I realized Lucas was a wonderful part of my life outside this mess, and now he was being recruited to a crucial role inside it. All my little stories, my private and intimate moments were being typed up and sent to Brock's defense attorney, available for reporters to read through, where the sweetness would be diluted and reframed. I already wanted everything I'd said back, to take every word home with me. The line between what was mine and theirs was blurring.

I was thankful to have Lucas. But it bothered me that having a boyfriend and being assaulted should be related, as if I, alone, was not enough. At the hospital it had never occurred to me that it was important I was dating someone; I had only been thinking of me and my body. It should have been enough to say, *I did not want a stranger touching my body.* It felt strange to say, *I have a boyfriend, which is why I did not want Brock touching my body.* What if you're assaulted and you didn't already belong to a male? Was having a boyfriend the only way to have your autonomy respected? Later I'd read suggestions that I cried rape because I was ashamed I had cheated on my boyfriend. Somehow the victim never wins.

And what if I'd been assaulted the summer before, in the aftermath of a broken relationship? What kind of questions would the detective have asked? *Oh, my dating life? Yes, well, I went to dinner at an Ethiopian restaurant with one guy on Tuesday, but slept with a different one on Sunday who's never taken me on dates, but was wearing cool socks that evening. Yes, I did go home with a guy who has a tattoo of a beheaded pigeon who still texts me at two in the morning. Yes, I did order four Moscow Mules, yes, they were all for me.* Would I have had any credibility? Would my private life have been exhibited to show that I was too loose, my lifestyle indecent? I would never have been able to explain they were my choices, but choices made during a period of sadness and low esteem. We all have different ways of coping, self-medicating, ways of surviving the rough patches.

To deny my messiness would be to deny my humanity. I don't believe there is such a thing as an immaculate past or a perfect victim. Yet now I felt I was being upheld to an impossible standard of purity, worried that failing to meet it would justify Brock raping me. His attorney would simplify, generalize, and mislabel my history.

In other blackouts, I was responsible for acting a fool. But waking up to an empty McDonald's bag and crumbs on my chest was different than waking up with dried blood and clothes missing. In the obscurity of the blackout lived a pivotal difference. Rape required inflicting harm on somebody. The moment I was violently dragged into his story, my story stopped. When I was finally out of his hands, or rather when his hands slipped out of me, I was released back into my life. But it was during that brief passing over, that period where he took the reins, where I lost everything.

I began showing up to work later and later, sometimes coming in at noon with no explanation. How did other victims manage this back-and-forth between worlds, the rotation of selves? You can't fawn over your coworker's photos of Maui by morning, slip away to battle your rapist by noon. It required two entirely different modes of being; different worries, rules, bosses, emotions. If this continued, I wouldn't be able to go and come back, but I was not ready to quit my job and give up my life yet. I prayed he would give up first.

Every time I received a call from an unfamiliar number, my head filled with heat. I was wary of investigators, tracking me, listening. Months passed. I had not told a single friend. Every email about the case brought on a surge of stress; it was not distracting, it was mind-wiping, I'd forget what I was doing, my mood sinking the rest of the day.

My hospital bill arrived, just short of a thousand dollars. My dad called me into the living room, asked me if I knew anything about getting reimbursed. I told him about restitution, how Brock would be court-ordered to pay it off, but only at the end. It would be paid back, I promise. But I wondered how many costs would accumulate. I learned it was expensive to be assaulted.

Another letter appeared at home stamped with The County of Santa Clara court seal. It asked if I wanted Brock tested for HIV and provided a form for me to fill out. I didn't know, was I supposed to? Would he be mad at me? Would he know I was the one who requested it? Can't you do these things without asking me? I never responded. When a friend came over, I quickly slipped the letter off my desk. My way of dealing with it was to not deal with it, to throw away the incoming letters, to refuse to research what this process might look like.

My rape kit still hadn't been tested in the crime lab. They told me it would be expedited due to media pressure, but months later I was still waiting. I figured it had something to do with results showing up slowly, some DNA sciencey who knows what. But I was told it was because of the backlog of kits. There were hundreds in line before me, some kits kept so long they grew mold, some thrown out, the lucky ones refrigerated. Immediately I felt ill. How could that be; this was not fruit rotting, it was little pieces of us in each one, an indispensable story. It also meant there was a population of victims in my vicinity, disguised in their everyday lives, going to work, refilling their coffee, eyes wide at night, waiting.

Most nights I avoided going home after work, wary of questions as simple as, *How was your day.* Instead I parked my car downtown, walking along the lane of lit-up trees on University Avenue, taking comfort from others while being alone. One night, I passed a metal newspaper box, saw Brock's name in the upper-right corner. I slipped out a newspaper and trotted to my car. I clicked on the weak light, flipped the pages open, found an opinion piece a Stanford student had written. She asked why, in the Turner case, there was so much focus and condemnation of the victim's alcohol consumption. I could hear the soft plops of water on paper as tears fell off my cheeks. She was asking questions, pushing back, a hand reaching out in an attempt to lighten the heavy thing I'd been carrying. I folded the newspaper into fourths, tucked it into my purse for safekeeping.

Every time I stayed out late, I received texts from my mom, *Mama can't sleep until you're home.* This was new. Growing up I'd never had a curfew. Now my parents asked where I was, how I was, who I was with, when I was coming home, the boundaries of my adulthood shrinking.

One day I received a call at work: no semen found. A tiny knot unbound in my chest; I was penis-free. *Thank you!* I said, my coworkers in close proximity. *You have a nice day too.* Since there was no penile penetration, five felony counts would be reduced to three; rape charges were dropped while sexual assault charges remained. My celebration died down as I realized how this would appear in the news. People would say, *See! They were wrong. Soon they'll throw out the rest of the charges too. How come the victim doesn't pay for the crime of false accusation? The DA is after him, sad his reputation was already ruined. Sickens me to see an innocent person used as a scapegoat. When will she apologize?*

The hearing was set for June 8, 2015. The preliminary hearing would be like a minitrial without a jury, to determine whether there was enough evidence to merit a full trial. Tiffany would be missing finals week, would need to take her exams early. She had planned on telling her professors it was a "family matter," but in three of the six tellings, she had broken down while the professor held her, stared at her, or patted her. *It was embarrassing,* she told me. *I'm tired.* I needed to tell my boss in order to request time off. I admired her deeply; still I was nervous. I'd now be perceived differently, aware of everything commenters had called me: sloppy, irresponsible, reckless.

Sitting across from her in a glass-walled room, I struggled with where to begin. *Have you read about the Stanford swimming assault . . . It was me.* Her mouth parted slightly. I could never get out more than eight to twelve words before the walls of my throat began to ache. I looked down at the table, my eyes burning. She asked a few questions in a gentle tone, but I kept shaking my head, holding my breath, until her voice faded away. I waited for something to happen, perhaps talk about scheduling. But when I looked up I saw a tear rolling down her cheek. I felt a small shock, something inside me awakening and softening. I was not in trouble. I was not stupid. It was sad, she was sad. I was stunned.

On May 5, Alaleh informed us we'd have to reschedule the hearing due to the defense attorney's unavailability. The options for resetting the court dates stretched into September. I didn't know this was possible. My company was small, how would I explain my strange absences? Everyone thought I was taking time off in June, but now I'd have to tell them I'd be gone in July or August or September. Tiffany would also have to inform a new set of professors during fall quarter. *I'll be in touch about the next court date*, Alaleh said. *If anything comes up, please feel free to call me.* We'd later discover the hearing would fall even later. This was part of the madness of the system; the illusion of structure, plans never followed.

How long would I have to live my double life, pretending things were going smoothly? I was behind on work, a pile accumulating on my desk. I couldn't catch up and I couldn't keep looking at that pile. Some days I would sit and stare at the screen and do nothing. Every morning, I had to work harder to talk my limbs into moving. Imagine a skeleton, tossing its organs inside its bony shell, sealing on its skin. Strutting into the world with a *Hello! Doing fine, thank you. How are you? I'll have it to you by the end of the day. Yes! That's too funny, ha ha, good-bye.* Holding myself together long enough to go home and fall back apart, rolling into the corners.

Home was no longer home. Home was hell, steering clear of the courthouse, the sprawling Stanford campus. I felt ridiculous fearing places I knew to be objectively safe. I could not stop reading comments online. By now I'd grown deaf to the warmhearted ones, while the harsh ones grew louder. I always told myself I wouldn't read any more. Then maybe one or two. But they trailed in like ants, a single one appeared, suddenly I noticed a line, and then they were inside all my bowls and boxes and left-out spoons. They were faceless dots, swarming, subtle, incessant, always reminding me I could never eliminate them. Me and all of these ants.

Lucas was about to move to Los Angeles for his MBA program's summer internship. He offered for me to join him. I thought of the jogs in the sand along Venice Beach, the late-night ramen. But I needed to prove I could find my own way forward.

In our living room there's a portrait my mom framed of the poet Pablo Neruda, who I always thought was my great grandpa. Why else did we have an old man on our wall? For my whole life, art and writing were my steady ground. Grandma Ann always said I was born with a pencil in my hand. I draw when I'm upset, when I'm bored, when I'm sad. My parents let me draw directly on my walls, inking sumo wrestlers crawling out of chimneys, eggplants with long arms. On physics tests when I blanked on an answer, I'd draw a man shrugging, saying *I simply do not know,* using test time to shade the bags beneath his eyes. In college, I stacked my bookshelves with Rumi, Woolf, Didion, Wendell Berry, Mary Oliver, Banana Yoshimoto, Miranda July, Chang-rae Lee, Carlos Bulosan. I slept in the library. I learned printmaking, spent nights in the print room carving linoleum blocks, inking the barrels, staining my apron, watching the sun rise. When I wrote, when I drew, the world slowed, and I forgot everything that existed outside it.

Growing up, there were times my mom left us for weeks for writers' residencies. I remember this vividly because my dad would serve the same canned peas and chicken and rice day after day, while we waited for her to come home. Finally, we would drive through unfamiliar hills to a gallery opening in a forest, the adults in flowy clothing and lipstick, crackers with those teeny-tiny neon-orange fish balls that made me gag. My mom told us how she'd write all morning, hike in the afternoon, ticks latching on to her socks, and I thought how could you leave us for blood-eating bugs and seafood caviar? One time I asked her why she'd left, and she said, *I want to be who I am.* It was sort of impossible to argue with that.

In Palo Alto, I was beginning to feel acutely that I was not fitting into old patterns of myself, who I was or who I thought I would be. I wanted a place where I could create, a corner of the world where I could disappear. I chose the smallest state, as far away as possible from California, to live with people I had never met. The Children's Book Writing class was full, but no matter. I would leave my job to enroll in a printmaking workshop, From Light to Ink, three thousand miles away, at the Rhode Island School of Design for the summer. The woman in the admissions office was named Joy, just like the nurse. I took this to be a good sign. My parents asked the usual questions, *what about safety, are you sure, what will you do when you come back,* but they understood. By now I had enough saved to pay my own tuition, rent, flight. I assumed the trial would conclude by the end of year, and my savings would last me until then. When I wrote my name on the RISD application form, signed the check, sealed the dark yellow envelope, I lay on my carpet, overcome. My dad peeked in to see how I was doing and I said, *I'm so happy.*

Before I left, there was one person I wanted to tell. Claire, a close friend of mine, with freckled skin and a tiny nose ring, was about to move to France to work as an au pair for a year. We had spent her last weeks sitting in her car, eating ice cream and listening to French cassette tapes. I was always waiting for the right time. But maybe there would never be a right time; all I knew was that I was running out of it and I would have to tell her now. She had gone through something similar when she was only eighteen, called the police, completed the rape kit, but even after she did everything victims are instructed to do, she was informed it was not enough to more forward. In my room I told her. She immediately leaned over to and put her arms around me, and strangely I did not have to say much at all. She understood. She pulled back, looked me square in the face, and said, *This is your opportunity.*

For months I'd regarded this case as a burden that had been placed on me, one I wanted to rid myself of. I was frustrated, why do I have to do this, I don't have time. But in her eyes this was a chance. This was what she'd tried to do four years ago, only to be met with impatience and apathy, only to be worn out and set aside by authorities, until her best choice had been to leave, to force herself to forget. There had been a time she had tried hard to get to the place that I was in now. I had somehow reopened the way forward. *You're the one who's going to do it.* And I thought of her at eighteen, and I thought of what the guy did, and I understood what I had to do, understood now what it meant.

4.

MY NEW HOME was a small yellow room in a dark green house that I shared with an illustrator and an oil painter; the dancer who had rented out her bed would be gone for the summer. It was located in the West End of Providence, four hundred dollars a month for a large backyard and a cat named Elvis. The dancer had left me a pillow, clean sheets, a soft yarn blanket, drawers with little silverfish. The morning after I arrived, I forgot for a moment where I was. I panicked until I noticed the butter-colored walls, the leaves pressed against my window. Nobody was home. I looked around. The kitchen had black-and-white tiled floors, large oil paintings of jungles. There were freshly picked tomatoes and carrots, their threaded roots clumped with dirt. A wooden shelf full of spices, a crusty container of honey, a green kettle, an alligator figurine. I followed strings of lights across a denim-blue couch, a mustard corduroy chair. A newspaper was flipped open to a half-finished crossword, beside tiny paintings of mountains and peach-colored yarn. I liked my absent housemates already.

The walk to school was two miles long. The heat in Rhode Island was thick, unlike the West Coast sunshine that kissed you on the forehead. My route took me along iron fences, weeds lining the sidewalk like black flames. Old furniture lay on the street like sea lions beached on the sand. People in lawn chairs sat outside liquor stores and laundromats, white cigarettes littered the curb. A cart stood on a corner; I'd exchange one crumpled dollar for a Styrofoam cup of coconut sherbet.

Closer to campus, the streets began sloping upward, the pavement smoothed, the trees spread their arms wide, providing gray continents of shade. The grass was lush, not the scrappy, dry California kind with blades yellow tipped and bent. There were girls and guys with flamingo pink hair, quilted dresses, pumps, feathered earrings. *I must look so boring*, I thought, glancing down at my old exercise clothes, fingering the cheap pearl earrings I'd added for flare.

Class was held in a small brick building, up two flights of stairs. Large single-pane windows. Corkboard walls with constellations of small holes where art had been pinned up for critiques. I saw the drying racks where our prints would soon be laid out. A room built to do nothing but create.

My teacher had a thick mustache, round glasses, and a long apron nearly down to his ankles. He had us go around and introduce ourselves, what brought us there. The ten students reminded me of elves, specializing in elegant crafts; glassblowers and weavers and pedal-less bicycle-builders. Everyone except me was an undergraduate, many of them using the summer to fulfill missing credits. And you? he said. *I just moved here, for this class, from California, I quit my job. I like printmaking, I took a class in college, mainly relief printing.* The teacher said, *Okay! That's exciting.* He had us write our names on pieces of masking tape, choose a drawer, and label it. I wrote my name in all caps, *CHANEL MILLER!!*, prepared to fill the drawer with new prints.

He passed around a supply list of everything we would need to buy and what would already be provided: *Single-sided frosted Mylar, acetate, Rubylith, X-Acto knives, dot screens or frosted glass, Hydro-Coat plate, rosin, acid, Rives BFK, starched cheesecloth, monofilament polyester, degreaser, direct emulsion, scoop coater, Caran d'Ache water-soluble crayons, blotters, etc.* After class I walked the aisles of the art supply store, picking things up and looking at the price stickers. I hadn't factored supplies into my budget.

The next class he had us follow him back into the darkroom. He showed us how to use the enlarger, to load the negative carrier, to rotate the disk to the right lens, expose test strips emulsion-side up, develop film, stop bath, fixer, water. How to place the transparency emulsion in the center of a positive photo litho plate and expose it inside a vacuumed bed, degrease the plate, rosin-dust the plate, aquatint the plate, soak it in nitric acid; to bevel the edges, lay the plate in the press, mix the ink, soak our papers, pat them dry, adjust the pressure. And finally to turn the wheel and pull the fresh print off the block, gingerly placing it in the drying rack. After hours of demonstration, a single print was born.

I watched attentively, standing on elevated toes behind my class-mates, furiously taking notes. In the end, I had no idea what had happened. I had been lost forty-five steps prior. Students began sketching out ideas. I sat on my stool, staring at my scribbles of tiny letters like trails of dead ants all over my page. When we were finally released, I hurried down the stairs out of the building.

By the third class, I was even further behind and too ashamed to ask questions like, *What is a cheesecloth?* I ate lunch alone. Ate dinner alone. I'd already ruined a photo litho plate by bringing it into a room where there was sunlight. Everyone else was well versed, purposefully walking from station to station preparing their materials. I stayed at their heels trying to glance at what they were doing. When class ended, I went to the administration office. I think I made a mistake, I need a different class. It was too late to switch. I nodded.

I pulled up Google Maps on my phone and identified a light blue stripe as a river. I walked and walked and found it, then walked and walked along it, and finally plopped down on a patch of grass and cried. I didn't know what I was doing. I didn't even know the name of the river

I was sitting in front of. I had moved to a state the size of a puzzle piece, far from everyone I knew, to learn outdated printing techniques. What kind of idea was this, why did I think I could do it? Emily had followed me, reminding me I was a go-nowhere, do-nothing, *VICTIM*. This life was too sweet. This kind of pleasure, creation, reserved for people who were not me.

But only one month ago my boss had offered me a raise, and something shook my head. My boyfriend offered me a room, but something shook my head. Coming all the way here seemed illogical and expensive and inexplicable. Yet here I was, sitting inside that idea, sweating inside that idea. It was the only thing in my life I'd ever truly chosen. No one told me I could do it, except me, which meant that no one could tell me I couldn't do it, except me. This would require trusting myself, fully for once. When I was little, I never asked anyone if I was an artist. I just cleared enough space on the table to make room for my paper. I picked up my things and walked slowly home, preparing myself for the next day.

I started coming in on off days. I told myself I wasn't stupid, and started asking questions. My teacher always took the time to help me, encouraged me to work on an even larger scale, and soon my prints were the size of tabletops. I was teaching myself to ask for help, and in return beautiful things were happening.

One evening, I heard my roommates and their friends in the living room discussing plans to go bowling. I sat still, afraid of going out to the bathroom and having to introduce myself to so many people. I was waiting for them to leave, so that I could take a long shower and chop a zucchini into disks to fry in the silence of the house. Then I heard a knock.

I waited a beat as if I'd been busy with something before opening my door. My roommate asked, *Would you like to go bowling?* I had no plans, of course I had no plans. My instinct was to reject her invite, worried it was born of pity or necessity, like a cashier asking if you'd like help taking your bags to the car. But before I could politely shake my head, the people around the table chimed in and said, *We're getting McDonald's ice cream after! What bowling nickname are you gonna choose for the screen? Don't forget socks.* So I nodded, put a wad of socks in my bag, and followed them out the door.

I was not homesick, as I was not ready to return home, but I felt the unease of being adrift, of having no footholds in the world. This and other small invitations saved me: Driving to the pond, to lay out on frayed towels amidst thunder warnings. Riding with Angie in the cranberry-colored van with missing seats, sitting on flattened cabbage boxes. *Purple Rain* projected on a hanging sheet. Eating cherry pie, listening to dubstep remixes of the *Seinfeld* intro. I was cast a minor role in their summer, and my presence may have barely registered in their memory reels. But I can't imagine those days without them, would never forget how it felt to be included.

I bought a desk on Craigslist. A nice couple arrived to deliver it. The woman called me, said they were outside. *We can help you carry it in, but I understand if you don't want us in your home, because you know, Craigslist people. I just don't want to—* The man said, *Well how else is she going to carry the desk?* I understood what the woman meant, that a transaction as simple as receiving a piece of furniture from a stranger possessed an inherent threat, that any time we met someone online, we must scan for signs of assault, rape, death, etc. We knew this. But the guy did not speak this language; he just saw a desk.

I walked an average of six miles a day, taking myself to parks, movie theaters, bookstores, intent on discovering my new land. No matter where I went, the same thing kept happening. At first it was an older man, who nodded and said, *Good morning, beautiful,* and I turned to see who he was addressing until I realized it was me. Confused, I said, *Good morning,* before even deciding if I should've said anything at all. Be kind to the elderly. A bald man said, *Hey, pretty girl, you sure are pretty.*

His smile spread slowly as if his face was unzipping, and I replied, *Thank you!*

These remarks peppered my walks, as common as birds in the trees, strange men asking me, *How are you*, and me responding, *Fine, how are you*. The comments felt too subtle to be consequential, like a tiny thumbtack inserted into a thick tire. I sometimes berated myself for being too friendly, for the way I smiled back too quickly. When a man honked at me, I instinctively waved. My default was to mirror every greeting. But I realized I didn't know the honking man, that I hardly knew anyone in all of Providence, and wouldn't need to wave next time. No waving, no thanking, no good morning, I told myself.

I passed three men sitting on a car who fastened their eyes on my legs, clicked their tongues, and smacked their lips, performing the sounds and hand gestures one might use if attempting to summon a cat. I felt all six eyes stroking the backs of my calves as I walked away. I couldn't tell if the nonverbal bothered me more than the verbal, did I prefer clicking or comments. I really just wanted silence. Once a few men clustered around a narrow sidewalk, not moving aside an inch as I walked through the narrow passageway between their stomachs.

I began avoiding certain streets. If I was spoken to going one way, I'd come back a different way, and found myself winding around many blocks. I trained myself to tuck my head down, avoiding eye contact, feigning invisibility. Instead of strolling looking up at the trees, I walked with unwavering conviction, or stared down at my feet. Once a man started walking next to me and said, *Can I walk with you?* I began walking faster. *Let me walk with you.* As his feet kept pace with mine, I just shook my head, my hands gripping the handles of my backpack, waiting for him to fall back. Some men would be offended when I didn't respond, one man saying, *I'm just trying to start your day right.* But the compliments didn't feel like compliments when my body language communicated I didn't want to be looked at, didn't want to be spoken to.

They didn't feel like gifts when they were thrown at me or whispered so only I could hear. Every comment translated into, *I like what I see and I want it. But I don't want it, I don't want it,* I thought.

Imagine you're walking down the street eating a sandwich and someone says, *Damn, that looks like a delicious sandwich, can I have a bite?* You'd think, why would I ever let you eat this sandwich? This is my sandwich. So you'd walk on and continue eating, and they'd say, *What? You're not going to say anything? No need to get mad, I was just trying to compliment your sandwich.* Let's say this happened three times a day, strangers stopping you on the street, letting you know how good your food looks, asking if they can have some of it. What if people started yelling out of their cars about how much they wanted your sandwich. *Let me have some!* they'd exclaim, driving by with a honk. Were you supposed to say, *I'm sorry, no thank you,* every time? Would you feel obligated to explain over and over again that you don't wish to share because it's your lunch and you don't know them? That you don't owe them any of it? That it's a little unreasonable that they're asking in the first place? All you would want is to walk down the street eating your sandwich in peace. Maybe I am making this worse by comparing a woman's body to a sandwich, but do you see what I mean?

I started using my phone to discreetly record videos as I passed clusters of men. I sent one to Lucas. *How often does that happen?* he asked. *Every day,* I said. He asked if I needed a car, said he would pay for me to rent one. I said I enjoyed walking; it was the only way to notice everything. Plus I had so much time and was never in a hurry; walking was really one of the only things I had to do.

One afternoon as I came home from school, a van drove by and honked; I didn't bother turning my head, familiar now with this game. But the sound of the engine didn't die out. I heard the wheels slowly turning on the asphalt as he U-turned and pulled up next to me. He rolled down the window. *Talk to me,* he said. I immediately crossed the street and began filming as I walked. He must've been around fifty, unkempt hair beneath a cap, with a thick, soft neck. *Come talk to me,* he said, *I'm lonely.*

No, I said.

Why not? he said.

I don't know you, I said, half laughing at his question.

Just for a little, I'm lonely.

No, I said, shaking my head and looking down at my feet. I didn't say anything more, too irritated; why is it my job to care if you're lonely? *Please,* he said. I quickened my pace as he continued to call after me. I pretended to turn into a house until he slowly pulled away, then ran to my real house, closing all my blinds. I sent the video to Lucas. He immediately called me.

I need you to rent a car, he said, *I'll pay for it. Don't put it off, go today if they're open. Okay?*

Okay, I said, *I'll go.*

Thank you, he said, *and don't send any more videos. I can't watch them, these guys make me too angry.*

I said okay and he went back to work and I sat on the bed. I felt like I'd done something wrong, upsetting him by sending them. It also seemed like he'd said, if they're bothering you while walking, why are you still walking? It didn't feel like a solution at all; they'd forced me to seal myself off in a car. I didn't want to give up my sidewalks.

I called Lucas back. *That's not fair,* I said. *I just want to walk home from school, I'm not doing anything wrong. I should be able to. You can walk anywhere you want. It's not fair you get to unsubscribe from the videos. You get to turn off the feed, you get to see it selectively, I don't have that option, to decide not to live it. I'm trying to show you what it's like for me. It doesn't matter what I do, it doesn't matter what I wear, how I act, it's constant, the harassment is constant. I have no money for a car, and even if I did, I enjoy walking, I want to keep walking.* I was crying.

There was resignation in his voice. *I feel powerless over here. I don't want anything to happen.* I knew what *happen* meant. He sounded pained, stuck across the country. One night, when I told him I was working late in the studio, some money was Venmoed to my account. *For Lyft,* he said. *Get home safe.* He was looking out for me and I understood. I agreed I wouldn't walk alone in the dark. But even in a Lyft, I never put in my real address, so the driver would never know where I lived. Safety was always an illusion.

Walking down the street was like being tossed bombs. I fiddled with the wires, frantically defusing each one. Each time I was not sure which wire would cause it to detonate, tinkering while sweat ran down my forehead. Women are raised to work with dexterity, to keep their nimble fingers ready, their minds alert. It is her job to know how to handle the stream of bombs, how to kindly decline giving her number, how to move a hand from the button of her jeans, to turn down a drink. When a woman is assaulted, one of the first questions people ask is, *Did you say no?* This question assumes that the answer was always yes, and that it is her job to revoke the agreement. To defuse the bomb she was given. But why are they allowed to touch us until we physically fight them off? Why is the door open until we have to slam it shut?

One day, I tried wearing headphones and reading a book as I walked, hoping to appear immersed, busy busy busy. I made it one mile. On the overpass, a man pulled over, said, *Hey, you look like a leader, I like that. I've never seen a girl walk and read at the same time.* I started laughing, up at the sky, like I see what you're doing, universe! I can't escape! What do you want, what can I do? I stopped, plucked out my headphones, walked over to his window, surrendered. The man asked me what I was reading, and I told him, he asked me what my name was and I told him, he asked me where I was going and I told him. He asked me if I was interested in attending the conference he was speaking at, and I said no, and he asked me if I was busy later, and I said yes, and then I'd worried I'd given him too much information so I lied and said I was actually moving back to California in the next three days, and he gave me his business card, and then I took it, and I thanked him. I later threw it away.

I did it, I gave someone the time of day. Can I be done wasting my energy, engaging in one-sided conversations. Once I saw a flier at a coffee shop that had a picture of a pouncing kitten, made by a group that aimed to stop catcalling. Attached were fake business cards that read 1-800-STOPTALKINGTOME, intended to be given to catcallers. Someone was feeling this too, had gone so far as to print fliers.

Lucas had a single day off that summer and flew across the country to visit me. I showed him my route to school. I showed him how incredible it was how much I sweat. I showed him the print shop and walked him through every step I'd learned. At night we unwrapped hamburgers by the river. I was proud to share my world with someone, the world I'd created myself.

As soon as he left I felt an aching hollowness inside my days, a peach with its pit missing, its strongest part, while I became the soft mush around it. I'd forgotten how it felt to have someone looking out for me, someone to buy me fresh smoothies, to kill the centipede in my room, to fan me with a piece of paper and dab my limbs with a cold washcloth. I'd forgotten what it was like to walk relaxed in the sun, to sleep with ease, to not be on guard every hour. Most of all, nobody on the street talked to me when I was with him; he'd silenced them with his presence.

Men had lines other men didn't cross, an unspoken respected space. I imagined a thick line drawn like a perimeter around Lucas. Men would speak to me as if no line existed, every day I was forced to redraw it as quickly as I could. Why weren't my boundaries inherent?

I continued going to the studio every day. I spent more money on art supplies and no money eating out, sticking to my microwaved pizzas and raw vegetables. Sometimes I spent hours working just to have my print come out murky or faint or blotchy. I started over. I didn't keep track of time. I flipped through my notes until I didn't need them anymore.

One night I left the studio around sunset, but the sun exited more quickly than I'd planned. I was a few blocks from home, passing the neon-pink glow of the liquor store, when a man in a silver car pulled over. Not now, I thought. I don't feel like it. I heard the window roll down, *Let me give you a ride!* He was smiling as if he'd arrived in a golden chariot, instead of a small Chevy the color of a foil gum wrapper. He was so excited, like we were long-lost friends, and he was elated to see me. I couldn't believe the width of his smile, so confident. I started filming, took three long strides toward his car, bending over and putting my head into his window. In the video you can hear me asking, *What'd you say?* Inviting him to say it again for the record. He replied, *Come in, let me give you a ride!*

GET IN YOUR CAR ARE YOU FUCKING CRAZY WHY WOULD I EVER DO THAT, I said. My voice was so flighty and high-pitched I hardly recognized it. FUCK YOU, I said. I remember how quickly his smile evaporated, like a drop of water on hot pavement, how fast he turned the wheel and accelerated away. *Good!* I thought. But my limbs started shaking, all that adrenaline, I walked unsteadily to the crosswalk. I looked at the stopped cars, trying to make eye contact with the drivers. If he comes back, are you going to help me? Do you see me? As the little glowing man of the crosswalk illuminated, I began running, panting to the tempo of my backpack slapping against my back.

I didn't send the video to Lucas. I promised myself I would be careful about coming back from the studio earlier. I was trying to save the six dollars that the ride would've cost. It's funny really, asking six dollars or safety. I knew I shouldn't have yelled at a man alone at night. Most of all I felt the eyes: this would not count as standing up for myself, this was not considered brave. If this got back to my DA I'd be reprimanded;

the defense would argue she's crazy, she acts out, screams profanities, provokes men. She should've ignored him, why was she walking alone? She endangered herself, asked for trouble.

Always she, always she. I never heard the voice asking why he pulled over, why he believed I'd get in, what he might do if I did. How much was I expected to take, to absorb and ignore, while they yelled and clicked their tongues so freely, with no fear of being confronted. Was I stubborn for wanting to walk, was I asking too much? The thick tire was now pockmarked with thumbtacks and nails. I felt the tire becoming misshapen, lopsided, deflating. It would not function like this.

One balmy night, I was far from my home, at a coffee shop on Thayer Street. When I was ready to go, I sat on a bench outside, waiting for my Lyft. An old man sat down beside me. He turned and said, *Would you like a slice of bell pepper?* He had glasses, a soft cotton shirt with a little notepad in his pocket, looked content and restful. He had a small knife in one hand, a sliver of green bell pepper in the other, a handkerchief in his lap where he had set the rest of the vegetable. I stared at the slice. What if he's poisoned the seeds? What if he's a pervert and rubbed his penis on the bell pepper and wants to watch me eat it? What if he slits me with his pocketknife? The little old man patiently held the bell pepper out to me. And that's when I thought, *I'm losing it.* There is a kind man wearing a fedora on a warm evening eating a bell pepper on a bench. You are allowed to be cautious but you don't always have to be afraid. Give yourself permission to enjoy this small vegetable. I took it, eating it in one piece, thanking him.

Every night, when the light disappeared in the sky, when the bells of the sherbet man's cart rolled away, and Elvis curled into a perfect circle, I could not fall asleep. I would lie starfish-limbed atop the blankets. *It's too hot to sleep,* I told Lucas in a tiny green text bubble. The next day a package appeared at my door; he had ordered me a nice fan, not the cheap propeller kind in a wire cage, but the kind with timed settings and glowing buttons, with a note that said, *From your number one fan.* But heat was not responsible for my peeled open eyes. What kept me awake was the knowing that soon Brock would be studying my face for the first time. In court, I'd be forced to forfeit my anonymity and all the protection that came with it. I wanted to remain unrecognizable to him. I wanted to sit behind a screen, to wear sunglasses, wondered if I should cut my hair, place a bag on my head. The day I'd show up in court would be the day I surrendered my safety.

On a Friday night in college, graduation a few weeks away, I was walking to a friend's house when two police cars tore past me. I thought nothing of it. It was common to hear sirens in Isla Vista: it was a town on the ocean bluffs inhabited solely by eighteen to twenty-two-year-olds, every street lined with shabby wooden houses, bikes abandoned on lawns, overcrowded balconies, orchids growing out of recycled Franzia boxes. On sunny days you'd see beautiful girls in swimsuits holding large rafts over their heads, like ants beneath a crumb, walking down the street to the water. Guys biked with surfboards tucked under one arm, their wetsuits peeled halfway off like a banana. Isla Vista was a network of couches to sleep on, a friend a block away in any direction. A wild, sunny village we called home.

But by the time I reached her apartment, the sirens had stacked, blossomed, erupted. When I walked in the door, all five of my friends were quiet, listening. We received an email from UCSB Emergency:

Shots fired in IV 2 detained, investigation ongoing,

That was it. A single line that dropped off with a comma. Texts began circulating; maybe it was gang related, a robbery, a drug deal gone wrong, a drive-by, no a shootout, a bomb, firecrackers, drunk driver. He was Persian, no Asian? It was two guys, one guy, in a car, a black one.

Someone may have died, one person, possibly three, maybe none and this was all a sick prank.

There was a video going around, someone said it was a guy, the guy, so we huddled around the phone, and there he was, sitting in the driver's seat, face saturated in orange from the setting sun. *Hi, Elliot Rodger here . . . I don't know why you girls aren't attracted to me but I will punish you all for it. I'll take to the streets of Isla Vista and slay every single person I see there. . . . I take great pleasure in slaughtering all of you. . . .* Panic erupted, one of us screamed to turn it off, one was convulsively crying on the floor, jerking as if her stomach were being yanked by a string. He was still speaking, contaminating our air. I shook my head, refusing to hear it. He is coming to Isla Vista to kill girls, we are girls in Isla Vista, but we can't be who he is talking about. *You denied me a happy life and in turn I will deny all of you life, it's only fair. I hate all of you.* We denied you a happy life? Hate fucking who? I was livid. I grabbed the phone, walked out of the room, set it on the bathroom counter, and walked out, firmly closing the bathroom door behind me. I felt I had trapped him in there, the video still playing, him speaking into the darkness to no one.

The next email told us to remain indoors. We bolted the locks, closed the blinds, *get away from the window.* Our phones kept chiming. Claire's housemate had been shot. Nothing pieced together.

At three in the morning, we stared at the news on TV, heard *mass murder.* The word *seven* was displayed in tall, white letters at the bottom of the screen. It seemed wrong to group the dead. It was not seven; it was one and one and one and one and one and one and one. Each an entire life, each with a name.

The morning light never came, the air unmoving and still. On days like these the fog slipped in from the ocean, erasing the water, the shore, engulfing our little houses. We blinked, exhausted, wondering if it was safe to leave. We kneeled on the couches and carefully parted the blinds.

I received a call from an eleven-digit phone number. It was my mom, calling from Beijing, on a trip to visit family. She'd seen the news, *I just wanted to hear your voice*. Our phones shook with calls from family members waking up to the news and we retreated into corners, *I'm here, I love you too, we don't know, grandma's calling*. Rumors circulated there'd be copycat crimes, some men glorifying Elliot's actions, hailing him as their leader, the *supreme gentleman*.

When we finally stepped outside, it was eerily quiet. On the street people traveled in tight groups, divided into herds and packs. The atmosphere was hushed, no one strolling, longboarding, no thumping music leaking from houses. The press conference was scheduled for 4:00 P.M. Before it began, we separated to privately unravel in our showers, to put on clean clothes. We regrouped inside the apartment, our safe house, refusing to be alone.

Elliot had lived in a brown apartment building, a block away from Sweet Alley, where I'd frequently buy bags of sour watermelon candies for long nights at the library. On Friday evening, he killed three people in his apartment, two Chinese roommates and their visiting friend; 142 stab wounds in total, bloodstains in the hallway, bodies dragged and covered in towels. He carried his knives and handguns into his black BMW, drove to the Alpha Phi sorority house, knocking hard on the door. When no one answered, he shot three women outside, two bled to death in the grass. He sped off, fired through the glass window of Isla Vista Deli, one male slid to the floor dead inside. He crashed his car on Del Playa, the main street, the nose of his car crunching in, before pressing his gun to his temple. Police found him with his head blown out, blood painting the curb. The ambulances were backlogged, students kneeled beside bleeding students. Bullet casings littered the street alongside sprinkled glass, large shards of window. The police found 548 rounds of unspent ammunition inside his car that he never had time to use. Six classmates had been stolen from us, Elliot the seventh. I do not include the victims' names here, for names are sacred, and I do not want them identified solely by what he did to them.

A month after my assault, I stepped out of work, unable to focus. I walked down the carpeted hallway, unlocking the supply closet to crouch behind the routers and chairs with broken wheels. I called the detective. *I was just wondering,* I said. *I know this sounds strange, but do you think Brock would ever hurt me?* I clarified. *I went to a school where a guy got really angry, there was a shooting.* I didn't know how to ask my question, he didn't know how to answer it. *There's no way of knowing,* the detective said. *But hopefully not and we are working hard to get ahold on things.*

Right, of course, I thought. I felt crazy. What was I looking to hear. You're safe forever. I didn't bring it up again. But it was a strange feeling having never met the man I was now up against. I had no idea who he was or what he was capable of.

I never forgot one of the opening lines of Elliot's 137-page manifesto: *This is a story of how I, Elliot Rodger, came to be. . . . This tragedy did not have to happen . . . but humanity forced my hand.* His cruelty had a narrative arc. He spoke like he had never wanted to do what he did, he was pushed to. And it was women who had made him suffer, who left him no choice but to execute his Day of Retribution. In his video, he'd said, *I've been forced to endure an existence of loneliness, rejection and unfulfilled desires all because girls have never been attracted to me.* His hostility was born of entitlement, self-pity.

I will punish all females for the crime of depriving me of sex. In Elliot's world, the unspoken law was that women owed him sex, we existed only to receive him. Those were the rules, that was our purpose. Sex was his right and our responsibility. The punishment in his world for breaking his laws, for rejecting sex, was death. When headlines first broke after the assault, Brock's smiling photo accompanied every article. *Unfair that he is publicly shamed while she gets to hide,* commenters said. Why would I want to humiliate him, when I'd seen what it could lead to?

As the months passed, I grew wary. He was out of school, I was out of work; we had both been untethered from society, aimlessly drifting. All those empty days. You change, you forget to eat, you don't know how to sleep, you drift far from yourself. What if in the time I was growing depressed, he was growing resentful? I asked if he was seeing a therapist and nobody could tell me. *College is the time when everyone experiences those things such as sex and fun and pleasure,* Elliot said. *In those years I've had to rot in loneliness, it's not fair. . . . . You forced me to suffer all my life, now I will make you all suffer.* Everyone needed someone to blame. He and I were both in some kind of pain, but what type of violence could his pain ignite? I could not live with myself if he hurt anybody. I contemplated it obsessively. What if he was angry at Stanford and wreaked havoc on campus. What if he really did believe his life was over and committed suicide. *You deserve to be annihilated and I will give that to you. You never showed me any mercy so I will show you none.* Whatever he did, I would feel responsible, although I knew it was out of my control.

I wanted accountability and punishment, but I also hoped he was getting better. I didn't fight to end him, I fought to convert him to my side. I wanted him to understand, to acknowledge the harm his actions had caused and reform himself. If he truly believed his future was ruined and he had nothing to lose, the possibilities were terrifying.

The scenarios multiplied in my head. I'd lodged wooden planks in my windows to seal them tight. I checked the backyard, looked for feet beneath shrubs. I hated how close I was to Ohio, he could come find me, could take the train. I turned off location tracking, deleted social media. I looked up gun laws. Elliot had legally purchased three semiautomatic handguns, fully loaded magazines, as easily as one buys grapefruit. I was losing my mind. What if the hearing was a trap. I imagined shootouts outside the courthouse, chaos erupting, ducking behind car doors, splintered windows, bailiffs sprinting, blood pouring out of bodies. I did not know whether this was reasonable or insane, just knew that insane things were possible. In my yellow room, I'd lie still so I could hear everything, my bulb always burning. I soaked myself in light. Sleep was no longer rest, but vulnerability. At six in the morning the solid black masses of trees finally split into individual leaves, and I'd feel relief. The light washed my thoughts away and I could be unconscious for a while.

I could barely wake up for class, after sleeping only one to two hours. I never made time to pack lunch, and unwilling to spend money on campus I starved myself for eight hours until I got home in the evening. At art galleries I filled napkins with free grapes and hummus-smeared chips. I was always exhausted, increasingly unhealthy. I wanted my mom's cooking. Wanted Lucas to hold me sleeping.

I taped the note from the fan above my bed, like a flimsy dream catcher. I taped a picture of my parents, young and holding hands in front of a blue wall of fish at an aquarium. A picture of my naked baby sister and me, side by side on a bedsheet patterned with tiny geese. They were my little protectors hovering above me at night.

It was on one of these nights, after hours of lying still, that I tossed off my blankets and picked up a pencil. I drew the two bicycles that had found me, bringing them to life, spoke by spoke. I had learned their names in the police report:

Carl-Fredrik Arndt

Peter Lars Jonsson

I drew smooth handlebars, tiny pedals, lumpy asymmetrical wheels. I stuck it to the wall above my pillow, pressing it flat. An omen of protection. Send help. I rolled back into the sheets and took a breath. If they were out there I could rest. I closed my eyes and drifted off to sleep.

The night before my final critique, I stacked my prints; a pile representing hours of trying and retrying and finally succeeding. I made thank-you cards for my professor and my TA. I set three alarms. I laid out my favorite red dress. I got into bed and wished to sleep this one night. Six hours passed. Sleep never came, so I decided to simply stay awake until I'd have to leave at eight o'clock. Instead my mind slipped away at seven in the morning, and I was so heavy in my stupor I didn't even hear the alarms. When I woke up, it was one o'clock in the afternoon.

There was no buzz of panic, only a deep welling of sadness. The critique was almost over. I had missed my classmates' presentations, the finale of the entire summer. Still I called a Lyft, pulling on my red dress. In the car I picked the crust out of my eyes and thought about everything in the world that was worse than missing an art critique. This was so small. But I was sad because it was so small, and I couldn't even do it. I would apologize to my professor, make sure he knew my absence was not born of disrespect.

When I walked in, the last person was presenting. Everyone looked at me. I didn't have an explanation and I didn't pretend to. I took a seat in the back, wanting to be invisible. I did not feel it was worth presenting. Yet my professor gestured that I should, welcomingly. I began one by one pinning them up, my back to the room, as people sat in silence. *It is no matter,* I told myself, *Soon none of this will matter.* I turned around to face them and introduced each piece.

I was met with quiet. Then the professor spoke, a warm smile beneath his large mustache, and said they were wonderful. Classmates pointed out my drawing of a two-headed rooster. They complimented my imagination, the sinister, the whimsical. They asked me about where I got my ideas, what kind of techniques I'd used, admired the coloring. I sat and marveled too, as they were commenting, and I must have looked tired, but I was beaming. Seeing all of my pieces up, side by side, the beautiful and bizarre things I'd created despite all of the struggling in the hours in between.

After class I bought a fresh roll of tape. I stood on a chair, hanging them all up in my room, even though I'd be moving out soon. I made a gallery, just for myself. I had gone from a clueless river weeper to a prolific printmaker. This was my evidence that while my mind had been shriveling in anxiety, my heart had been busy, thankful to have been given a chance. I saw the part of me that insisted on surviving.

To celebrate, a friend I'd made in class invited me to a block party where there'd be snow cones and dancing. I arrived early. Eventually my friend appeared with another girl, a sculptor, and they both blinked a little slowly, having had some whiskey. I treated myself to a vodka pineapple, watching kids catch lightning bugs and drink cream sodas out of red vine straws. We hopped around the makeshift mosh pit; I tied the sleeves of my jacket around my head like floppy bunny ears. A few guys came over in a musty cologne cloud of oakmoss and burnt logs. They asked if we were art students. I wondered if he knew because of the clothing tied to my head. *Just for the summer,* I said. *Are you from here?* he asked. *No, California,* I said, *how about you?* But his friends were already moving on, calling his name and wildly gesturing they wanted to go. He looked at them and turned back to me, leaned in with a serious look, *If I stay here, will you have sex with me later?* There was no segue. We'd gone from small talk smaller than a peanut to this blunt question. *No,* I said, unblinking. Without a word he trotted away to his friends as I stood there, my sleeves dangling from my head. The three of us were left bristling. His friends had asked them the same question. Was that real? Why would he say that? His friend asked you that too? The one with the gelled hair?

We called it a night, heading back to my friend's apartment, craving buttered toast and cold water. As we walked we exchanged stories of ludicrous encounters with guys, the things they would say and do. *One time this guy at a coffee shop, one time my friend's brother, one time my philosophy professor, one time . . .*

Where are you ladies going? A black Mustang was rumbling at the stoplight with three heavyset guys inside, snug in their seats. *Do you want to come to the club?* The club! I felt dehydrated, vodka and tiny pineapples streaming through me, my mind filled with stories of *one time*s, and suddenly I was delusional over how much I was expected to tolerate. The street was mostly empty, we were blocks away from the bars, nothing but houses with black windows and dormant Greyhound buses. I walked into the middle of the empty street, clenched my fists, threw back my head, and started screaming.

I screamed with my chest open, ruthlessly. My friends were stunned, began laughing, and the men grew testy, looking around uncomfortably, stuck at the red light. They began peppering my scream with *Crazy bitch! Crazy bitch!* But I didn't care. Their polished Mustang, their specks of hair, their dumb logistics; even if we did want to come to the club, we couldn't all fit in the tiny car. I don't want to have sex with you, I don't want to go to the club, I don't want you walking next to me, asking me where I'm going, how I'm doing, in a tone that wraps around me and pulls my shoulders up into my ears, making me want to go deaf and disappear. The tire full of nails had burst, tinkling like rain down onto their car. I felt powerful, intimidating, insane. I didn't care if the entire world woke up. The light turned green. *Chase them,* my friend said, and we began running.

We were three girls sprinting after a single black car. She caught up with them at the next light and slapped the taillight. *Get the fuck away from my car. Don't you dare fuck up my car.* They were angry at us, these women turned menaces, stepping out of line. I was still yelling, the adrenaline flooding, *you stupid-ass pigs.* But when I looked in the window, I saw the way one of the men glared at me.

Suddenly it didn't feel like a game, and I snapped into defensive mode. Stop, stop. We stepped back and they sped away. Witness, if they come back we need a witness. My head swiveled around. There was a young guy with glasses about thirty feet behind us. He seemed taken aback, hands in his pockets, as if we were going to turn on him too. I was secretly thankful he was there. I held my forehead, out of breath, our chests still rising and falling.

That night, though I had planned to stay through August, I decided it was time to go. Home was not an option, anywhere but home, the hotbed of assault, festering memories. I needed to continue my route of avoidance.

The day Lucas's internship ended, he boarded a plane and arrived in a rental car. He helped me pack up, gently rolling my prints, my whole life in this blue vehicle. We would drive down to Philadelphia, where I could stay with him until the hearing. He waited in the car, giving me time to say good-bye. I stood in my yellow room, my refuge, my chamber, remembering all the nights of suffocating heat, the terror that coated the walls, then melted away every morning. I left the fan, standing alone in the middle of the room, hoping it would bring coolness and quiet to whoever came next.

5.

THE HEARING WAS set for September 27. I had three weeks. In the last eight months I'd never spoken the full story aloud. If anything, I'd become less and less ready, my anxiety swollen inside me. I was standing at the edge of a cliff, tissue paper and sticks in my hands, being told to build something that would fly me and my sister safely to the ground.

Alaleh had arranged a call with me to begin preparing. In the month I'd been in Philadelphia, Lucas asked me many times, *Do you have questions for her? Yeah,* I said. *Do you want to write them down? Not right now,* I said. *I don't want to talk about it, maybe later.* On the day of the call, he handed me a list of questions he'd typed up, outlined and categorized; *Hearing vs. Trial, Timing, Communication with Other Party, Range of Final Outcomes, Settlement, Witnesses, Support for Chanel?* I had scribbled a few words in pencil, slanted and trailing off the corner. I had questions, but all of them lacked neat answers: can I take Xanax on an empty stomach, will I ever be employed, is he mentally stable, am I losing my mind.

The call was scheduled for 5:00 P.M. I'd asked Lucas to join me, another set of ears to absorb the information. At five, my phone rang, but it was Tiffany; she was walking home and wanted someone to keep her company. She was telling me that she'd seen a documentary about how albatross couples mated for life, can you believe it. Lucas tapped my arm, gesturing toward the clock. He whispered, *Time for your call.*

I shook my head.

Hang up, it's time! He motioned again.

I looked at him. *Tiff can I call you back? Thanks.*

I stood up. *What'd you say?*

It's time for your call, he said.

You think I don't know I have a call at five o'clock?

He was still.

What, you think, you think I can't tell fucking time? That I can't see the fucking time on the fucking stove? That you get to decide when I can and cannot talk to my sister? Hey, who was there that night? You? No? Who? Oh, her? That's right. You know what kind of shit she's going through? I will take every fucking call from her, EVERY FUCKING CALL FROM HER. You want to help me? You think SITTING here is fucking HELPING me?

My anger came pouring out, vile and immediate. My voice rose as if someone else's hand was steadily turning the dial. He backed away, stood transfixed across the room, staring at me, scared of me, I was scared of me too. My words bled freely with nothing to clot them, *How could you know anything about what this is like, what the hell can you do about it.* I slammed my phone onto the counter. We both heard it break.

The screen had not cracked, but shattered, glass spilling onto the stools, the floor. Humiliated, I screamed at him to get out. He offered me his phone, I said, *Get out.* He paused. *I'll be downstairs if you need me,* and the door clicked shut behind him. Trembling, I ran to grab a sock from my drawer, slipped it over my hand, used it to push my shattered phone into a ziplock bag. I locked myself in the bathroom with his list of questions and curled over my knees on the bathmat. My bag of glass was glowing, Alaleh was calling. My sock puppet slid and slid across a shard of glass, there was hardly enough surface left to accept the call. SHIT SHIT SHIT. *Hello? Yes! Doing well! How are you?*

When the call was over, I laid down with my sock on my hand. I didn't recognize who I was becoming. Volatile, enraged, touch the topic and I'd explode. Soon I'd fly to California alone, while Lucas continued his life at school. I imagined a gap between us widening, my gradual unraveling, our relationship collapsing. What if when I returned I was even more fragile, destructive.

When I was ten, I attended a sleepaway camp, atop a hill dense with sugar pines. My dad gave me his down sleeping bag from his college years. But it had a tiny hole. When I woke up, little white goose feathers rested in my hair, all over the place, like it had snowed. Instead of asking a counselor to repair it, I decided to wait until we were scheduled to go to the art room, to get tape. I took one long piece, about six inches, and held it at the tip of my finger. After art, we had swimming, so I hid it, dangling off a bench, away from backpacks and legs and water. At night, I delicately carried the flappy piece all the way up the hill. But by then it had become wet and dusty, didn't stick on like I hoped it would. For months after the assault, I'd been carrying around this little piece of tape, planning to patch everything up on my own. But it would not be enough. You need to tell somebody, you need to seal the holes, restore your warmth, stop cleaning up the feathers. The next day, I agreed to go to therapy.

It may seem strange I had postponed it for so long, considering my dad's a therapist. But I was still in complete denial about the magnitude of the role this case would play in my life. Only when it was staring me in the face did I succumb to addressing it.

Growing up, all I understood about therapy was that on *take your kid to work day*, I never got to go. My dad was busy helping people with divorce, marital issues, alcoholism. When I was young, I thought my dad was a doctor for head injuries; if you bumped it, he gave you a Band-Aid, etc. I also wondered how he knew all the answers. Did he have a secret guidebook? *I don't tell them the answers, I guide them.*

We used to stop by my dad's office every Sunday morning. I'd dust the wooden bookshelves. Spray the ficus. Rake the sand in the stone garden. Stack his yellow legal pads. Feed his fish. I loved the teal and pink pebbles, silver striped minnows, orange billowing cheeks. Then I'd collect my payment; when people reclined in his cushioned chairs, coins fell out of their pockets, so I'd stick my hands in the crevices, scooping out pennies and gum.

I wished I was a fish so I could listen to these strangers who trusted my dad with their secrets. For one hour they could safely unravel and cry and say the things they would never say in their daily lives, and when time was up, they'd bind themselves up again, setting off into the hum of the world.

But the people I imagined in his office never looked like me; they were adults who wore ties, women with large purses, finicky hands. I was the one who fed the fish, never the one in the seat. I called and made an appointment with a therapist who had worked at Women Organized Against Rape. A tall building. A sign-in sheet where I scribbled my name illegibly, afraid to be traced anywhere. A cream-colored couch. Deb, a woman with wavy brown hair, blue eyes. Notes on her side table, a family of small flowering cacti, quilted tapestries depicting branches. So quiet, at ease. I would do well here.

I needed to show her Emily, needed to bring her to the scene where she was found beneath the trees. For the first time, I was handing someone a flashlight declaring, *Come with me.* She followed me, pulling back branches, as I shined the beam of light on her body. The therapist looked with me. I told her we had three weeks to get Emily on her feet, get her ready.

The telling was a doozy, but afterward I felt lighter, like I'd left some of the weight up in the building, which made it easier to walk in the streets. I bought a small, red notebook and wrote, *It feels better when the story is outside myself.* I remember at Costco, my dad would buy tissues and toilet paper in bulk that Tiffany and I stacked to create a cushioned throne inside the shopping cart. Maybe he needed so many because people kept crying, their insides coming out, like me.

When my therapist asked me if I'd noticed the assault affecting other parts of my life, I instinctively shook my head. *The whole point is that it's entirely separate from my life, I've kept it that way for a reason.* She didn't respond, the two of us sitting in silence a moment. Sometimes I wondered if my testimony would work better for the defense, because if he asked, *So you haven't been affected?* I'd want to say, *Nope.* I sat on my hands. *Maybe, I've noticed some things. Anger, I've noticed. The way I carry myself, more nervous I guess. I wear this pretty much every day.* I lifted my arms, the black sleeves of Lucas's jacket extending past my hands like empty sushi rolls. As I spoke, I realized the assault had moved from the periphery to the very center.

I railed off all the worst things I'd heard about myself, judgments made and memorized from reading comments. *They think I'm, they tell me, I shouldn't have,* on and on. She said, *Can I ask if you've ever heard any of this in person?* I thought awhile, pinching my mouth together, then shook my head. *No, not once.* It had never occurred to me that I'd given the opinions of online strangers equal weight to actual people. This was a powerful revelation. I had never heard those horrible things spoken; when the news was relayed to a person, silence enfolded them, a palpable sadness, a teardrop, a hug. I began to distinguish real experiences from online ones. I repeated mantras in my head, when I washed dishes, before I slept.

I did nothing wrong.

I am strong.

I have a voice.

I told the truth.

. . .

Alaleh called. The hearing was called off for September 27, moved to October 5. There was a sadness in the way I was able to say *no problem* without a second thought or a glance at my planner. For the past month my schedule had been empty, therapy only occupying a small chunk of every week. Take any day of mine you like, I have emptied them all for you. *Great,* she said. *Can you let your sister know about the schedule change?*

I was always the first to be updated, the one responsible for keeping Tiffany in the loop. I sat on the bed with the phone in my hand, knowing that in normal life, the date changes meant upheaval, collapse. She'd already rescheduled her finals the last time. Now she had six classes and two jobs. I dreaded the call. *I'm sorry,* I said.

I was met with a long pause. *But I've already rearranged everything,* she said. *I can't keep explaining.* I could hear the strain in her voice, the stress spreading, turning into *I can't, I can't,* could hear it all stacking in her mind, *but I already.*

They will understand, I said. *I'll talk to them. I'll help organize your schedule. You can quit one of your jobs, I'll help you with your readings, we'll get everything fixed.* But she said no and no, that she could figure it out herself. I could hear her retreating, going quiet. *I'm fine,* she said, *I don't want to talk anymore. I need to go now.*

I'll make it up to you, I said as she hung up the phone.

I knew there were already times she'd stepped out of class, pacing the hallway, too unstable to reenter the room. I knew she'd abandoned plans with friends to go look at lineups at the police station, gave up concert tickets, missed birthdays and makeup quizzes. Knowing all of this hurt me the most. My life overshadowing hers, claiming to be more critical. The coldness of the court system, picking off pieces that make up a life.

A minute later my sister called back. *I just wanted to make sure you know I'm not mad at you, just the situation. I didn't mean to yell at you. I'll figure it out, okay?* My eyes blinked wet and taut. I nodded, I understood. I knew what it felt like to have nowhere to put the frustration, the way it infected our lives, caused us to lash out at one another, all of us lost.

I was ready for October 5. On the night before my flight, my small suitcase sat packed and zipped by the door. My red notebook was stocked with grounding techniques and encouragements: *You are more powerful than anyone who has ever hurt you. It is not pathetic to feel and react. You are stronger than you know, even if you can't feel it yet.* I had soft pants laid out for the plane, clean socks. I stood in my flannel pajamas in the kitchen with a pair of scissors trimming the bonsai tree I'd bought to liven up Lucas's apartment. My phone rang at 11:00 P.M.

I'm sorry, the hearing has been postponed, my DA said. *Don't get on the flight tomorrow.* I held the phone without speaking and stared at my suitcase by the door, bloated and sealed. I tried to envision myself rolling it back into the bedroom, the exhale of it unzipping. Taking the time to tuck each piece of clothing away into its respective drawer, returning my toiletries to the sink, curling up into bed. Waking up to another vacant day, waiting to be told to pack up again. Preparing for court had become my sole purpose, all this momentum now halting. She also said since they'd paid for my first flight, I'd have to buy the ticket when the time came. I couldn't afford it.

I'm coming home, I said. I told her I would stay in Palo Alto until whenever it started. *All right,* she said. *I'll keep you updated. Just let your sister know it's off for now.* That night, I did not call Tiffany. I would wait a couple of days to hear the final plan before rearranging her life. I was done jerking her around.

My parents' home is a sun-infused sanctuary, one story, made of old wood, two brick chimneys, built in the seventies, painted a burnt salmon color, with a cracked cement driveway. Out front there are lava rocks, small banana trees, large palm fronds and lavender bushes my dad planted. Our door is lined with small nails for Christmas lights we keep up year-round. But when I got out of the car, I hated the neighborhood, hated the sunshine, the way time never seemed to pass, the green leaves that never changed. I hated the palm trees, so damn spunky. I missed the cluttered streets of Philly, the way lives overlapped, the crowded elevators and shopping bags bumping into my legs and the smog of buses and flimsy boxes of red chicken smeared in white cream from silver halal carts. My street was empty, the park empty, my house empty. I hated it.

I went to visit Gong Gong, my grandfather, who lives close by my parents' house. He didn't know about the assault, my mom said if he found out he'd be too heartbroken. He came to the United States when I was four to help raise me and Tiffy; once I saw him in my room, squishing my pillow between his hands. *No good,* he said. Next thing I knew we were at Ross and he was squishing all the pillows, finding a firmer one that would better support my neck. When he says "Chanel" it comes out sounding like "xiao niao," which means *little bird* in Chinese. He hand fed me and my sister like little birds growing up, and every time I am in Palo Alto his is the first meal I eat.

I sat at his low table covered in Chinese newspaper and free calendars from banks as placemats. I ate a few bowls, helped translate his mail. The call came in. The hearing was back on. Alaleh said I could come see the space if I was free. I threw my empty bowl in the sink, hugged him, sprinted toward my car.

The courtroom was small, much smaller than I'd anticipated, dark and cramped and musty. Natural light came in from mold-spackled squares in the high ceiling. In the corner was a withered flag that never rippled, only hung, permanent in its formation of folds. Everything was stagnant and dreary, like the air had been stored there for years. I would be entering from the doors at the back, walking down the aisle like a bride. I didn't like this period of vulnerability, everyone's eyes on my back as I approached the witness stand. I would have preferred to emerge before them, more of a *ta-da* moment. The judge would be sitting to the left of me, perched above, a bigger bird in the same nest. My DA would stand before me at a podium. I would be looking directly at her.

Here's where you will be sitting, get a feel for it. Brock will be sitting there. She pointed to an empty chair close to my stand. I nodded but it seemed impossible, that soon those seats would be full of bodies. She laid out the guidelines: I would first be sworn in. Be sure to speak loudly and clearly. I cannot respond with a nod, must give an audible yes. If there's an objection, I must stop and wait for the judge to grant me permission to speak again. Only answer directly what is being asked. It's okay to cry, but avoid being overly emotional. My advocate would sit in a chair adjacent to the stand, but during testimony she was not allowed to talk to me. I would be asked to identify Brock. They'd be using my first name in court, referring to me as Chanel Doe. Do not take his defense attorney's confrontations personally. His questions will help her figure out his angle and prepare for the trial. You must always tell the truth.

I heard it all, but mainly I stared at the chairs where Brock and his attorney would be sitting. I felt a pinch in my throat, as if, were I to blink enough times they'd materialize. She said I didn't have to look at his defense attorney, even when he was speaking to me. I could look into the audience, lock eyes with a friend. But I knew no friends would be coming.

Claire was in France. Tiffany was not allowed in the room as a fellow witness. My mom was going to be in the courthouse, but I refused to let her watch, knowing my focus would shift to protecting her. I feared I'd withhold, unable to disclose the full truth, not wanting to hurt her. I would do it alone.

Alaleh handed me a thick manila folder, filled with transcripts of my interviews from the hospital and police station. *You don't need to study as if this were a test,* she said, *it's just to freshen your memory.* The court reporter walked in to introduce herself; she had short hair and sharp glasses, walked with an ease like she ran the place. She would be sitting at a desk slightly adjacent to the judge. *Don't be afraid,* she said, smiling, dipping her glasses down so I could see her eyes. *If you get nervous, just look at me.* She winked.

A part of this felt familiar. When I was eighteen, I took a Spoken Word course with Professor Fulbeck. Before every show, we would go to the venue, check out the lighting, the stage, test the mic. Day to day I was shy, but onstage I was different. When I stepped out, I became another person.

Freshman year, a classmate told me she'd woken up to a guy having sex with her, her virginity lost, as she faded in and out. She said that's why she hadn't been to class in a few weeks, but it was okay, she shrugged. Within a week, I'd written a spoken word piece called *Nice: I'm tired of being good, being nice, in this life, where rebellion is not wearing my retainer for one night. I want to evoke feelings, create enemies, appear a little corrupt, I want to bitch out some bitches, I want to fuck some shit up.* At this point people would be laughing and clapping as the piece swelled, amused as punches were thrown, until I dropped the line, *To the dick who stuck his dick in my passed-out friend.* Sudden silence.

Are you self-conscious because your dick is shorter than a ruler, so you got her drunk and gone enough to rule her? Because your fleshy dangler didn't find your hand that handsome, your wang banger needed a real companion, so you got her alone, put the sword in the stone, you had her violated, she's degraded while you're the one shallower than a kiddie pool, I pity your lack of dignity, pity your— I reeled it off while making eye contact with each person in the audience.

I'll have you bawling about your balls while you're calling me the meanest, and that is how I'll vanquish your fetus-sized penis and to top it off . . . I'll shoot it. People erupted, hollering and stomping. When I competed in slams with *Nice,* tens went up from the judge's table. My parents were stunned, but supportive. Each time I hoped he was watching.

Writing and performing this piece was easy, because at the time I was in a relationship with the first boy I loved, made powerful because I was safe, and sex was kind, and the piece was for her, not for me, and I could use fancy wordplay and speak fast and bring down the house by verbally annihilating a dick. Now that I was the one assaulted while unconscious, I could hardly speak. Sitting in front of that microphone in the empty courtroom, I just nodded my head, and I thought of my young self, bold, parading around the stage, wondered where she had gone.

Tiffany drove home the evening before the hearing, would be in Palo Alto for less than twenty-four hours before she rushed back to class. She'd never seen the courthouse or met Alaleh. Strange that we were suffering through the same process, but there was nobody looking out for her or helping her prepare. I would argue that testifying would be harder for her because she remembered; would have to describe what he did while he stared. And still she had homework, would have to be in class the next morning, as if she'd never lived this day.

What are we supposed to wear, she said. Images we'd Googled of *women's court clothes* displayed tall women with hands on their waists, long hair twisted into soft tendrils, pencil skirts, legs slender as stair banisters on pointed heels. *How the heck are we supposed to look like this.* It was dark out, we were at Kohl's, wandering around the gleaming white floors. I texted my advocate for guidance; *something comfortable, respectful.* Got it. My sister emerged from the dressing room in a large shirt with a Minion on it, pantless. *What would they do if I showed up in this.* I said, *Tiffany, this is serious,* and walked out in diamond-encrusted capris, a visor, a shirt that said BLESSED.

As the closing announcements droned overhead, we abandoned our game, succumbing to the business casual section, our arms growing heavy with earth-toned sweaters. She stepped out in a maroon crew neck with a dipped hemline. *Are you testifying or giving a speech at your child's spaghetti dinner fund-raiser?* The floral button-ups transformed us into frumpy secretaries. *Damn it, Janice, did you remember to fax my W-9?* Finally I found the one, a sweater the color of old milk, soft and quiet. Emily's new uniform. I looked like someone who would lend you a pencil. My sister nodded in approval.

It was dark now and time to study the transcripts. We sat at opposite ends of the dining room table with our stacks of paper. I heard my dad say to my mom, *Aren't you happy our girls are here?* It was true I was grateful for these impromptu family reunions. Still, the reason we were all brought together loomed. We read in heavy silence, broken only by the occasional scrape of a page turning. One of the most important rules established early on was that Tiffany and I could not discuss the case. If our facts aligned too closely, we would be accused of conspiring. But her presence alone was a gift, made it possible for me to begin reliving the night.

As I pored over the pages, the feelings began leaking in. To read each line was to be in a room slowly filling with water. It filled and filled until there was a space just big enough to keep breathing, a sliver of air between water and ceiling. Just when I thought I was going under, it stopped. I knew it could not drown me again. It was in the past, the assault stuck inside these papers. The water began to drain.

I stayed focused, typing up notes, putting all my facts in order. I ingrained the details until I could recite the night backward and forward in fifteen-minute time frames, from the moment I decided to go to the party to the moment I was released from the hospital. *I'm nervous,* my sister said. *It's okay,* I said.

If you get nervous, look at the court reporter. She winked at me. *They don't expect you to remember everything, it's been ten months! It's simple, we just tell the truth. Everyone's gonna be like wow, she's an angel, but that guy gives me the heebie-mother-freaking-jeebies. Plus we spent seventy dollars at Kohl's so we kind of have to make it worth it, you know. We don't have to be afraid because we have nothing to hide.*

It was true, and I felt it when I said it. She was smiling now. I let her look over her notes, and then walked to my room. My eyes began dripping. There was one thing I didn't add. *I'm nervous too. I have no idea what's going to happen.*

The plastic security frame was my portal, a doorway into this unfamiliar world. The security guards escorted my mom, Tiffany, and me into the tiny victim closet, which was furnished with a dirty yellow couch that looked sculpted out of earwax. A metal-legged desk piled with torn, expired magazines. A cloudy bag of markers with uncapped, dry heads. Dusty stacks of domestic violence brochures. A laminated red poster with bold yellow lettering read: VICTIMS HAVE THE RIGHT TO BE TREATED WITH FAIRNESS AND RESPECT FOR HIS OR HER PRIVACY AND DIGNITY, AND TO BE FREE FROM INTIMIDATION, HARASSMENT, AND ABUSE THROUGHOUT THE CRIMINAL JUVENILE JUSTICE PROCESS. Papers left behind with kids' drawings; a drawing of a heart, cramped lettering inside, *Because I'm scared.* My mom was uneasy in the sordid space, wanting to make it better somehow, and left to get us warm milk at a nearby café, some cookies, chopped honeydew.

Anne, Julia's mother, was on her way, had offered to come and be in the courtroom, my sole supporter. Julia was abroad that quarter. I'd later learn that when she returned to campus she'd begun suffering from panic attacks every time she walked past the fraternity at night. This would happen for the next two years.

As we waited, my advocate Bree arrived. I noticed she'd gotten a haircut. It was nice to talk about her hairstyle, like we were friends in a normal context and she had not been assigned to me from the YWCA so I wouldn't be alone. When she saw me fidgeting, she told me to press the soles of my feet to the floor, a grounding technique. She reached into her purse and pulled out a toy; a long, bright-blue wiener dog that had fur like rubbery spaghetti. *It may be helpful to have something to squeeze while you're up there,* she said. I stretched it out, shook it around. My sister got a squishy skull.

Alaleh would come get me when they were ready. An hour passed. My steamed milk cooled. At the knock, my sister squeezed my hand. I followed Bree and Alaleh down the hall. Do I raise my right or left hand to be sworn in, what if I forget everything, is my fly zipped, do I look okay. I began pacing, breathing in and out audibly. I was self-conscious of the noise I was making, embarrassed I could not disguise my panic, but figured she'd rather have me breathing heavily than passed out. *Take a look,* she said. Through a thin rectangular window in the door, I scanned the room, a small audience, the back of his head. I froze, locked on the bare skin of his neck. I wanted to hold on to my last moment of being hidden. But Alaleh was pulling the doors open, and there was nothing left to do but walk through.

At this time the people call their first witness, Chanel Doe. Heads turned as I came in, I didn't know where to put my gaze. I switched the blue wiener dog to my left hand, so I could raise my right hand to be sworn in. I said, *I do.* Words I thought I'd speak first at my wedding, not my rape trial. I felt the eyes taking me in. I wondered if they were surprised I was Asian, if I looked like a woman, or a girl, if I appeared mundane, less pretty than imagined, why didn't he choose someone better looking, stop, what are you thinking, be quiet. As I stepped toward the witness stand I wanted to keep walking and walking, but when I touched the back of my chair, I sat to face forward, here I am.

I was told to make myself comfortable. I did not understand what that meant; I tried lifting my chair to scoot it forward, everyone watching as I thrust haltingly forward an inch or two. Alaleh reminded me to speak loudly and clearly. With shaking hands I tilted the thin stem of the microphone toward me. I heard someone clearing their throat. Bree sat in a chair down to my right, facing the audience in solidarity. The audience was sparse, but the smattering of bodies was enough to make me anxious, wondering who they were and why they were here. I noticed Detective Kim next to Alaleh, a familiar face, a small relief.

In my periphery on my left, Brock was just a mass. I rested my eyes on Alaleh's face, letting everything around her melt away. She was smiling at me from behind her podium, the way I've seen mothers smile encouragingly at their toddlers, beckoning to take their first step, and I smiled as best I could in return.

If you could tell us your first name and please spell it for us.

Chanel, I replied, *C-H-A-N-E-L,* I said. It felt like cutting off a large portion of hair all at once. A loss swift, irreversible. My name no longer mine, a secret I'd now have to trust everyone in the room to keep. There was no time to dwell, we went on to my age, education, area of residency. I spoke about Arastradero Preserve at sunset, Tiffany and Julia, the taqueria, my open-faced chicken taco, drinking water because it was spicy, going home, my dad's dinner. *Other than the stir-fry and broccoli and the taco did you have anything else to eat that day? No,* I responded, then paused. *Well, that day, that day I don't remember anymore.* I must have had lunch that day ten months ago, but what could it have been?

She asked why I was going to Stanford, I said I was going to the fraternity party to meet up with Julia; *And, apparently, that's what was going on that night. But if they had said let's go get frozen yogurt downtown, I would—it's a different party at Stanford by the International club, I would have gone to that. I had no incentive to go to a fraternity party.* A man's voice appeared to my left. *Your honor, I'm going to move to strike the last, approximately two-thirds or three-quarters of the answer. The question was answered at the very beginning.*

I looked over. The defense attorney sat cube faced, white haired, black suited, hunched over his notes, speaking as if I weren't there. The judge replied, *All right. I will strike the last two sentences of the answer as nonresponsive to the question.* I watched my words fall like birds shot out of the air. I was unaware he had the power to erase my testimony without moving a finger. The most disconcerting part was that he'd objected against a line about froyo. What would happen when we got to what mattered?

Alaleh continued questioning me about the decision to go to a frat, and again and again he sliced off my sentences. *All right. So stricken.* I was a dog with an electric collar around my neck, the remote in the defense's hand. Every time I spoke I felt the shock, turned around confused. I became wary of overstepping my bounds, wanting to avoid being cut off. He was teaching me to be afraid of speaking freely.

Alaleh broke down the questions so I could flesh out my answer. *Did you want to go to a fraternity party? No,* I said, nervous to say any more. *Why not?* A chance to elaborate. *Because why would I want to go to a fraternity party?* My irritation surprised me. *I had no incentive to go to a fraternity party and meet anybody in a frat.* How hard it was to get a single point across. Eventually we fell into a nice rhythm, tapping words back and forth. Soon every inch of the evening was coming to life. The courtroom dissolved, as I began to see the worn linoleum floor of my kitchen, the black-rimmed clock, the thinly striped blue-and-yellow wallpaper. When asked what I had to drink, I could see the auburn liquid in its glass bottle, mugs on the wooden countertop. When asked what kind of whiskey, I squinted as if I could focus the memory to read the label. Down the stairs, stacks of red cups, wide wooden tables, spilled juice, basement filling with heads, bodies flooding out the sliding glass doors to the back, squatting beneath the trees, trying not to sprinkle on my shoes, returning to the soft din of the cement patio, play by play by play.

It stunned me how seriously all of these questions were being asked, as if it were normal to recall every trifling detail, to divide the murkiness of casually drinking into a chronology of consumption, marking minutes between sips. Time was dissected down to the minute, length down to the yard, liquid down to fluid ounces. How long did it take to drive there (*7 minutes*), when did we arrive (*11:15*), who I was with, where were we dropped off, if we'd gone to any other parties, how many people were there (*60 people, 20 minutes later there were 100*), how far outside I'd walked to go to the bathroom (*15 yards*). My assurance felt almost comical, how could anyone be so sure? I was so consumed by the staccato rhythm of her questioning, the humming contemplation in my mind, that I didn't notice us edging closer to my final memory. I saw myself, beer in hand, smiling, shoulders loosely swaying. Tiffany was there, a friend or two of hers floating around. I had been watching them, thinking about how I missed college, but didn't really, how even if I could return, it would never be the same. I saw Tiffany now, running around in the sweet wildness of it, happy for one night that I could be part of it.

What was the next thing that happened?

The little movie in my head stopped, the music fell away, the crowd in the glow of the porch light disappeared. Black, just black. I looked at her; a silent panic, a blinking, I have no answer. She had held me by the belly, letting me paddle around the water, and now she released her grip, watching me slip beneath. *I woke up in the hospital.* As the words left me, my head dropped forward, my thoughts scattered. She asked something, but I did not respond; in the transcript, the court reporter had only typed *(shakes head)*.

I heard a sound, a long wail, a high cooing, that sailed and fell. It was growing louder, I could not stop. I wanted someone to hold my shoulders, but I realized nobody was coming. A room of strangers, sitting unmoved, as I cried into nothing. I had kept loved ones outside these doors, had made a grave mistake. I put two hands over my face, clenched my eyes. If I couldn't see anyone they could no longer see me.

JUDGE: *Would you like to recess?*

DA: *Yes.*

JUDGE: *We're going to take a brief recess. So I will step off the bench.*
  Thank you.

DA: *Oh, here's a cup.*

I heard everyone scuffle out of the stillness, as if to say, *Shut it down, we've lost her.* I imagined all the gazes on me broken, snipped like threads. I heard the judge stepping off his bench. I could hear the click of my DA's heels toward me, pouring water into a Styrofoam cup on my stand. I stayed covering my face, the blue wiener dog squished against my cheek. Bree got me to stand up, led me out the courtroom doors, down the halls to the bathroom.

The door swung closed. Finally quiet. *This is hard,* I said. My voice was tiny, dim. This wasn't how it was supposed to go. I was embarrassed by who I was to everyone in that room, the one who drank herself to limpness, and now made wet gasping sounds into the microphone.

Alaleh had touched some soft center, pulsing and nebulous, the portion of lost memory between that night and morning. She would have to play the game of stepping around that center, knowing when and how to enter, for if she entered abruptly, she'd lose me, again and again, I was sure. I imagined her growing frustrated, *We got a weak one.* My confidence was waning.

You're doing great, Bree said. I looked at her. She was smiling, not with pity, but something bordering on admiration. Holding the wad of paper towels, she seemed hopeful, excited by this morning. It meant something to her that we had made it here. I felt only fatigue, charcoal smears of makeup on my cheeks. Maybe in this context, this is what great looked like.

I was surprised to be carried by my own feet, following Bree back through the courtroom doors. As she settled into the chair on my right, I felt the two of us had returned from a secret clubhouse. I was great. This fact became as solid as her presence.

When we resumed, Alaleh went back to my final memory of standing outside on the patio, then touched the soft center again. *Can you describe how you were feeling when you first woke up?* Her gaze locked into me. I could not describe that feeling. I don't know that many survivors can. I would argue that I was still in the process of waking up. But I understood we were not going anywhere until I could start giving answers, that we would recess and return for as long as it took. So I tried.

I wept through the blood, the underwear, gone, my face contorted, chest heaving. My words were breathy, I felt ugly, making a mess of myself, but beneath all of this I heard that rapid clicking, the hands of the court reporter carrying me, little footsteps of the keys, running forward, we were moving. *You need a moment? Take a deep breath. Okay. Can you describe was it just one pine needle, how many pine needles were in your hair?* Pushing and pushing, every detail, every feeling. *Did a nurse perform an exam on your genitals? It was a fairly invasive exam?*

At this I paused, sat for a moment, wiping my face. If I shared too much, I'd make everyone uncomfortable. But she was asking me. Why should I carry the shame for the things that were done to my body. *I had a plastic beak stuck in me*, I said, *I had Q-tips in my anus. They painted my vagina blue I think to look for abrasions. They spread my legs. Photographed me. They photographed me naked. So yes.*

I felt a little lighter. I'd stated my truth unapologetically, and for a moment I'd held the power, made the men fidget, cast their eyes down. I wanted to say into the microphone again, *anus.* I'd let go of my posture, my hair was out of its clips, I was exhausted. We must be almost done.

Chanel, I'm going to ask you to take a look at this exhibit, and tell me if you recognize the items that are photographed in the exhibit. Photographs? The assault in my mind was always a scene constructed by dialogue narrated to me. She shuffled through a few large photos on her desk and I caught a glimpse of my naked wrists and ankles folded over. She approached my stand with one large photo, a square of reality sliding onto my podium, and I pulled back from it instinctively.

The entire rectangle was a bright auburn color filled by a crosshatched texture. I studied it for a moment, realizing it was thousands of pine needles. Among them was a small, white scribble of fabric and a blue phone cover. My two tiny possessions left behind. So this is where I was found.

Up until then I'd tried to stay present but detached, the blond guy to my left a stranger. That mystified morning in the hospital, the snag of pulling needles from my hair, was the only reality I had. But here now the scenes were beginning to connect, the black fragment of my mind filling with this bright, auburn color. A stranger looking at the photos would see white fabric; I saw my underwear, knew that if you looked closely you could see the faded black polka dots, thread loose on the waistband. The victim is you. Which meant there was a point in time I had been there, and the man in the suit sitting feet from me, had been running his hands over the bones of my bare hips, as I was pinned beneath the weight of him, my hair mopping the ground, his palm pressed against my exposed nipple, his mouth opening onto my neck. He is spreading my legs, worming his fingers into me. The reality of it all was too large, expanded too quickly, panic rising. I stared at the photo, fully aware now of the presence of him.

Alaleh pulled the photo away, replaced it with another, this one an enlarged screenshot of my phone, displaying nine missed calls from my sister. Next, a screenshot of Lucas's texts: *Tell Tiffany to take care of you, please, I'm worried about you boo.* Evidence of their panic. I pressed my arms against my sides, my face dry, chin shaking. *Chanel,* I heard my name. *Did you have any interest in hooking up with anyone in court today?* I lifted my head and looked directly at him, at the top of his head, as he looked down into his lap. He is real, it is really him. I wanted to make sure he was listening. Pick up your head.

No.

Silence rippled out around this word. My mind became clear, all the questions faded to nothing. *Do you recognize anyone in court that you may have hooked up with?* The way he refused to look at me told me we both knew the answer to this question.

No.

This single syllable on my tongue felt like nourishment, tasted like something new. I wanted the two little letters to slip inside his ears like seeds, to settle inside his gut, to expand, pushing on his lungs, his heart, suffocating him from the inside out, until he was overcome, bursting out of his buttoned shirt.

My DA smiled, gave me a nod, tapping her papers on the podium. *I have nothing further,* she said. I had completed part one. Fatigue seemed to have beaten out the fear in me. I had been taught to be intimidated by the defense, told he was reputable, distinguished, one of the best, but as I waited for him to get all his papers in order, I softened to the fact that he was quite old, maybe someone's grandpa, and I imagined him tossing a baseball underhand. Only when I watched him rise did I feel a slight prickling. His face naturally sagged in a frown, and I was reminded he was here to dismember me.

Good morning, Chanel. He smiled, but I believe a smile has to appear for more than a beat to be considered a real smile, and his dropped too quickly. Still I smiled warmly back, teaching him how to hold one. *I wanted to ask you some questions mostly based on the questions that you've already been asked. Just clarifications,* he said. He had a light air about him, as if this were just friendly talk, we were going on a stroll together. This bothered me, this feigned politeness, a baseless cordiality.

His questions began again at the taqueria. In retrospect, I would never have gone to the taqueria that day if I knew there were going to be so many questions about it. *You stopped before you got home at a taqueria to have some dinner? That's where you ate one taco? You had nothing to drink, not water, or coke or anything?* He looked up from his notes to kind of squint at me, then nodded and returned to his notes as if confirming something. His approach was unexpected; taking long pauses, flipping back and forth slowly through his legal pad, writing while we waited. I had anticipated a rapid-fire cross-examination, instead he seemed to be taking his time deliberating, evaluating my every word. I grew uneasy during these long silences. I continued to stare at him.

His questions mirrored my attorney's, repeating everything we'd already been through, it sounded like: *Stir-fry, you testified, whiskey, help yourself, broccoli? Who prepared that, drinking with, that's where you, four shots, half hour? Correct? Alcohol? The whole period? With your sister, believe you, number of shots, champagne, I believe, so how much, was she also, consumed, roughly? The party? Before? You say? She wasn't? Did you both? How much? During? Excuse me? Stanford? Same time? Approximately? Or with her? With whom? When you? That you saw?* Not hard hitting, but hole poking. I made sure that every time he looked up my eyes were still holding his, showing him I'd be with him every step of the way, while he made it increasingly difficult. Unlike Alaleh's, his questions became increasingly nonlinear, making it harder to keep a visual narrative in my head. *When you consumed the amount of alcohol you poured into the red cup between the first and the second lines, was that before or after you went outside to pee? You mentioned that day when you went to Stanford and went to the KA house you were wearing a beige cardigan, correct? That's a sweater?* Was he asking me if a cardigan was a sweater? I grew unsettled by his frivolous questions posed in a serious light, the idea that they somehow bore weight. He asked me if I had been singing at the party. Quizzed me on how many liquid ounces are in a handle. *At one point in your testimony I believe you described your actions as standing on a chair on a table and dancing by yourself?* At this question, I smiled, imagining the furniture stacked, my head grazing the ceiling. *On a chair on a table?* I said. *Yeah,* he said. *Did I get that wrong?* He looked at me, deadpan. *On a chair,* I said, *on the floor.* I waited a moment to let him write it down. *Everyone else was on tables.*

Okay, he said. *So you were just on a chair? When you were at the hospital you didn't notice that you were injured in any way on your body, did you?* I almost said yes, quick to agree, until I realized I'd never said that. Why was he asking me like I'd said it. He had seamlessly transitioned from furniture stacking to bodily injuries, consistent in his tone and pacing, and I suddenly wondered if the joke was on me, for getting too relaxed by his easy questions. In response I began talking about the dried blood, but he quickly dismissed this, attributing it to the needle from the IV drip. *So other than that you didn't notice any injuries on your body?* His questions were disguising statements; *you didn't notice, you didn't notice.* He was forcing me into something. *Except for a scratch on my neck,* I said. He snapped back, *That was the only injury you noticed, right? Yes,* I said. He'd gotten what he wanted. I felt him feeding me the answer, framing it in a way that made me want to agree, to keep things running smoothly.

A memory surfaced then, of standing in the bathroom mirror at home, turning and pulling down my sweatpants to reveal the red patch on my bottom. I'd quickly pulled my pants back up, washed my hands as if something had rubbed off on them. I hadn't thought of this incident in months, and it now showed itself to me, freed the memory from its anchor. But how do I explain this? That a repressed memory has bubbled to the surface? I had already said yes; testified to not having any injuries, permanently on record, as I was swept off into questions about shotgunning a beer, if the person used a key to puncture the can, was it actually a key, like a key on a key chain.

The end was abrupt. He sat down. I was free. Was I free? I looked at

Alaleh as if to say are you sure, if I walk out now, no one will stop me? And when she nodded, I was gone. When I got back to the victim closet, there were two things I noticed. First, my wiener dog was strangled in a tight knot. It alarmed me that I'd almost killed my small friend. I gingerly untangled him. Then I saw the skin on both hands between my thumb and forefinger marked with deep, red crescents that trailed down to my wrists. While the upper half of my body had remained still, my thumbnails had carved into my skin, digging into the meat of my palm and forearms, releasing the tension. This habit born in court has never died; now when I'm thinking hard or in a stressful situation, my hands involuntarily curl tightly and I begin pinching. At night, I ache in my hands and forearms, fantasize peeling them open, scooping out the hot, thick, pain buried there, until my arms and fingers are limp and empty.

I was done, but my sister was not. Her friend Elizabeth had arrived to watch her. Tiffany planned to make eye contact with her the entire time, even during Alaleh's questioning. She did not feel the need to stare down the defense in an act of self-redemption and reclamation, she simply wanted to get through it. I loved this about her, always knowing what she wanted, surrounding herself with good forces. It was sweet to imagine the two of them anchored in each other's gaze, ignoring whoever was talking.

When the two of them returned, the first thing I noticed was their eyes, glazed over, unresponsive. That told me everything. I was reminded of the night I went to pick up Julia; saw her standing with her notes, disoriented and despondent. It was time for Tiffany to drive back to school. I told her, *I am going with you.* I was afraid of what would happen if we separated, like we would not heal correctly. I had not planned to go to Southern California, did not have a way of getting back. All I understood was that I needed to be in the passenger's seat. I told my mom that I'd see her and dad whenever I returned.

There were very few situations Tiffany and I couldn't convert to laughter. When I had arguments with my first boyfriend, Tiffany would blast soap opera sound tracks from her room, so any time we paused we were left staring at each other while dramatic piano riffs played in the background. But sitting in the car, neither of us could think of anything to lift the dampened mood.

That night, lying on my sister's frameless mattress on the floor, the churning laundry machine in the background, I could finally rest. I was content to have earned this moment of peace. I pulled out my small red notebook. I illuminated the pages with my phone, and wrote, *I feel like I've already won.* It was a small nod to myself; I had done the impossible, showed up. Those who watched me cry on the stand might have perceived me as fragile, but I believed it to be the quiet beginning of my strength. I did what I'd never thought I could do, had somehow been spit out on the other side, still far from the finish line, but alive. Side by side, we went to sleep.

The next morning, I woke to the headline: WOMAN IN STANFORD SEXUAL-ASSAULT CASE TESTIFIES. I eagerly clicked on the link. Emily was described as giving *emotional testimony.* It was reported she and her sister *drank beers that three men gave them* before Emily woke up in the hospital. *Alaleh pressed Emily, asking her again if she remembered anything that happened in between those two events. Emily responded, "No," and started to cry. Cry* had never looked like such a tiny word, a drop of water. Everthing felt flattened out and simplified.

In one article, they mentioned my university, my boyfriend in Philly, and included Tiffany's name eight times. For them to have sat in the room with her, with me, and then so casually expose us, I could not understand.

Emily described her level of intoxication as "so drunk that I didn't think I was drunk." Looking at the transcripts I can count all the *Q*s: two hundred and twenty questions asked by my DA. One hundred and two asked by the defense. I sat and answered three hundred and twenty-two questions that morning, and this was the notable quote they had chosen. I scrolled down to the comment section: *I have young daughters and I hope they make good decisions in college and after.*

There would be no change in the tide. No reason for celebration. I felt punished for showing up. It was exhausting to be under constant review, the judgment I always feared confirmed. My pride dissolved quickly, made room for the voices that critiqued, scoffed. I knew now that I could do it. I also knew how much it would cost. If the goal was to heal, move on, this was not the way to proceed. Healing needed privacy, needed patience, needed nurturing. Healing required planting seeds in the soft, dark underground. Reporters arrived like shovels tearing into the earth, scooping seeds out, bare-skinned, back onto the surface. I was left on my knees in the dirt digging holes, placing the broken shells down deep, patting the soil with my hands. But there would always be more shovels, more disruptions, looming court dates. The more it happened, the less energy I had to keep digging; a deadening faith that something would grow.

That week I stopped speaking, stopped writing in my little red notebook. I slept for hours. I folded piles of Tiffany's clothes, hung her necklaces, tossed out old dried tubes of mascara, flattened crumpled paper. I would not allow the case to wipe us both out. I planned to go back to Philly, un-becoming Emily, so lonely in drab clothing, crying always crying, and returning to myself.

Alone at night, when I felt the weight of twenty sandbags on my chest, I would open the police report and read:

JONSSON caught up to TURNER and did a leg sweep and tripped TURNER. TURNER fell to the ground and tried to get up. JONSSON said it looked like he was trying to get up and run away again, so he tackled him to the ground. JONSSON straddled TURNER and held his arms down as ARNDT held his legs down. . . . He told TURNER he was not letting him up until he figured out what was going on and he wanted to make sure that VICTIM was ok.

I reminded myself this was not simply a fight between perpetrator and victim; there was a third element, the Swedes. They represented the seers, the doers, who chose to act and change the story.

It should be noted that several times throughout giving his statement, JONSSON became very upset, to the point where he began crying while recounting the incident. He had to stop and take several deep breaths before being able to resume giving me his statement. He said it was a very disturbing event for him to witness and be involved in, but he just reacted to the situation at hand without really thinking.

What we needed to raise in others was this instinct. The ability to recognize, in an instant, right from wrong. The clarity of mind to face it rather than ignore it. I learned that before they had chased Brock, they had checked on me. Masculinity is often defined by physicality, but that initial kneeling is as powerful as the leg sweep, the tackling. Masculinity is found in the vulnerability, the crying.

At the hearing, both Swedes had shown up to testify. I discovered that the night of the assault, they'd bolted him to the ground, and said: *What the fuck are you doing? She's unconscious.*

Do you think this is OK?

What are you smiling about?

Say sorry to her.

I do not attribute surviving to willpower or optimism because none of this I had. It would take weeks to recover, depression would take over. But that October, the Swedes had introduced this new voice inside me. I had to teach myself to talk like them. To one day face my attacker and say, What the fuck are you doing.

6.

LUCAS LIVED ON the sixteenth floor on Walnut Street in Center City, Philadelphia. I loved the stacked squares of gridded lights on every building. The warm steam that billowed up from grates in the street. The Italian delis encasing speckled sausage and pink meats, the butchers' smocks covered in rosy fingerprints. Soup with matzo balls as large as fists. Milky marble museum floors. Small bookstores. College students with wiry limbs running in jaunty packs by the river. Amish families selling wildflowers. When we walked together, Lucas pointed out the main streets, *Chestnut Street, Walnut Street, they should name a smaller street Cashew.* He introduced me to Big B, who sat with a chess set every day in the park, showed me his favorite place to get roast beef sandwiches. He gave a list of all the clubs at his school I could join, paraded me around to meet his friends. *He's acclimating me,* I thought, *he's telling me he wants me to stay.* I liked fantasizing about this becoming my home for the year, but I did not retain the names of the parks or the bus lines, feeling it pointless to get familiar with a world I would soon be ripped away from.

Winter break was approaching and Lucas talked about taking us someplace warm, Indonesia maybe. I told him to travel with his classmates, I couldn't leave until a court date was set, plus I needed to save my money. *If we go and have to come back, we'll come back,* he said. I imagined us on a moped along a dirt road beneath the mottled light of banana trees, receiving a notification the trial was back on, the warmth of the dream vanishing.

For a long time I told myself I was not allowed pleasure. I began calling all the things I'd hoped to do *sugar-cube ideas*. The court case was a pot of hot water that quickly dissolved all semblance of a regular life. During the month I'd been home, I'd applied for a few administrative jobs, but when they replied I was already in Philly.

It had almost been a year since the assault, but I found myself exactly where I'd started. An anniversary for a couple celebrates a year together, a birthday marks a year of growth. The anniversary of the assault marked a year of treading water. At the trial, we'd start all over again.

Trauma was refusing to adhere to any schedule, didn't seem to align itself with time. Some days it was distant as a star and other days it could wholly engulf me.

I'd expected the legal process to be composed of a back-to-back sequence of dramatic court scenes. Nobody had warned me about the waiting, the floating formless months in between, the way it demanded all of you, then none of you. It seemed impossible that in this year I had only spent a single day testifying in court, while around that day my life had disintegrated. It had taken me nine months to process, a few weeks to prepare, a day to testify, all this time to restore, and we had yet to get into the meat of it.

I finally received an update, but it was not one I was expecting. My advocate called to tell me she'd received a job as a counselor at a university and would be moving away. I would be assigned a new advocate, someone she trusted. She was calling to say good-bye, say she was proud of me, and would be rooting me on. After we hung up, I was hit by a moment of sadness, reminded that in life, people moved on. That's what you do, that's what was supposed to happen.

My DA was also reassigned to a new department. When she called to tell me this, my mind drifted away from the conversation, until I heard her say she'd asked to keep my case, to see it through to the end. I remained quiet, shaken by the idea that if she hadn't made it a point to stay with me, I would have been handed off to a new attorney, a new advocate.

Had they both left I imagine it would have been hard to keep myself committed. Why would I continue? At this point, who was I doing this for? Me? If this was for me, then why was I sitting on a bed alone, unemployed, in an unfamiliar city. We were fighting for closure, for justice. It was not for me, but at the expense of me, that we'd be able to get there.

Lucas bought the tickets for January 1, 2016. The idea of Indonesia still seemed abstract, too far away to grasp, but the ticket itself offered me a little hope. Even victims go to Indonesia. Victims have sun on their skin. He kept reminding me I was a person who deserved life.

Every morning, when Lucas left for class, I'd feel his lips briefly press into my forehead. Next I'd hear the click of the door, the signal that for the next eight to ten hours there would be silence. I would get up, stare at myself in the mirror while brushing my teeth for ten minutes, sit on the couch wrapped in a bedsheet, put my pants on, put them away again, and crawl back into bed. Occasionally I'd hear Lucas's roommate come in, use the kitchen sink, flip on the television. Even more reason to burrow deeper into bed, making no sound, erasing my existence. In the afternoons I would go up to the roof of the building to read, watching people on adjacent balconies take smoke breaks. Sometimes I would slip on clean clothes ten minutes before Lucas arrived home, to suggest I might have left the apartment, gone out, done something. But often this was not the case.

The lounging may have looked like laziness. But the days didn't feel like Sunday afternoons. The parts of my mind I'd left untouched for so long had been awoken; the jars I'd stored away in January uncapped, broken, contents released. I remembered all the days I'd spent in the office, counting down the hours until I could return to bed. Now I'd successfully rid myself of work, could lie in bed uninterrupted, but that freedom came with emptiness.

For one hour a week I saw my therapist, a contained realm where I could talk about what was on my mind. But outside that hour I preferred silence or easy conversation. If Lucas brought up the case, I grew agitated. *Why would you even ask me that?* I corralled all of our conversations into the realm of normal life; deciding where to go to dinner, if we should take a jog to the river. I wanted easy decisions, situations I could manage.

Every now and then, Claire Skyped me from France. My day was her night and she whispered, careful not to wake the kids she had tried so hard to put to sleep. She wore bright pink headphones in her windowless bedroom. I called her the little DJ in the dungeon. She told me about learning to drive a stick shift, a toddler's diarrhea that dripped into socks, the kids and their silk pajamas. I told her about my fear of lawyers, the relief of cool nights in Philly. If I was miserable, I told her I was miserable. She did not say, *Really?* Or, *I can't imagine. That must be hard. How unusual.* She just nodded, verified. Strangely it made me feel right on track. She too had visited these emotional landmarks. Even though she was thousands of miles away, it was a comfort having one person in the world fully aware of me, who still told me funny stories, who didn't treat me any differently.

One morning, lying in bed, I noticed a little clump of my hair in the carpet. Then I noticed one strand curled around the leg of the couch. I picked it up and it lead me to some dust on the floor, lining the baseboards of each wall. Soon I was on my knees with a roll of paper towels going over every inch of the apartment. The silverware drawer was rid of plastic sporks and soy sauce packets, the paper take-out menus alphabetized. I stuffed trash bags into the metal trash chute at the end of the hall, like Santa's sack down a chimney. This was all very satisfying. By the time Lucas came home, I was red faced and shimmering, and he was stunned, everything polished and citrus scented. *Wow, you didn't have to do that,* he said. *I did,* I said. It was the first anything I'd done in weeks.

The next day there were no dishes to wash, no counters to wipe. I had to make the dishes dirty. I'd grown up coming home to my mom sitting at the dinner table surrounded by twelve women making dumplings, their hands fluttering to produce mountainous piles of doughy delicacies. I never participated, just sat in my room as bowl after bowl was delivered while I did my homework. Now I walked to Chinatown and back again, my arms looped with plastic bags sprouting long green chives and pink ground pork sealed in plastic. Usually I avoided raw meat, unnerved by touching the wet insides of animals. But I was chopping the chives into tiny green circles, sprinkling them into the flesh, dipping my finger in water and tracing the crescent rim of each circular coaster of dough, plucking a morsel of meat to place in the center, sealing them into soft pouches. I didn't have a factory line of women, but I sat humming to myself, hunched over the counter, making over two hundred. My loneliness was turning into something edible, something nourishing, something good when dipped in chili pepper and soy sauce.

Having two mouths instead of just my own to feed was enough motivation. Every day, I would rip off a blank sheet of paper, write down a recipe, tuck it into my purse, go collect the required vegetables and meats and spices. It was over stir-fry that Lucas told me he was going to a rugby tournament for three days. *Just three days,* he said. *Three whole days?* I said, shifting the bell peppers around the pan. Seventy-two uninterrupted hours could bring me down quickly. I needed to be taken out of my own head. Coffee shops would not be enough.

I found a coupon online for a twenty-dollar haircut. On the day he left, I walked through a construction site up the stairs into a room with bamboo plants and plastic washing bins, a small statue of Buddha flanked by tangerines. *Just a trim*, I said, which is easier to say than, *I'm here because I need to talk to humans, I need you to gently touch my head.* I missed my mom's soft hands, the feeling of her care. My neck was craned back. The woman had black bangs and wore an orange apron. She cradled my head beneath a hot stream of water, my hair wet and heavy and full of lavender. I asked her questions about her life and each one of her answers pulled me a little up out of myself, her worries, her relationships, her pregnancy, her bunnies, one which happened to be named Tiffany. She guessed I was Thai, I said I was half Chinese. *I'm from California, yes the beach is nice, but the water's actually quite cold.* The day was saved.

Day two. I had never gotten my eyebrows done. Another tiny salon, mirrors bordered with plastic cherry blossoms, a small glittery fountain on the counter. I sat in a line of ladies in chairs along the wall. *Sorry for the wait.* No worries, I said. I meant it, I had nowhere to be. When it was my turn, I reclined into another woman's soft hands.

Day three. Fingernails, fifteen dollars. It was raining. I scanned the wall of colorful glass orbs, choosing orange. My large hand looked like a dead pancake held by the woman's nimble fingers. I was warm inside the glowing salon, the sidewalks dark and wet outside. The girl next to me was celebrating, had just gotten a job at Applebee's. *Everything's starting to go right,* she'd said.

Lucas returned, and my hair was smooth, my nails the color of traffic cones. I fell back into my self-made rhythms and routines. One afternoon, I was on the floor next to the laundry machine, trying to figure out which compartment I was supposed to pour the bleach into, when I paused. *What am I doing.*

I had become the little cleaner fish, he the whale. We both enjoyed and benefited from each other, but the difference was that he was a majestic creature in his element, and I was tiny as a minnow. He was getting a master's degree and I was picking lint out of the dryer.

Lucas had mentioned a comedy club on campus, run by his rugby teammate Vince. One evening as Lucas was going out the door, he invited me to join. At the first meeting, there were about fifteen guys and two women sitting at a round table. Everyone was pitching ideas, revising jokes about the pope's upcoming visit, cheese hoagies. The atmosphere was loose and forgiving. I sat in my black snow coat, wound up and silent, my chair slightly tucked behind his, observing.

After the second meeting, Lucas and I walked home across the bridge and ran into one of his rugby teammates. *Where you guys coming from?* he asked. *Comedy club,* Lucas said. *We might try out for the show,* I said. *Nice!* said the friend. *Wait, you?* He turned to me and cocked his head, as if I'd told him I was going to the moon. Instinctively I shrugged my shoulders, quickly adding a small shake of my head to sweep the idea away. And he nodded as if to say, right. It was subtle, but his toe had slid over the line. He had not been aware of my one rule: I decide what I am capable of. Whenever I am underestimated, I think, you mistake my quietness for weakness. If you can't imagine me on a stage, I'll get on one.

The next morning, I got out of bed as soon as Lucas left. I sat on the couch and wrote about everything I didn't understand about *B-school*, all the conversations I had quietly listened to. How I mistook Ali Baba for a character from Aladdin. How it turns out the guy in P. E. does not, in fact, teach physical education. How when Lucas asked me if I knew what microfinance was, I said, *Yes, tiny finance.* I contemplated my newly acquired role as a "partner," the label given to significant others. The way partners stared out the window like cats waiting for their owners to come home. I pointed out that what they considered a signing bonus was more than my actual salary. I detailed the ways I struggled to pronounce the Schuylkill River. I read it aloud to myself in the bathroom, laying each word down like a brick, until I memorized ten minutes of material.

On the day of the audition, I walked alone to campus, across the bridge, all the while speaking quietly to myself. Lucas had drawn me a little map. I arrived at Huntsman Hall an hour early, shutting myself inside a bathroom stall, reciting my routine. When it was time, I rode the escalators down, scanned the doors for the right room number. The two presidents of the club, Vince and Liz, sat with hands clasped. I closed the door, set my backpack on the floor. I spoke slowly from memory, watched their eyes enlarge at times, a laugh spilling here and there. Smiling wide, they said, *Thank you, we'll be in touch.* I nodded and left. *If I don't get it, it's okay,* I thought.

Two days later the email surfaced in my in-box. The lineup had been released. I scanned the names, the jumbles of letters, trying to locate mine. I found it at the bottom: I was one of two females among eight males, the only nonstudent, and they had saved my act for last. I was going to close. I remember inhaling and clenching my fists, making running motions with my feet, swiveling in my chair, and opening my mouth as if to tell someone, turning back to the screen remembering no one was there. *Look where they put me.* If they had given me the challenge to top off the show, they must believe I was going to succeed. My nerves shot up in flames, but for the first time in nine months, anxiety did not cause me to shrivel up and shut down. It fueled me to begin.

We rehearsed in the evenings at an apartment near the river. Some people arrived late from class or buttoned up in a tie coming from an interview. I was always early, freshly showered, my material prepared, my backpack empty except for my comedy notes; this was not my fun thing on the side. We took turns holding the TV remote as a microphone, butchering delivery, tweaking and repeating jokes until we'd memorized each other's sets. For a few hours in the night we lived in the world of the absurd, where every hardship translated into material. A small part of me waited for a tasteless rape joke to emerge, prepared to conceal a flinch, knowing I wouldn't voice discomfort for fear of becoming the sensitive one. But a rape joke never arrived. Instead we talked about hairless cats and told Vince it wasn't funny he saw a June bug in July.

One night, our meeting glided past midnight. We left as a group and shuffled through the cold, discussing the highlighted flops of the evening. At every intersection, one or two people peeled off to go home. It slowly occurred to me that I lived the farthest away. The group dwindled, my steps accompanied by fewer feet. I remembered a song at summer camp, singing as friends flapped their arms and flew away one by one, until I was left standing alone; *only one short neck buzzard, I said one short neck buzzard, sitting in a dead tree.*

I began planning; I would stop in the bright cone of a streetlight as soon as the last guy veered off. I would call Lucas to come and get me. But what if he was already sleeping? I would run. I looked to see if the rest of the street was well lit, if there were people around to be my witnesses. All the stores were closed. I scanned the sidewalks, evaluated which route to take to avoid cutting through the park. If I needed help, I could run to the CVS two streets over. There'd be people there. But I could already hear the questions: *What was she doing alone at night? Why didn't she just ask someone to accompany her? Where was she coming from? Comedy? Is she even funny? How many beers did she have? What are her jokes about? Where was her boyfriend? Is there a call log? What was she wearing?* The voices had amplified since the hearing, unfurling endlessly in my head, so maddening I didn't realize the final guy had stopped walking.

I'm that way, he said. *Are you sure you're going to be okay walking home? I can walk with you.* I looked at him, a little stunned; for a second I thought I may have been speaking out loud, my face contorted and exasperated without me realizing. I wondered if he was only asking out of politeness and really wanted to get home. But he stood patiently, shrugging his shoulders up in asking. *Happy to,* he said. And like that the voices dispersed, scuttling back into the shadows, and the two of us walked down a regular sidewalk on a regular street on a regular night in Philly.

There were many subtle moments like this where I paused to look the person in the eye in an attempt to say, *If only you knew how much this meant to me.* A small gesture, just remembering my name, or asking if I needed a little assistance, felt like warmth on my skin when I spent most of my time being numb. The custodian of my building, Anthony, was always refilling the hot cocoa machine on the fifth floor because he knew I drank two cups in the evenings. The Korean mother who worked at Sue's Market, oval bun and tiny round glasses, would look up and smile when I came in and say, *Hi, Chanel, everything okay? Haven't seen you in a few days.* And the three doorwomen, Alicia, Khadijah, Joda, who circulated at the front desk of my building, twenty-four hours a day. When it was quiet in the lobby, I'd ride the elevator down in my slippers with two coconut popsicles, to spend a couple of hours conversing. They were the ones always telling Lucas to take me to dinner or yelling at him if they saw me carrying too many groceries. I watched them stay calm when people accused them of mishandling food deliveries, blamed them for late packages, a drunk man telling one that he liked her hair better longer, why'd she have to cut it? I watched them respond in level tones, even when they had every right to be angry, their shoulders held back, a skill I took note of for my testimony. And finally there was the comedy crew, who made sure I got home safely in the evenings. These were the pockets of the world where I was regrowing. They called me Chanel, not Brock Turner's victim, not Lucas's girlfriend. Just Chanel.

The day of the show I was too nervous to eat, too deep inside my head to make conversation. I told everyone at Sue's Market and the employees in the building that I was performing at Helium Comedy Club and they wished me luck, asking me to record videos for them to watch. There would be two shows, at 7:00 P.M. and 10:00, hundreds of tickets sold out, a packed house. When deciding what to wear, I came across the oatmeal sweater I'd worn in court. I threw it on with a pair of jeans. I had spent all my time trying to bury Emily, to forget and repress her. Now I wanted to show myself that the one crying in court was the same one who would be funny onstage. Both existed in me.

The ten of us gathered in the cramped greenroom, looking like a ward of mental patients; muttering to ourselves, talking to the walls, huddled in the corners passionately whispering. We heard people filling the venue, the room humming. The time had finally come. Vince, the emcee, stepped through the door, the point of no return.

Every time someone went out onto the stage, the door closing behind them, we listened in quiet anticipation, knowing the exact moments the muffled laughter would rumble through the walls. Each person returned relieved, their shoulders relaxed, half laughing, as we greeted them with high fives.

I began to notice that each person who stepped onstage had been greeted by the giddy screams and barks of friends. Lucas was only going to be at the later show. Who would be calling my name? I had nobody. It was that feeling again, sitting alone on the stand. *Who was that girl they put last? She was so depressing.*

But then I saw the guy's face from that day on the bridge, looking at me dumbfounded. *Wait, you?* I saw the defense attorney, raising his eyebrows, jotting down my words. I saw the reporters looking bored in the courtroom. I saw the light filtering through the feathers of down blankets, all the hours spent beneath them, days so lonely I thought I could dissolve into nothing. I remembered the pain, acute in my chest.

Then I saw myself in the shower, my routine taped to the glass, memorizing my lines, animated speaking them. How hungry I'd been to get here. I could hear the final bits of the set before me. Applause. I heard my name announced and stepped out.

It was completely dark, the lights blaringly bright, and the smattering of applause trickled into silence. I looked out into the audience, a mass of black. In the quiet, my mind became clear. I was alone again in front of a microphone, but this time I spoke, and they listened, no objections. As I began talking, I heard my voice leading hundreds of people exactly where I wanted to take them, and all at once they erupted into laughter. My mind went briefly blank. I fought to remain deadpan, while I was smiling like a child inside. I had to wait for the noise to die down, but I was in no rush. I felt whole, standing on my own. It was like holding the room in my hands, I could turn and lift and drop them. For the next ten minutes, you are going to listen to me, and we are all going to be happy.

After the show, everyone dispersed into the audience to be congratulated by friends. I hesitated a moment in the back room, drinking water. *Just go,* I told myself. Tentatively I drifted out.

For many months I'd been greeted by professionals who spoke to me in quiet voices, with sympathetic eyes. People were always passing me tissues, patting me gently like I could easily break. Now as I moved through the crowd, I watched people's faces light up. I quickly became the Katniss Everdeen of the partners, swarmed by women and hailed as a leader. This time I was not pitied, but revered. *Wow, you were wow,* someone said. *I am wow,* I repeated in my head.

After the second show, I ran out to meet Lucas. He picked me up, turning me in circles. *I didn't even recognize you,* he said. I felt I'd been born anew, the timid self shed, the transformation witnessed by hundreds. I heard someone ask Lucas, *You're her boyfriend?*

My therapist once told me to *hold your wounded self.* When I finally left the crowd, I thought of her, felt she must be proud of me.

The next day when I woke, Lucas was already in class. The afternoon light was muted. As I lay in bed, it slowly dawned on me that I had no more comedy meetings, no rehearsals, no mantra to put on loop in my head. Auditions for the next show wouldn't be until spring. The whole thing felt like a dream. The previous night had been a seven-course dinner, and now I was staring at a blank plate, licking the crumbs. All at once the sadness hit me, like a well had been opened in my chest I remembered my reality, the one I was never going to escape, and dropped back into sleep.

I opened my eyes hours later to Lucas sitting on the bed, holding my shoulders, shaking me gently. His eyes were radiant. *Everybody is talking about you,* he said. *Do you know how many people came up to me on campus today? Look, look at these emails. I don't even know these people! Look what they said.* But I saw him register there was something deeply wrong, my eyes red, my mind having already been dragged under, and just as quickly he was pulling me into his chest, stroking my hair, rocking me, in an attempt to bring me back again.

The next day, I called my mom, no speaking, only crying, and she began telling me stories: When she was little and the Cultural Revolution began, libraries were closed, pages ripped from books and used as toilet paper. She would find individual pages, construct her own stories. She had watched her mom deliver babies in rural China, saw the young mothers who didn't make it. In university, she'd studied literature, became editor in chief of the campus magazine. She told me about her first job as a bartender in America, learning her first swear words, while locals called her Suzie Wong, a fictional character. How she met my dad at a New Year's party, they kissed at midnight, got married. How he taught her to drive. How they raised two daughters in a pink home with two Border collies. What may seem ordinary to me was never lost on her. There were a million ways things could have gone differently, but somehow she had made it here, the very fact of my existence some kind of miracle. When she was young, inventing stories, she never imagined a life full of swimming pools, daughters drinking iced coffee, California coastlines full of wild poppies.

When I listened to her, I understood: You have to hold out to see how your life unfolds, because it is most likely beyond what you can imagine. It is not a question of if you will survive this, but what beautiful things await you when you do. I had to believe her, because she was living proof. Then she said, *Good and bad things come from the universe holding hands. Wait for the good to come.*

As winter approached, I was grateful for dark red and yellow leaves plastered over wet, gray stones, for the rugby players who ate my tortilla soup, for the students who invited me to coffee. I joined the Storytellers club, went to drag shows, and chocolate-themed parties. I occupied myself writing stories, printing them on campus. Sometimes I went to class with Lucas and spent the hour drawing. But I could never lose the feeling that this was not my real life, that reality awaited me back in the courthouse. Mentally I always felt isolated, I just got to choose my surroundings.

Alaleh called, said the trial wouldn't be happening until *sometime next year.* Tiffany called me crying, *I can't do it.* I'd been assaulted during the winter quarter of her junior year. The trial would likely be in the spring of her senior year. Every quarter she had a heavier workload she couldn't afford to adjust if she wanted to graduate on time. The damage was unremitting.

One night, I'd gone alone to a Storytellers event, where a woman named Elizabeth spoke about a small team called Rise, a civil rights nonprofit, that was drafting the Sexual Assault Survivors' Bill of Rights, which included free forensic medical examinations and preservation of rape kits. I felt my heart sputtering, my skin clamming up. Afterward I approached her, my words tripping over themselves, the rape kits, so invasive, you wait for so long, the injustices. I talked nonstop like a faucet had opened, it was the first time I'd wanted to discuss any of it. She was receptive, excited. *You know so much about this.* I lied and said I used to work as an advocate, and excused myself. I was too nervous to get in touch with her again, worried I'd out myself, but for the first time I felt a new kind of hope.

Throughout the legal process, I felt like I was always trying to keep up, to not mess up, learn court jargon, pay attention, follow the rules. I wanted to fit in and prove I could do whatever was expected of me. It had never occurred to me that the system itself could be wrong, could be changed or improved. Victims could ask for more. We could be treated better. Which meant my onerous experiences were not useless, they were illuminating. Being inside the system would give me insight; the more I encountered issues, the more I'd be able to see what needed to be fixed. I could convert my pain into ideas, could begin brainstorming alternate futures for victims.

I was walking on campus when I saw the statistic on the front page of a newspaper: one in four women, one in five? I don't remember, it was just too many, too many women on campus had been sexually assaulted. But what got me was the graphic, rows of woman symbols, the kind you see on bathroom signs, across the entire page, all gray, with one in five inked red.

I saw these red figures breathing, a little hallucination. My whole life had warped below the weight of the assault, and if you took that damage and multiplied it by each red figure, the magnitude was staggering. Where were they? I looked around campus, girls walking with earmuffs, black leggings, teal backpacks. If our bodies were literally painted red, we'd have red bodies all over this quad. I wanted to shake the paper in people's faces. This was not normal. It was an epidemic, a crisis. How could you see this headline and keep walking? We'd deadened to the severity, too familiar a story. But this story was not old to me yet.

A word came to my mind, *another.* I remember, after learning of the third suicide at school, people shook their heads in resignation, *I can't believe there's been another.* The shock had dimmed. No longer a bang, but an ache. If kids getting killed by trains became normalized, anything could.

This was no longer a fight against my rapist, it was a fight to be humanized. I had to hold on to my story, figure out how to make myself heard. If I didn't break out, I'd become a statistic. Another red figure in a grid.

Our trip to Indonesia was approaching. It was December in Philadelphia, the cold air nibbling the rims of my ears while we walked, when Lucas brought up scuba diving. *I don't know how to scuba dive,* I said. *Neither do I,* he said. *We will soon.*

A week later I found myself standing at the edge of an indoor pool with a heavy tank on my back, murky goggles suctioned to my face, the air baked with the smell of chlorine. The number one rule of scuba diving was to breathe continuously. This sounded intuitive, but I remembered panic attacks where I felt I was sucking air through tangled straws, times breathing did not feel so simple. *Always remember to breathe.*

Before resurfacing, a diver must stop twenty feet below the surface for three minutes, in what's called a safety stop, to let your body decompress. Ascending too rapidly could cause bubbles to form in your blood, and I imagine a sort of painful champagne running through your veins, making you sick. After surfacing, you must wait forty-eight hours before flying, as the drop in air pressure could make your blood frothy enough to be fatal.

These rules were fascinating to me; the body dictating what you must do. I had fallen into the habit of neglecting my body, often forgetting to feed it, and when I was assaulted I refused even to look at it. Now my body was saying, you have to listen to me. You have to respect my needs. We have to work together or you will end up hurt.

The instructor showed us the octopus, a backup regulator on each pack that a diver's partner can breathe through in case of emergency. The instructor pointed to me. *Pretend you are out of air and signal to Lucas.* I nodded, and Lucas and I submerged. I sliced my hand back and forth across my throat, signaling, *I'm out, no more.* I removed my regulator and tapped my fingers to my mouth, showing I needed his air. In two wide strokes of his arms, he was next to me, offering the octopus attached to his pack, and I brought it to my mouth, my lungs expanding in relief as I inhaled. Simulation complete. We sat at the bottom of the pool, breathing from one metal lung. Suddenly my eyes were hot, blurred with a lining of tears. *This,* I thought, *is what the past months had felt like.*

It was early January when we arrived on a peanut-shaped island of Gili Trawangan in Indonesia. We sat floating on a long wooden boat, the sun licking our necks, smearing sunscreen on our cheeks. I stood up and strapped the belt of weights around my waist, perched on the edge of the boat, and threw my legs up into the air, tumbling backward into the ocean. Lucas dropped in beside me.

I slowly released air from my buoyancy control device, deflating my jetpack, gently slipping below the surface. My ears were popping as I descended, a sharp pulse in my eardrums, my goggles tightening. I told myself to be patient letting my body adjust, as I sunk lower and lower.

All became quiet. I opened my eyes and was hovering inside a room of luminescent blue, as if the sun had sat inside the ocean like a tea bag, diluting the water with soft light. I could no longer hear my thoughts, could only hear the sound of my breathing, like a calm wind filling my whole head. The giving, the taking, the coming, the going; my breath smoothing, as I floated in blue laced with golden light.

The fish appeared like confetti, pouring around me, darting freely. There were massive stones, glowing spaghetti anemone. Long, slender bodies of white-tipped sharks slunk close to the sand. The reeds swayed, long and lazy. I made way for a potato-shaped fish with large green lips, bumbling by in a hurry like he was late to a job interview. *Tink tink tink.* The instructor was tapping his oxygen tank with a metal stick to point out an eel wiggling its head, like it was in an argument and couldn't believe what you just said. *Tink tink tink.* A crab was combing his mustache. *Tink tink tink.* A little sleepy-eyed fish was munching on a spongy algae cake. I watched all of these creatures going about their daily lives, completely unaware of my existence. What a relief to feel so small, to go unnoticed in this wordless world.

Down here there was no snow, no hallways, no buildings, no cement, no shoes, no paperwork, no emails. No ringing, shouting, clicking of pens, beeping of machines. It all meant nothing. The whole world was muted, noise forgotten, save for the sound of my breathing. I felt I had melted into the water, nothing but a beating heart with two eyes.

I imagined the defense attorney bobbing in the water in his suit, glasses dripping, with a sunburned forehead, his tie undulating like seaweed, one polished shoe drifting slowly to the bottom. He'd be kicking wildly, while I stayed safe below, moving through constellations of pink and yellow fish, in silence. *You cannot touch me.*

I swam deeper. If a stressful thought emerged, I let it out with a long exhale, letting the fish gobble it up, released and dissolved. I was seventy feet down, the depth of six pools, one hour gliding by, then two. I left the pain, the kind that blinded me, that had me dreaming of sinking into nothingness, the kind that made me want to disappear. How could you want to leave the world if this is the world. All this beauty and strangeness. I felt it had been holding a secret, that just below the surface there were neon mountains, clams the size of bathtubs. All I had to do was equip myself to go deeper, to push past the initial pains, to teach myself to breathe.

When it's winter in one place it is summer in another. When I return to Palo Alto, to the pallid walls of courtrooms and legal documents and media headlines, hearing the echoes of heels on tiles, I would also hear the *tink tink tink*. I would remember that this world also exists, and that I can exist in it. This world is just as real as that one.

7.

I STARED THROUGH my oval window at the yellow carpeted hills of California, spotted with dark shrubs. I wished the plane was like a bus so I could miss my stop, could fall asleep and wake up in Honolulu. As we landed I watched the dotted trails of cars along the highway grow larger, the gray bay water expanding out below us, plane belly skimming the surface, until everything became detailed and loud and crisp, and I was small again.

I had arrived to fight the hardest battle of my life, but nobody in Palo Alto knew I was home. I pushed open my parents' door with a bump of my shoulder, my suitcase teetering over the door ledge, wheels slowing on the carpet, hanging my oatmeal sweater on a plastic hanger in the closet, placing my toothbrush in a ceramic boat.

I had yet to be told what day I would testify. I emailed my new advocate, Myers, whom I had never met. She wrote, *Jury selection will occur next week, starting 3/14 and likely ending by 3/16. There is the possibility that you will need to testify the 17th or the 18th, but most likely it will be the 21st or the 22nd.* How does one plan for this? Alaleh told me it would take as long as it needed to take, three weeks or more. How should I ration out my energy, how much was I expected to endure, what if I couldn't last? I felt I shouldn't be in the courthouse too long, the same way you shouldn't be in a garage with exhaust, brain cells being killed off.

Tiffany's winter-quarter finals would start the day jury selection began. After her last test, she would pack a small duffel and drive through the dark hills to spend her senior year spring break in court. Lucas would fly in the day before his testimony. After testifying, they would leave to begin their final spring quarter before graduation. I would stay behind awaiting the verdict.

Two weeks before trial there's something called a *trial readiness conference;* a meeting between judge, prosecutor, and defense to ensure they are ready. While this is happening, the victim is off somewhere, lying on her bed, peeling string cheese into limp shreds. No readiness conference exists for her; the witnesses do not gather into a room for a pep talk, putting hands into a pile, to yell out a team cheer. I was not allowed to attend other witnesses' testimonies, which meant that for the next few weeks I'd spend most days waiting aimlessly at home. I would later learn eighteen people testified, but I had no idea most of them existed. We were like horses, lined up in separate stalls with our blinders on, unaware of those in our periphery. When you heard the bang, felt the smack, you ran for your life.

I was nervous about not having enough people in the courtroom. Brock's parents and older brother and sister would be flying in, his rows of the courtroom stocked while my side remained sparse. *His grandmother will be there,* Alaleh had said. She delivered this like bad news. I was unaware the jury was going to be keeping some unspoken tally. Both Swedes would be testifying, along with Detective Mike Kim, Deputy Jeff Taylor, Deputy Braden Shaw, SART nurse Kristine Setterlund, Julia, Colleen, Tiffany, and Lucas. Any witnesses I had were not allowed to sit in the courtroom. Only Detective Kim would be allowed in my audience. My mom and Grandma Ann would come to watch my and Tiffany's testimonies. My dad would drive over when he could between work. Anne would come and sit through all eight hours every day, for as long as it took. She was the single constant in all the fluctuation; calm, sharp, a mother, a fighter.

When looking into my empty seats I'd have to remind myself there were plenty of people who cared for me. I wanted to explain that Chanel's social life was healthy and well populated, but it was lonely being Emily Doe, my world much smaller, a shrunken circle of confidants. I wondered how it happened that I was now spending more time with my rapist than my friends.

It was warm outside, white blossoms fell, reminding me of the white dots of paper that'd fall when you emptied your hole puncher. I wore my black down jacket, a sleeping bag that went down to my ankles, less for warmth, and more for insulation from everything else. One evening a few old friends from high school were getting tapas. I joined them wearing my floor-length snow parka, they poked fun, I didn't mind. I was careful to gently shift the conversation away from myself. If there's anything I've learned, it's how much you can get away with by saying *work*. It's almost concerning. *Why are you home? Work. It's been awhile since I've seen you. Work. We should get lunch next week. Can't,* I said, *work. You look tired. Work,* I said. *Totally,* they said, *I feel you.* What I wanted to say was *trial.* When they said, *How are you,* I wanted to say, *Terrified.* When one said, *You look tiny!* I wanted to say, *That's not always a good thing.* They walked away thinking we had caught up, while I held the quiet knowledge they knew nothing.

I grew worried I'd bump carts with someone I knew at the grocery store or cross paths on a jog. Very quickly my world was reduced to my room; the floral bedding I bought when I was sixteen, a ceiling fan that could only be turned on with a remote I'd lost long ago, my brown carpet, my desk coated in half-peeled stickers. I needed to clear my head.

One night, I slipped out of my house in old sneakers and a worn hoodie. I jogged down Alma, my feet carrying me miles down to the railroad tracks where the guard sat. I tucked myself out of the glowing circumference of a streetlamp, resting on the sidewalk, skin prickling with heat, my breathing heavy, elbows resting on my knees, out of his view. I panted and stared and watched and waited.

The guard stood up. The dots of light shielded by metal visors began blinking red. Two tall, thin vertical planks slowly lowered into horizontal position, blocking off oncoming cars. I heard a distant clanging, a clumsy chaotic bell, like a huge cow barreling down the tracks. The screaming of the horn shattered the air, the stabs of white light, the silver nose shooting into the intersection. An elongated silver body, belted with yellow windows, blurring and streaming into one strip of passengers' heads, tilted this way and that, reading or eyes closed, blinking by, head head head head head, then gone. Stillness. A residual, clumsy banging of pots and pans. The planks gave a tremble and a lurch, rising to point up toward the sky, to announce the performance was over. The guard made a note on a clipboard, took his seat in the plastic chair, and all at once the red lights shut off, the intersection dark and quiet again.

I sat, the hair on my head blown to the other side. Death had breathed on me, had rattled me back into being. In high school, death had become a classmate, a constant presence, returning to collect us from our short lives. I'd begun to see a black hole, a dark oval the size of a puddle, above each kid. Beneath that black hole, the color and texture and everydayness of life glowed. What I prayed was not that the black hole would disappear, but that all of us would have a chance to grow up beneath it first, to experience all the things people talked about in my dad's practice, marriage, divorce, heartbreak, mortgages, because all of that too was life.

There were times now when I felt like crawling into the hole. In bed some nights, I stared up at it hovering above me. Wouldn't it be easier? I took inventory: I was twenty-three, assaulted, unemployed, my only accomplishment being a nameless body in the local paper. When I thought of my future, I saw nothing. I wanted to stop.

But as I sat on the street, staring into the portal where kids had disappeared inside a cacophony of glowing red lights and bells, I told myself what I wished I could've told them: *You have to stay here.* I told myself this was just one point in the long life I owed myself to live before I was swallowed up. I knew that soon I'd be humiliated and torn open, feared the denigration that awaited me. But I also knew I would always choose the cold cement of the sidewalk, the finicky pulse of my heart, the sweat in the folds of my stomach, the thinned-out fleece hoodie that'd been through the wash too many times. I would always get up, turn around, and jog home, because it was the only thing I knew how to do.

Alaleh and I were back inside the empty courtroom. I stepped into my assigned box like a trained animal. I scanned the rows of padded seats, like a sad, small movie theater. Soon they'd be filled by my rapist's family. The court reporter who winked was not there. When I asked where she went, Alaleh responded that someone else was on duty, and I nodded to say of course, but swallowed the sadness that I'd lost one of my few supporters.

So much had changed in the last fifteen months, but in court, everything remained stagnant. Strange the way time did not move, but deepen. We had revisited that same night over and over again. Questions branched out into more questions, a root splitting.

This time I wondered what behavior was acceptable for a victim. What tone? She warned me not to get angry. I learned that if you're angry, you're defensive. If you're flat, you're apathetic. Too upbeat, you're suspect. If you weep, you're hysterical. Being too emotional made you unreliable. But being unemotional made you unaffected. How should I balance it all? *Calm,* I told myself. *Collected.* But during the hearing I'd lost control. What about when that happens? My DA reminded me that the jury understood what I was doing was hard. *Just be yourself,* she said. *Which self,* I wanted to reply.

She said the defense was going to confront me with theories, reminded me it was his job. If he tried to walk me in another direction, steer it back. I imagined myself a donkey, defense attorney dangling the carrot, don't follow the carrot. If you don't know an answer, just say you don't know it. Be honest. The preview was brief and bland; she never brought up graphic details or warned me about what evidence she would show me. Looking back I wonder if she'd been careful not to cook the emotions out of me too early, keeping them raw for the jury to see.

The only statement Brock had ever given was on the night he'd been arrested. That night he'd admitted to fingering me and denied running. He would be testifying for the first time. I expected Alaleh to say, *Don't worry about him.* His initial interview had been recorded, he could not unsay those things. But since then he'd learned I could not remember. So instead she said, *He's going to get to write the script.* I stared at her a moment, wanting to say that's not fair, what about the truth the whole truth, he can't just come in and say whatever he wants.

In the beginning, I thought this would be easy. The first time I was told Brock had hired a prominent, high-paid attorney I thought, *Oh, no.* And then I thought, *So?* Even he could not change the truth. The way I saw it, my side was going to convince the jury that the big yellow thing in the sky is the sun. His side had to convince the jury that it's an egg yolk. Even the most eminent attorney would not be able to change the fact that it is a massive blazing star, not a ludicrous floating egg. But I had yet to understand the system. If you pay enough money, if you say the right things, if you take enough time to weaken and dilute the truth, the sun could slowly begin to look like an egg. Not only was this possible, it happens all the time.

Walking out of the courtroom I noticed a piece of paper taped beside the door reading: PEOPLE OF THE STATE OF CALIFORNIA V. BROCK ALLEN TURNER. I thought, *What people? There are about three people in California who know I'm in here.* Strange that he was the one supposedly up against a large state, but I was the one who felt outnumbered. Alaleh handed me the stack of transcripts in a manila folder, now thick as a phone book. Every word I'd said in the last fifteen months had been recorded and typed up. I would be sitting on the stand with three other selves; the hospital, police station, and preliminary hearing selves. All four tellings had to align. She said I didn't have to memorize them word for word. *Know them,* she said. I understood that memorize is different than know; to know them meant to feel it in my bones. It was not a stack of papers, it was the night itself. I held its weight in both hands. You'd think this is when I'd start preparing; a montage would show me fervently flipping through pages, running through questions, sitting head-to-head with my DA. Instead you could see me rolling my red cart through Target, where I go to calm down, where the world is organized in aisles. Is it time for a new flavor of deodorant? I was squatting in the shampoo aisle, accidentally squirting shampoo onto the tip of my nose to get a whiff. Should I buy a new pan? Do I need a hat? I bought my parents a Swiffer, bought myself a magnolia-scented candle, cookie dough. I would eat half the package of uncooked dough before falling asleep. The trial would start on Monday, March 14, 2016.

MONDAY

All my life I had heard adults sigh about this *jury duty* business. Twelve people taken away from their own lives. Twelve people who would rather be anywhere else than in the courtroom. Twelve people who I needed more than anyone in the world. The vote would have to be unanimous. When I was told this I wondered if I had heard incorrectly; *did you mean to say anonymous?* The alternative seemed impossible. I would need all twelve of their votes to win. In the news articles I read, I had never found twelve positive comments in a row.

If a prospective juror had been sexually assaulted, she or he was immediately eliminated. I would later learn that when this question was asked, several women got up to leave. There would be no survivors in the jury.

My DA would later tell me women aren't preferred on juries of rape cases because they're likely to resist empathizing with the victim, insisting *there must be something wrong with her because that would never happen to me.* I thought of mothers who had commented, *My daughters would never . . .* which made me sad because comments like that did not make her daughter any safer, just ensured that if the daughter was raped, she'd likely have one less person to go to.

My friend Athena had just returned home to Palo Alto. We have been friends since sixth grade—she is Vietnamese American. After college she'd gone to work on a lettuce farm in Hawaii. I picked her up from the airport and she told me how it felt to sleep in a tent, to hitchhike to the ocean, to see clarity of the stars on the Big Island. We went over to my house. When the conversation floated off her island back to my little room, she asked me what I had been up to.

There was always a moment, right before telling someone, that felt like I was peering over the edge of a cliff into water. I was taking a few final breaths, swinging my arms, telling myself I could do it. As I told her about the rapist who swam, about the victim that was me, I was free-falling, preparing for impact. After graduation, we'd gone out to a bar with live music. Drowned in noise she told me she had been assaulted. *It happened early in college,* she yelled loud enough for me to hear.

I just haven't told many people. I just thought you should know. I said, *Are you kidding me. What an asshole.* At the time anger was the only thing I knew how to do, more than empathy, more than comfort, more than contemplation. Now I was sorry I hadn't known how to take better care of her. She leaned forward to wrap her arms around me, just like Claire had done, like she could see in an instant how my whole year had been. We stayed hugging on the floor. Falling and falling and suddenly caught. I said I needed her to come with me, and she said, *Tell me when.*

TUESDAY

Jury selection continued. No word from Alaleh. I'd still refused to touch the transcripts until I was insulated by the presence of Tiffany and Lucas. I got a haircut, just a trim. I took my car to Lozano's Car Wash, where there was free popcorn and lemonade and the meditation of watching my card glide through the soapy, moppy-headed beasts. I looked for jobs on Craigslist, wrote three sentences of a cover letter. I biked to get a burrito, drank from an expired coke can, sat wearing my helmet on a bench at the park. I took a photo of the burrito and posted it online. I received thirty-two likes. It was a joke with myself, playing tricks on the world. People believed I was enjoying my afternoon, when in reality I was about to face my rapist. How creepy it was that we could conceal these stories. How easy it was to pretend. The slivers we show, the mountains we hide.

Over dinner my dad told me he was proud of me. *I'm so proud of you, sweetie, truly proud.* When he said this I never responded, it never absorbed. I was almost irritated, dismissive of his unfounded comment. Proud of what? The large gap between his pride and my current reality embarrassed me. Didn't he see me in my pajamas, shuffling around the house? I got assaulted, there are no trophies for that. What dignity is there in being discarded half naked? I smiled, but said nothing.

WEDNESDAY

Final day of jury selection. Lucas would land in the evening. I arrived at the airport early, didn't mind looping. He trotted to the car, suit bag slung over his shoulder. He made quick circling motions with his fist, gesturing to roll down the window. He came to the driver's side to kiss me, and the traffic lady in the yellow-highlighted vest barked at us to keep moving. *Give me this one moment, lady.*

Usually I immediately relaxed into him, donning his large clothing, like a hermit crab tucked inside its new home. But I knew he would only be here for four days before he'd fly back to school. This time, I could not afford to make him my center.

Alaleh said she was relieved the first time she met Lucas. I wondered what that meant. I had a feeling my boyfriend would have to make Brock look like a downgrade rather than an upgrade. I imagined the back walls of the court parting, Lucas doing a light jog out in his suit, waving to a clapping audience. *Here we have a twenty-six-year-old attractive, employed businessman! In his spare time he enjoys woodworking, scuba diving, and rugby. He's taken her to Indonesia and they live in a high-rise in Pennsylvania. He plans to romance her by engaging in consensual intercourse.*

The spotlight would turn sharply, the cone of light encapsulating Brock. *He's just turned twenty and dreams of becoming an Olympian! She's never met him, but he swims faster than a fish and enjoys fireball whiskey. He plans to romance her in the great outdoors, on a bed of pine needles.* Then there'd be me, in a floral dress, smiling wide. *She's wild, compassionate, silly, but not the kind of girl who gives it up so easily! Or does she? Let's find out!* The trombones would be blaring, lights polka-dotting. *Now your host, the honorable judge!*

Over the year, Lucas had witnessed me screaming, dissociating, leaving the apartment, crying under the covers, in the shower, whenever the case was brought up. And each time, when my breathing finally stabilized, he would excuse himself to go on a run. It never mattered if it was nighttime or raining, I would watch him disappear into the dark, running. I thought him thick-skinned and was so consumed by my own emotions that I'd never paused to question how this had been affecting him. I wondered if there was something raw inside him too, a rage that made him sprint. That night, as I watched him get ready to testify the next morning, I was made still by the seriousness with which he polished his shoes, ironed his clothing, all playfulness evaporating.

THURSDAY

When I woke up, Lucas's hair was already combed, face clean shaven. He would testify today and I would testify tomorrow. I planned to drive him to the courtroom, go to Gap to buy business pants. Tiffany would arrive in the evening, and with both of them home, I would finally open the folder and study it all in one straight go. I understood that I should have been studying them sooner. But you can't do a little at a time, can't dip in and out of it each day. I did not possess the ability to control the surging overwhelm and agitation it brought up. To read a small part was to drop dye into water; you could never stop the dye from spreading, a whole day ruined. So I preferred to do it all at once.

I pulled on some jeans. I was looking for a sock. A chime: a text from Alaleh. *There may be some extra time left over, so be ready to come in.* I sunk slowly to the floor, panic ticking like a stovetop burner, about to ignite into flame. *I'm not ready. I don't have pants. I can't, how many hours do I have.* I raked my fingers along my scalp, *I have to wash my hair.* I began throwing clothes out of my drawers. I sat, cheeks wet, madly blinking, kicking my feet back and forth to peel off my jeans. All of this was escalating in my mind, calculating how long I had to get ready. If I testified today, nobody would be there for me, my advocate was scheduled to come tomorrow. *I'll be alone again, I can't.*

Lucas came in and saw me in my underwear kicking, clothes lumped like washed-up sea life across the floor. *What's going on,* he said. *I have to get ready,* I said. *I'm going today and I don't have any pants. This jacket is too wrinkled.* I was seven years old again, small and helpless, remembering school mornings, inconsolable, *I have nothing to wear.*

Tell her you'd prefer to go tomorrow, he said. I looked at him like he was crazy. *I can't,* I said. *There's a schedule. You don't know how this works. I have no control. Why aren't you helping me get ready. I need to study, I don't have enough time.* I was exasperated until I heard his voice, loud and firm, *No one can make you do anything. They can't do this without you. If they have to wait, they'll wait. You're in charge. Tell her you can't go until tomorrow.*

I sat with bare legs, wild hair. It hadn't even occurred to me to assert myself, to do anything other than blindly obey. I had been conditioned to accept every schedule change, every question asked, no matter how upsetting or personal or sudden. I had forgotten it was possible to have limits. I drafted a message: *Hi Alaleh. Hey Alaleh! Would it be okay if. I would feel more comfortable if. Hello hope all is well. I would like for my mom and my grandma to. Apologies. I will not be able to come today. Good morning. If it's all right I would like go tomorrow as planned.*

She said that would be fine; if it went too quickly she would try to stall. It was so simple, all I had to do was ask. *Better?* he said. *Better.* We had an hour until Lucas was scheduled to testify, so we drove to the Driftwood Deli on El Camino. I sat in the sun in my jeans and wrinkled jacket, crappy shoes, awash in relief. I had gotten my day back. I dropped him off at the courthouse, waiting until I saw him walk through the front doors before pulling away. He would text me when he was done.

I walked into Gap. *Anything I can help you with,* an employee said. *A lot,* I wanted to say. Three hours passed and I hadn't heard from Lucas. I purchased gray straight-leg pants, cheap black flats. Finally I got the text to pick him up. *How'd it go,* I asked. He said they hadn't even reached his cross-examination, they'd resume tomorrow. At the start of the day it was predicted there'd be extra time, when in reality, they'd run out of it. The testimonies before him had run longer than planned and he had been waiting in the victim closet for three hours. I felt awful nobody had been there with him. *It's hard to keep your adrenaline up,* he said. It was the first time I'd heard him admit to anything being hard. Tiffany came in late that night, sleep deprived after her final exams.

With everyone home, I was ready to submerge, to go back and meet the three selves. Memory is often perceived as the victim's weakness, but I believe memory is a victim's greatest strength. Trauma provides a special way of moving through time; years fall away in an instant, we can summon terrorizing feelings as if they are happening in the present. I spread my transcripts across the floor. My carpet was the equivalent of a rope tied around my waist as I lowered myself into the past. I was brushing the carpet gently with one hand. In all of these memories, there was no carpet. I could see long, wet clumps of hair enclosing my face as my head hung. I am at the rape clinic. The water filling my ears, smearing my vision, sealing my nose and running over my mouth. Outside, there is a highway, a steady stream of cars, one pulled over on the side of the road. It is my sister, heaving cries so hard she cannot see. She is trying to come get me. Carpet. I am in a plastic chair in the rape clinic, hair dripping wet. Tiffany is sitting next to me, frayed, upset. How do I make her feel better. Carpet. I am telling the police woman, please don't call my home. I do not ever want to see this man again. Carpet. I see the yellow curls of his head as he looks into his lap, I am crying, looking out into empty seats. Carpet.

I wiped my nose. Tears were drawing lines down my neck, slipping under my collar, down my chest. For five hours, my chest folded over my legs on the floor as I flipped through pages and typed. I laid out the framework, every minute of January 17, every sip, location, remark, observation, infiltrating my mind. Chaos was slowly giving way to order. On the front page I wrote encouragements: *Shut it down with truth.* I plugged up all the tiny holes in my memory. I ignored the gaping hole. This was not the time for self-pity, for dwelling, for second-guessing. Study it hard. Know the timeline. Go back to the carpet.

FRIDAY

Lucas woke up at sunrise to be grilled by the defense, while I was scheduled to testify at 1:30 P.M. I was supposed to drive him, but he kissed my forehead and told me to go back to sleep, so I rolled over into the warmth his body had left. Hours later I felt the sun soaking my bed, heard him come through the door, watched through squinted eyes as he peeled off his polished shoes. He crawled back into bed fully dressed and held me. I didn't ask him how it went. If it was bad, I didn't want to know yet.

I ran my arms through my oatmeal sweater, becoming Emily, hair clipped back on both sides. I hesitated with my mascara wand in hand, painted my lashes lightly. Pretty, but not too pretty. Makeup would turn my tears into dark blots, eyes dripping with ink. But going blank faced would make me look fatigued.

Lucas drove. I was mute, sitting on my hands, studying the printed guidelines in my lap. My appetite was nonexistent but I knew better than to leave my stomach empty. There was nowhere to park at the bagel shop, so he pulled over while I went inside. I located the glass display of beige circles. I forgot all the names of the bagels. She asked me what I wanted, I just pointed. I took a white paper bag, unsure if it was mine. I stared at all the strangers around me, separated inside their warm reality of conversation and coffee. I pushed out the door, shuffled back into my car of silence, my notes. The bagel was hard to swallow, dry and thick.

We pulled up to the courthouse. I folded down the small mirror to check for seeds in my teeth. *Are you sure there are none?* Lucas nodded. He and Tiffany would be waiting for me on the outside. A kiss on the cheek. I stepped out of the car and he was gone.

I wanted this scene to open with me striding down the halls, shoulders back and head lifted, but when I walked through the plastic security frame, I felt a bristling on my skin, something was wrong. I'd seen those guards before. I stared down the hallway. Empty. But I sensed the cluster of bodies above. I ducked into the first-floor bathroom, squatted in the corner of the handicapped stall, my papers rolled into a scroll, whispering to myself to hold it together. My DA texted me, *Are you here?* My hands were shaking, *On my way.*

I closed my eyes. I could see the inside of the courtroom, the judge like a floating bald head above a black trapezoid, the mediator of this game. Teams would be divided into two sides, obeying an unspoken rule never to cross over. I was mentally prepared, but my body braced for pain.

No amount of preparation could protect me from the erasure of self, the unbecoming. Even after I'd leave, I knew my mind would stay there a long time, depleted for weeks.

I let myself out of the bathroom, urgently pressed the elevator button. Alaleh slipped out of the courtroom to let me into the victim closet. She had to return to wrap up a couple of testimonies; the SART nurse was testifying before me. My heart lit up; the nurse, a protector in this game. I wondered which nurse it was; I remembered three of them huddled around the peaks of my naked knees. I liked to imagine them as a three-headed dragon in a white coat, snapping mouths and metal tools, fighting off anything that came after me.

My new advocate, Myers, stepped out of the elevator. She had perfect posture, neat hair, a level demeanor. I liked her immediately. Soon my mom arrived with Grandma Ann and Athena, *Hi, Chanoodle.* Anne was already inside. All of us were scooting our chairs around to fit. I could hear my grandma asking Myers where she was from, how long she'd been working at the YWCA, how she got into this field. I tuned out, flipping through my notes beginning to end. As soon as I finished, I went through them again. Every ten minutes I'd excuse myself to go to the bathroom, to pee one last time, to smooth my hair down, fix my clips, check and double-check that my pants were zipped. One hour went by.

I reminded myself it was simple; the jury would respond to authenticity, what is real. My advocate handed me a small ball covered in acorn patterns, my new toy to squeeze on the stand. Athena told me to envision a rose before me: all of the defense's bad energy would be absorbed into the rose instead of me, allowing me to sit and observe his words at a safe distance. My therapist had said, *Visualize women around you, behind you, touching your shoulder, walking with you.* I could even summon Maya Angelou if I wanted. Grandma Ann took out a bag of dark chocolate. She was also wearing a pin I'd given her of a tiny red wagon. When Tiffany and I were little, she'd pull us around the cul-de-sac in a red metal wagon. I recalled something else my therapist had told me: *Remember who you are, what you like about yourself.*

Any minute now, I thought, *stay ready.* Two hours passed, all of us crammed in the room, touching knees in our small circle of seating. I must have peed twelve times. Finally a knock. The room was cleared, everyone guided out by my advocate to get settled in their seats. I had a few minutes alone. This felt right. When I took the stand, I knew I would be on my own. If I needed help, I would have to turn inward. *Everything I need to get through this, I already have. Everything I need to know I already know. Everything I need to be, I already am.*

I set down my packet and stood in the silence with my eyes closed. For a moment, the fidgeting stopped, the nervousness simmering away. In the past year, snow had fallen and melted, my hair had been cut and grown, the world kept moving, and I could've continued to move on with it, yet I had returned. What did it mean, that I kept finding myself in this tiny room, abandoning an orderly life to keep fighting. Didn't this count for something?

I left the packet on the desk, stepped out, the door locking behind me. I walked down the hallway, rubbing my damp hands on my pants. Alaleh and Myers stood outside the courtroom doors. *Are you ready?* I nodded. *Tink tink tink. Breathe as you descend.* She pulled the door open. I clasped my hands together, inhaled once more, and walked through.

The fullness of the room made me shrink. Walking into coffee shops is anxiety inducing. Walking into court, everyone stared at me. I didn't look anyone in the face. What I sensed were shapes, the landscape of formless bodies filling the room along the sides and in the stands, a denser presence than I'd felt at the hearing. I kept my eyes on my feet and told myself to walk. *Get to your box.*

I could not tell you how many males or females, ethnicities, kinds of outfits were in the courtroom. Half the jury could've been wearing tiger face-paint and I wouldn't have noticed. It was my second time seeing the judge and I still couldn't tell you what he looked like, only knew the pale curve of his smooth head and his gown, a looming shadow in my periphery.

I heard, *Do you solemnly swear . . . nothing but the truth,* my hand floated up, *I do.* I tucked myself into my chair in the hollowed-out stand, fixed my eyes on Alaleh's. I was told to spell my name into the microphone. I worried I would jumble the letters, began slowly.

DA: Can you just do me one favor and try to pull the microphone a little bit closer to you? You've got a soft voice.

It was true. It's as if my throat was padded with insulation, my voice a notch above a whisper. Still I could hear each word drop into the silent room, swallowed by dozens of eyes and ears.

The first questions were always easy; born in Palo Alto, one sister, UCSB, majored in literature, height is five foot eight. I was doing okay. *How much do you weigh? I'm sorry to ask you that question.* It is the question no woman wants to be asked in front of a microphone. I worried that if I guessed a number too low they would think, *no chance.* My driver's license said 140, but I weighed 163 in college. *Probably 158,* I said. Later I realized I was much lighter, my wrists slimmed, my body never hungry, my pants had dropped two sizes. Whatever weight I'd been, I shouldn't have been ashamed to declare it; a rock weighs differently than a lion weighs differently than a pile of mangoes and none of it matters.

Okay. Now, I want to draw your attention to January—the weekend of January 17th and 18th of 2015. I took a deep breath, nodded, refocusing on what we'd come here to do. We started at Arastradero Preserve, then moved on to the taqueria, *which taqueria,* she asked. I had never looked up the name. *Minus one,* I thought. She asked me what I ordered, one taco. *Plus one.* Then we were off, the questioning brisk as skipping stones; which of my sister's friends had come over to my house prior to the party, if I knew them, how many times I'd seen them, what time we started drinking.

I talked about never going to parties with Tiffany because I felt more like her mom than her sister. I talked about Lucas, who was Lucas, when'd you meet, where is and was he living, how do you maintain your relationship, do you visit him, how would you describe your relationship. She asked if I'd ever been involved in Greek life, if I'd ever been a member of a sorority, no and no. Back to Stanford, where exactly was the party located, name your mode of transportation, exact time of arrival.

Me: There was a table by the door, and Julia, Tiffany, and I stood behind it, like a panel, and decided to be a welcoming committee. We were just singing songs and acting really goofy. I was embarrassing my sister but definitely not trying to impress anybody.

DA: How were you embarrassing your sister?

Me: Singing out loud and dancing funny.

DA: Okay. And could you tell if your sister was getting embarrassed?

Me: Yeah. She laughed in spite of herself.

I heard the jury lighten, not so much laugh, just blow air out of their noses in amusement. I was smiling, I always smiled when I talked about my sister, even when boxed in by a witness stand. I felt myself loosening up, questions tedious but harmless, what brand of vodka, into what cup, was it a free pour.

DA: When you were dancing, how were you dancing?

Me: Ridiculous. The opposite of sensual. . . . Arms flailing, very wiggly.

I could already see it in the news, victim reported to be *very wiggly.* I talked about going outside to pee.

DA: Okay. And I know this is kind of graphic, but did you guys just squat behind a tree? . . . Did you guys shield each other from view of the people from the outside?

I tried to make it clear that even when I peed I'd done it discreetly. A woman who peed outside would be judged differently than a man who peed outside. She asked if it had been near a basketball court. I'd never been back to the scene. Maybe it would have served me to visit, but I could never get myself to go. *I do not recall,* I said. *It was very dark.* Back to the patio, seeing Caucasian guys who were shorter than me. The diluted beer I gave Tiffany, the guys shotgunning beers.

DA: *Have you ever shotgunned a beer?*

Me: *I can't.*

DA: *Why can't you?*

Me: *Because it's hard.*

A small chuckle. They could hear my honesty. By now about two hundred questions had gone by, reporters scribbling away in the back row. I admitted to not knowing a few of them, but had missed nothing too egregious. She asked about my next memory. *I woke up in the hospital,* I said.

It happened before I knew it was happening. My eyes went blurry, my breathing suddenly choppy, I couldn't speak, couldn't see.

DA: *Do you have any memory before that?*

Me: *(Witness did not respond audibly.)*

Tears were coming out of my eyes, out of my nose, I was worried they would somehow leak out of my ears, my mouth. Everything warm and wet and slimy, my inhaling erratic. I was mortified, as if I was soiling myself, everyone watching me wipe my face, I just needed a moment. I heard his voice.

Defense: *I'm sorry. Could we get a verbal answer?*

I had already forgotten the question, something about memory, did I have memory.

Me: *No.*

Defense: *Thank you.*

DA: *Do you need a moment?*

Me: *I'm okay.*

DA: *There are some tissues right there.*

I wanted to stuff the tissues into my mouth and nostrils, clog up all the holes in my face. Wanted to drag my hands down my cheeks and smear off my features. Alaleh tried to keep things moving, I could detect the defense's irritation. Get ahold of yourself.

DA: When you woke up in the hospital, can you tell us—do you have any idea what time it was?

I was awakening inside that feeling again, my mind trapped in that white hallway. I stared out, trying to come back to the present, seeing suits around me, tasting snot, my tongue cleaning my upper lip, salty.

DA: How were you feeling when you woke up, your physical feelings?

I was sputtering breath and wetness, suddenly found it impossible to craft a single smooth sentence.

Me: And then the—I saw the dean of students and the deputy, and they asked me—

Defense: Objection. Hearsay.

I was struck silent.

DA: It's not coming in for the truth, Your Honor. It's coming in for her state of mind and her level of understanding where she was.

Judge: All right. I'll allow the—the—question asked.

DA: When you say "they," can you specify who asked you?

Me: Sure. The deputy and the dean of students were speaking to me and asked me who I was and asked me if I could give them a number for them to contact. They told me, "I have reason to believe" that I had been sexually assaulted.

Defense: Objection. Move to strike. Hearsay.

I was suddenly aware of the defense's palm wrapped firmly across the top of my head, holding me underwater, saying, *Don't you come up.* Perhaps he'd realized this was the most agonizing portion, wanted to silence me before the jury could hear it. I told myself kick, you must kick hard.

Me: I had to use the restroom. . . . And they said that I had to wait because they might need to collect a urine sample. And that's when I—I—that sounded serious to me, because I still didn't—I thought they were—

Defense: Objection. Hearsay. This is a narrative as well.

DA: So when you indicated that you wanted to use the restroom, were you allowed to use the restroom?

Me: Eventually, but first denied because they might have to collect my urine sample.

Defense: Objection. Move to strike. Personal knowledge.

Judge: All right. I'll strike everything after "Eventually."

Personal knowledge? Isn't everything personal knowledge? My memory was being flicked on and off like a light. She's wrong, shut up, hurry up, stop talking, so stricken, keep going, narrative, objection. I couldn't get oriented. The interruptions felt like being hit.

DA: Other than being confused about where you were, what were you confused about?

I lost it, throwing open my arms, pleading, *I didn't know where my sister was. I didn't know where I was. I didn't know what they were talking about. I didn't know anything. There was no explanation. And they tell me, and I thought, "You have the wrong person." I thought they must be confused. I thought, "I just want to find my sister and go home."* I let go, emptying my lungs into the grape-sized microphone. Guttural sounds crawled out of my throat, long and loud. I didn't collect myself, didn't take my little sip of water, didn't daintily dab at the tips of my eyes, didn't say *I'm okay,* just decided, you will wait for as long as it takes. This is it, everybody. Here it is, you did it.

Not a single person in the room knew what to do with this unhinged wailing. But I had finally come out of the end of an answer without interruption. I felt manic, it was intoxicating, everyone forced to swallow my siren sounds. *Calm, collected, centered, strong,* bullshit, I abandoned all of it, had no intention of stopping, had lost the little voice that told me to reel it in, could only think release, release, release.

I heard my DA say, *Your Honor, can we take a break please?*

I know what that meant, the bathroom, my favorite place, escape! I

stood up, a fragile shell, following Myers down the aisle, cries sputtering out of my chest. A wave of humiliation passed over me as I brushed
by my row of loved ones, wishing they'd never seen this. I tucked my
face in the cave of my hands as she led me out the dark wooden doors.

At last, my tranquil refuge. I was calmed by the salmon-colored
tiles, the old toilets. I was grateful for Myers, who stood by the door, my
guardian. Part of me wanted to pull out a small white flag and toss it
through the courtroom doors. I felt spineless, depleted. My face looked
like it had been rubbed in poison ivy and Vaseline, shining, smeared,
patchily red. The metal sink creaked as I turned on the faucet, holding
the brown paper towel under the cold water. I rubbed it beneath my
bloated eyes, smelled the earthy pulp. I rinsed my mouth, draining my
head of mucus, spitting, blowing my nose. Looking in the mirror, a
small laugh tumbled out of me.

I realized this was it, rock bottom, I was touching the bottom. It
could not get any worse. I was standing in a ratty bathroom with single-
ply toilet paper in the middle of my rape trial. My dignity had diminished, my composure gone to shit. Everything I feared would happen
happened, was happening. Now there was nothing to do but slowly
crawl back out. When Myers opened the door, the compass in my body
led me back to my seat.

*DA: So, Chanel, just before our short break, I was talking to you about
waking up in the hospital. Do you remember?*

Each time, I could see myself sleeping on the gurney. Present me did
not want to wake her up and tell her what happened. I could see myself
lifting up my loosely bandaged hands, blinking and looking around. I
wished to approach her and say, *good morning, go back to sleep.* I'd quietly
roll the gurney back into the ambulance, we'd speed in reverse. I'd be
asleep again in the bumpy vehicle, delivered by paramedics back onto the
ground. Brock's hand would slide out of me, my underwear shimmying

back up my legs, my bra tucking over my breast, my hair smoothing out, the pine needles swimming back into the ground. I'd walk backward into the party, standing alone, my sister returning to find me. Outside the Swedes would bike past to wherever they were going. The world would continue, another Saturday evening.

But as much as I wanted this scenario, there was always the unsolved problem: Brock. I was out of his hands, but if he didn't get what he wanted at that party, then he would at the next. We are taught assault is likely to occur, but if you dressed modestly, you'd lower the chances of it being you. But this would never eradicate the issue, only redirecting the assailant to another unsuspecting victim, off-loading the violence. I never wanted to see him again, but I'd rather have him watch me wipe mucus onto my sleeve than roam free. One small victory.

I got all the way to the part where my underwear was missing and another organ seemed to burst in me like a water balloon. I surprised myself with how much water my face produced. I described being given a blanket, falling asleep. I worried that the fact that I had slipped so quickly to sleep that night undermined the shock I had felt.

DA: And I'm going to show you a couple photos at this point and ask you if you recognize them. I'm showing you People's 15, 16, and 17. . . . Chanel, I'd like you to take a look at People's 15. Tell me if you recognize that photo.

I was unaware there had been photos of me unconscious at the hospital. Now being pushed across my podium was my head, my brown scalp threaded with long auburn pine needles in a room I'd never seen. My stomach seized. It's me, that's me. I felt cutting pains in my stomach, put these away.

DA: What's—what's People's 15 depict?

Me: My hair.

DA: And when you went to the bathroom and realized there [were] pine needles in the hair—in your hair, does People's 15 depict what you were describing to us?

I was transfixed, my lower jaw shaking so hard my teeth felt like they'd tumble out. What other pictures did they have?

DA: I'm going to show you People's 16, and you can tell me if you recognize People's 16.

Me: Yes.

DA: And what are you—what is it?

Me: My head and my hair.

DA: Do you have any memory of being in that position in the hospital?

Me: No. I didn't know there were photographs.

DA: Have you ever seen these photos before?

Me: No.

DA: Just so the jury can see that picture, Chanel, I'm going to publish the exhibits again.

Before I could say anything, she turned, walking toward the projector, the large screen against the left wall. I stared straight ahead at my family, tried to lock eyes to warn them, *Don't look at it, just look at me, look at me,* but I watched their gaze follow her, heads turning in unison as if magnetized by her heel clicks. *This is People's 15. Is that you, Chanel?* I turned to my left, and there was my head, a brown planet filling the room, strapped to some sort of backboard.

I watched my mom cover her mouth with her hands. I wanted to whisper "Mom" into the microphone, but everyone would hear. I looked around, everyone's gaze fixed on the photo. My eyes became hot, my head pulsed thinking *can somebody cover her eyes please.* I wanted to say, *That's not me, me is right here, sitting in front of you.* I clenched my hands, flexed my feet, trapped in my stand with no power to stop what was happening.

DA: Is that you, Chanel?

Yes, I said.

When my DA returned to the stand, my anger had drained, my tears dried up. I sat detached in some strange, sad resignation. The defense could've screamed at me and I would've sat mutely. Brock could've thrown his water in my face and I wouldn't have moved. I thought I could protect my family, tried to hide the damage. But I had failed. This is all I am to everyone here and nothing more. It did not matter what questions followed. I did not care about the outcome, about impressing a jury. I didn't believe in the rose, could not summon Maya Angelou. All I could think was *home,* I was ready to go home.

She asked me to describe the SART exam. *Invasive,* I said. My voice was flat as I talked through the spread legs, metal needles, red Q-tips propped in a row. The gruesomeness no longer scared me. I had nothing left to hide.

She showed me the picture I had seen at the hearing, of my under-wear at the scene. *Do you have any recollection of being in this area where your cell phone and underwear is: this shrubbery and pine needles?*

Me: No.

DA: Did you ever willingly go with anyone to an area like that?

Me: No.

Defense: She has no memory. She can't testify about—

DA: Your Honor—

Defense:—personal knowledge. Objection.

Judge: Overruled.

DA: Thank you.

Me: I would never want to go somewhere where my—

Judge: The—there's no question pending. So next question.

I finished the answer in my head: *where my sister couldn't find me.* It didn't matter, what I said or couldn't say.

DA: Now, that night, when you went out to Stanford, did you have any intention of meeting anybody?

I felt a flicker, a kick, a branch emerging in the stream to grab on to.

Me: No.

DA: Did you have any intention of hooking up with anybody?

In my head I always go back. Many times I have tried to envision the moment he had me on the ground, and every time I imagine my eyes bursting open, blaring. My body coming to life below him, twisting, pushing him off me. Crawling on top, rising above, swinging my arms back and slamming them into his chest, my knee digging into his crotch like a battering ram, eliciting a cry, a whine, his harsh exhaling. I imagine leaning over his face, using my thumb and index fingers to peel his eyes open, dirt sprinkling into the wet pink slivers below his blue pupils, saying look at me and tell me I *enjoy this*. You think I am soft, you thought this was easy. I'd shove my palm into the center of his face, blood leaking from his nose, wetting my wrists. I would get up, land a final stomp between his legs, and walk away.

DA: Did you have any intention of kissing the defendant?

I looked up at Brock, his eyes already on me. I stared back. The thing about victims is that they wake up. Maybe you thought I'd never be able to go through with this. Maybe you thought, *She has no memory,* but I will never let you forget.

DA: Did you have any interest in him at all?

I wanted to climb onto my stand with a large red paintbrush, to paint *NO* across the back wall of the courtroom in long red strokes, each letter twenty feet tall. I wanted a banner to unfurl from the ceiling releasing crimson balloons. I want everyone's shirts lifted, *N*s and *O*s painted across hairy stomachs, NONONONONO, doing the wave. I wanted to say, *Ask me again.* Ask me a million times and that will always be my answer. No is the beginning and end of this story. I may not know how many yards away from the house I peed, or what I'd eaten earlier on that January day. But I will always know this answer. I was finally answering the question he'd never bothered to ask.

Me: No.

DA: I have nothing further.

Judge: All right. We are going to take our recess.

I felt my surge of adrenaline wash away, tired to my bones. It was time for the cross-examination, but I didn't want to speak. I needed fresh air, to sit beneath a tree, get out of this building. My DA informed me that it was already four o'clock, we'd run out of time. A miracle. I was free to go, we would resume on Monday. I collected the wad of tissues on my stand, flew out the door, returned the acorn ball to my advocate, gave her a hug, *Have a good weekend, see you Monday.*

I stood alone in the parking lot with a young deputy, still shaken. Where was Lucas, Tiffany. It was overcast, everything gray, no shadows. I made no effort to engage in small talk, feeling rattled and light, too tired to make a show of politeness. My phone dinged. *We're waiting for you by the courtroom, at the pizza place.* I said good-bye to the deputy and walked away. He insisted on escorting me, walking briskly to keep in step. He asked how I was doing. I told him I was nervous about Monday, the defense attorney. He said, *Don't worry about him, he's an asshole.* His honesty surprised me. I'd grown accustomed to everyone's formalities. When he saw me laugh, he smiled too. *You can take him,* he said. *You'll be okay.*

I turned into the doorway, saw Lucas and Tiffany in crewneck sweaters, a hot pizza between them, beaming, *You're alive!* I rested my head on the table, my cheek pressed against the cool wood. Their arms enfolded me, relief. My sister was rubbing my back, tucking the hairs away from my face. I was starved, began feeding one warm slice after the other into my mouth. I closed my eyes, tasted melted cheese, crunchy pieces of olive and onion. Cold sips of coke, crunchy blocks of crust. Lucas surprised me with a bag of gummy worms, made one worm dance and peck me on my cheek. I was safe, growing sleepy. They had carved out a warm place to collapse into, without having to ask or explain anything. I felt fear dissolving, the world a gentle place again.

When night fell, my mom insisted we use the sparklers left over from Chinese New Year. I said I was too tired, didn't feel like it. But she insisted we use them that night, like they were bananas on the brink of rotting. The sky was black. The sparklers were ignited, flurries of crackling light. My dad had a sparkler in each hand, standing on the diving board, waving his arms, wildly conducting. Lucas was chasing my mom, who ran in slippers around the pool, shooting nonsensical spells at the plants, the small yellow flowers, the oval towers of cactus. I was running through the house to get Tiffany, telling her to come out because our parents had gone nuts. My mom gave me the last sparkler. I was watching the sizzling light crack and sputter down the stick. In its final glow my mom said, *To the new year, new beginnings, to all of us healthy, all of us happy, all of us together, may the future be bright!* A small prayer, a new year ceremony in March, five sparks of light in the moonless night.

Lucas flew back to school. I spent the weekend distracting myself with banal tasks, but there was something I could not shake. The thing is I feel embarrassed on an airplane when I wake up and realize I've been sleeping with my mouth open. I was slow to realize how many men had seen me naked that night. I counted: Peter (1), who chased Brock (2), Carl (3), who squatted beside me. Guys from the fraternity (4, 5, 6, 7), who called the police. One guy (8) had been seen standing and shining a light over my body, before fleeing the scene. Deputy Taylor (9) was dispatched, a guy (10) led him to me. Next came Deputy Sheriff Braden Shaw (11), partner Eric Adams (12). Followed by paramedic Shaohsuan Steven Fanchiang (13), his partner Adam King (14), pinching my fingernails until I briefly opened my eyes, responding to the pain before slipping back out. The whole time I was lying there, left nipple out, ass bare, stomach skin folded, while polished shoes stepped on mulch around me. The deputies were crouching, taking notes, *entire buttock visible, left breast was exposed, clothes all messed up in a various array, bra area completely a mess.* I was photographed on the ground. These photographs, included the ones at the hospital, would be put up on the projector for everyone in the courtroom to see. Here I lose count.

I dreaded Monday's cross-examination. I remembered a night in college when my drunk guy friend dragged a cinder block all the way home. When asked why, he said, *Because I needed a doorstop!* We laughed because it made no sense, but in his world it seemed like the perfect idea at the time. Imagine presenting this in court. *Well don't you find a cinder block a little unreasonable? Why wouldn't you choose something lighter? Or get an actual doorstop, small and rubber? Approximately where was the cinder block located when you found it? Did you steal it? How drunk did you feel when you found it? Do you sleep with your door open or closed? What's your motive for propping it open?*

The first time I watched *Grease* I was nine, I loved Sandy, in her peach-colored skirt and silky ponytail. The entire movie was going smoothly until the final scene. Suddenly this woman in black leather pants and purple-lidded eyes emerged and I was in a panic thinking, *Where did Sandy go? Is she okay? She must have transferred schools. Does she know John Travolta is cheating on her with this huge-haired tobacco-smoking woman? Why is no one else worried?* I was watching the group of friends running through the carnival, while Sandy was nowhere to be found, and I was devastated. This is why, for so many years of my young life, I hated *Grease*.

It took me years to realize I was seeing two sides of the same person. At the time it seemed inconceivable. They looked and acted nothing alike; how were we expected to recognize one in the other? How do laced-up white sneakers become black heels snuffing out cigarette butts? Now the defense would be creating a new persona; the version he would show the jury would be someone I'd never seen.

MONDAY, WEEK TWO

Everyone was back in place, as if we'd never left. Before the cross-examination began, my DA had me stand in my new blue blouse with a red marker in my hand at the front of the courtroom, a large white pad of paper behind me. I had the urge to draw, wanted the jury to yell out objects and animals I could bring to life before them, to give them a glimpse of my real self before turning back into Emily.

On the paper was a timeline that looked like a vertical spine, marked up in green and blue notes from those who'd testified before me. My DA instructed me to write in the times I had tried to call Julia and Tiffany. I hesitated, reluctant to turn my back to everyone as I wrote. So I backed up, shoulder to shoulder with the white pad, awkwardly curling my wrist to mark the paper with the times I'd remembered from my call log. My red numbers came out crooked, squeezed in between other time stamps. She had no further questions. I took my seat.

The defense attorney stood up without raising his eyes from his notepad. He was a compact, rigid man. There was no greeting, no good morning, no smile. *Chanel, with regard to the testimony you've just given this morning as to those screenshots and—and what you saw on your phone the next day, not only do you not remember any conversation, you don't remember making any of those calls, correct?*

I flinched, my red marker lines wiped away in one stroke. He was staring at his notepad like it was my résumé and this was a job interview, wondering why I thought I was qualified enough to show up.

Do you have any idea what time it was when your last memory at the Kappa Alpha house occurred when you were standing on the patio with your sister?

I stated a time.

You don't have any way to know what the time is. That's your best estimate, right?

I already felt I knew less than I originally thought.

Now, you testified—at the beginning of your testimony Friday, you gave us your height and weight. Were those numbers that you gave us what your height and weight was on January 17th, 2015?

My mind went blank. I didn't know what I weighed on January 17.

At one point in your testimony, you said—about the possible plan of going to the KA house—you said something about going with your sister, but you felt more like her mom than her sister. What do you—what do you mean by that?

Had I been wrong to say that? He sounded irritated, as if he had a hundred people in line behind me waiting to talk to him. He asked if I'd been dropped off that night at the Tresidder Memorial Union parking lot. I'd never heard this name, had only thought of it as an area of asphalt.

It was the parking lot by the Stanford bookstore, I said.

Is that behind the bookstore or in front of the bookstore?

But the answer was neither; it was the lot adjacent to the bookstore, which was in the center of campus. How to explain this. He asked me what the closest building was to where I was dropped off. But I didn't know any names of the nearby buildings on campus.

Defense: You also talked about, fairly shortly after you got to the Kappa Alpha house, pretending to welcome people and singing and embarrassing your sister. That's what you decided to do at that time, right? That was an intentional thing.

Me: Intentional to welcome people or to be silly?

Defense: To be silly.

Me: Yes.

Was that bad? Was silly bad?

Defense: Okay. And it would be the same thing when you drank the quantity of vodka in the red cup. You drank it all down at once, right? Like, chugged it.

Me: Yes.

Defense: Okay. And that was a decision you made, right?

I cast my eyes down, aware this was a bad decision.

Defense: And you did a lot of partying in college, right?

He read this off his notes like an accusation, not a question.

Me: I did a decent amount. I would not consider myself a party animal.

Defense: Well, you did tell the police when you were interviewed that you did a lot of partying there too, right?

Which police? Detective Kim? Did I say that?

Me: Sure. I—

Defense: Okay.

Me: I'm a social person.

Defense: And all—

I was being trampled. My DA intervened.

DA: Your Honor, I would ask they not talk over each other—

Judge: Yes.

DA:—and allow her to explain her answer completely.

Judge: Let's—let's go one at a time. Next question.

Defense: Okay. And you've had blackouts before, right?

I wondered where he was taking me.

Defense: And when you've had them before, it was usually at the end of the night, right?

Me: Or fragmented parts of my night that I do not remember—

Defense: And—

Me:—not necessarily at the end.

This was a game of speed, stepping stones disappearing beneath my feet. I could not move as quickly, but I was determined to keep up.

Defense: Well, when you were interviewed by the police, you told Detective—or Officer DeVlugt that it's usually at the end of the night when the blackout happens, right?

The name DeVlugt didn't bring a face to mind, was she the deputy with long hair? I watched his eyebrows lift, heard his loud exhales, angry when I took too long.

Me: Right. Yes. But then I'll remember other parts.

Defense: Okay. During that same period of time, do you recall ever hearing your phone ring, as if somebody were attempting to contact you?

Me: I think I had silenced it because I don't like the clicking sound it makes when I take photos, and I was taking photos.

Defense: Do you have a specific memory of silencing it that night?

Me: I silence it often. It's very easy to do if it's a slide that can let you just slide.

Defense: I understand, but that's not the answer I need for my question.

He set his legal pad down, his arms now bent at the hip. He cocked his head, wearing an expression of bewilderment. I did something wrong. Everything in me registered alarm, my body tensing as if watching a snake begin to coil. He was visibly upset. Were we still talking about the phone?

Defense: The question is: That night, do you have any specific recollection of having done that, silence it?

Me: I'm telling you, I always silence it, especially when I'm taking photos.

He dropped his arms, shaking his head, began hastily flipping through pages.

Defense: All right. Do you remember testifying in the preliminary examination in this case in October? You were asked this question—Counsel, this is page 50, lines 10 to 21. You were asked this question: "That night, while you were at the party and you had your cell phone in your possession, it was set so that if it rang, you would hear it. It was an audible ring, correct? Answer: I believe it was set so that it could ring. Sometimes I turn it off because, if I'm taking a lot of pictures, I don't like the sound it makes every time it takes a picture. So I set it on silent. I believe it was auto. It was also loud." That was what you said at that time, isn't that correct?

Defeated, by my own words. Humiliation. I didn't study hard

enough. I had failed to anticipate the way he could make me my own enemy. The way he could step back and say, I'm not accusing you, I'm just repeating what you previously said. Suddenly I was staring myself in the face and thinking how could I argue against me?

My DA stood up for redirect examination.

DA: You were just asked, Chanel, a question about the preliminary hearing and regarding your cell phone. Do you remember that?

Me: Yes.

DA: Counsel left out the last part of that sentence. Did you also say, "But it's also possible I could have silenced it"?

Me: Yes.

She had caught him. He had deliberately stopped reading the passage early, had cut off my quote. She began coaxing me out of the corner I'd been backed into. She asked if my previous blackouts had been different than my one on January 15. I said that in previous blackouts, *I've never been half naked outside.* I wanted to curtsy. She gave me more opportunities to clarify:

DA: When you moved back home, how would you describe your level of drinking?

Defense: Objection. Relevance.

Judge: Sustained.

DA: Had your tolerance changed at all from college—from your college experience days?

Me: Yes.

Defense: Objection. Relevance.

Judge: Overruled.

DA: How had it changed?

She was trying to give me the chance to state that at the time of my assault my tolerance level had significantly declined since my college days, while he knocked her questions away. I was attempting to tell the same story through two different filters; through the questions of my

DA and the questions of the defense. Their questions created the narrative, building the framework that shaped what I said.

When I'd been questioned by my DA, I felt gutted, forced to come face-to-face with my painful memories, reliving it for the jury to see. Being questioned by the defense was stifling. He didn't want to open up the emotional territory that she did; he wanted to smother it, to erase my specific experience, abstract me into stereotypes of partying and blackouts, to ask technical questions that tied my shoelaces together, tripping me as he forced me to run.

Something else was happening that I'd recognized in the hearing; the frequency of the word *right*. He'd planted answers in his questions rather than leave them open ended: *Right? Isn't that right? Correct? Right?* To an observer, it would seem he was just verifying facts. But so much of it had not been right. It made me self-conscious, disagreeing with him repeatedly in front of the jury; wouldn't they believe the suited man who seemed to have everything in order rather than the woman with fragmented memory? Who was I to keep saying, *wait a minute, actually.* The entire time I felt he was pulling my hand in one direction and I was digging my heels into the ground attempting to resist.

When asked how many times I've blacked out, I'd said four to five. I detected a sudden shift in the room, heads tilting down to make note of this remarkable fact, a pause while pens scribbled around me. *Goddammit,* I thought. I knew immediately that by evening I'd be reading this fact in the news. I wondered whether, when my DA told me to be honest, she didn't mean this honest. Whether I should have said two to three. They never would have known. But it wouldn't have felt right, because it didn't matter how many times I'd blacked out before. This blackout remained different. I was not here to lie about who I was or to apologize for my past. Still, I berated myself, my character flaw burying my whole team deeper.

The final question the defense asked me, stern faced and level toned:

And your dinner consisted of broccoli and rice. I stared at him, waiting for some punch line, but did not detect a glimmer of amusement.

The end was abrupt. When I was excused, I sat for a moment, like I'd been spun in circles, instructed now to walk in a straight line. I hurried out of the courtroom, down the stairs, locking myself in the car, reclining my seat back until I lay flat.

I was supposed to feel a wash of relief, but I felt unease. I couldn't tell if I did well or ruined my credibility. In a setting where every word was deliberate, why did he end with the broccoli and rice? After I left I realized that my dad may have made quinoa, not rice—and quinoa may have lowered my alcohol tolerance. I typed out a text to my DA to clarify it was *quinoa, not rice, could she please let them know,* but hesitated, knowing she was already busy questioning whoever was next. I'd lost my chance. And what was the importance of the phone ringing? I will never forget the way he looked at me like I'd insulted his mother. Why so angry? Is it better if it rang or was on silent? Which one would win my case? Quinoa or rice? Bookstore in the front or back? Three blackouts or five? We had tiptoed around all of the heaviest moments and fixated on minute details, many of which I seemed to get wrong. The defense had months to come up with questions I only had seconds to respond to.

I shut my eyes and remembered something else he said; *That's not the answer I need for my question.* I felt naive as it dawned on me he was never interested in my responses. He already knew the answers he wanted; he just wanted me to say them. I had also heard an underlying pattern: *That's what you decided to do at that time, right? That was an intentional thing. And that was a decision you made.* He littered my night with intentions and poor decisions, suggesting they had everything to do with the final act. If you decided to go to this party, intentionally got wasted, is it really that hard to believe you intended to get handsy, fool around? I tapped my forehead with the heel of my palm, a small tempo, telling myself, *idiot, idiot, idiot.*

I was done with my testimony, but it was time to steel myself and be strong; in a few hours Tiffany would testify. As I put my hands to the steering wheel I saw them again; cuts like scarlet parentheses. It looked like red cough syrup had spilled beneath my skin. No matter how composed I had appeared, my stress had found an outlet, hands clenched beneath the stand, fingernails pinching each other like crabs fighting to the death, while I had felt none of it.

At home there was a note on the counter from my dad: *Girls, Will be thinking of you today. Remember, the truth will set you free. Mac & cheese, salmon, and chicken soup for the heart. Be strong!* A glass casserole of macaroni and cheese had gone cold from sitting out. I dug into it with a metal spoon.

Tiffany was in the bedroom getting ready, wearing a scarlet blouse, changing into a black one, back into the scarlet one, sweating through, then lifting her arms as I blow-dried the dark areas. I busied myself helping her; if I sat and thought too long I knew I wouldn't let her go back to that place.

Earlier in the day, before leaving the courtroom, I'd seen an Asian man in dress pants and a messenger bag standing in the hallway. I'd been told a DNA expert would be testifying and I wondered if that was him. I would later learn his name is Craig Lee, a forensic biologist, followed by Shaohsuan Steven Fanchiang, the paramedic, and Alice King, the criminal analyst, who all testified on my behalf in the time I was at home making sure Tiffany and I were fed and ready. While I was taking care of her, they were fighting for us both.

She drove us back to the courtroom. I asked her how she was doing, but she was distracted by a caterpillar clinging to the windshield, its fine white hairs blowing in the wind. She said we needed to save it. I said we were going to be late, but next thing I know she was pulling off the road into a parking lot, cutting the engine. I was unbuckling my seat belt, sifting through the middle console to find a crumpled receipt. I stepped out and wedged the receipt bit by bit below its tiny feet, and lowered it into the grass. When I got back into the car, she asked me if I saw it crawling away to make sure it was still alive. I got back out, confirmed it was moving. Only then was I allowed back in the car.

My sister had two friends, Elizabeth and Anusha, in the waiting room. I was grateful for the way they made this foreign world feel a little more familiar. The self that cried only hours ago had already transformed into a different person, upbeat and reassuring. When it was time, I sent my advocate with her.

I was no longer needed; this was the part where I was supposed to go home. But I didn't want to leave yet. I walked down the hallway that led to the courtroom. I wondered if someone would see me and accuse me of trying to listen. I peered through the sliver of window in the courtroom door.

When I was ten, my sister eight, we were in China and had gone to an indoor pool, vast and empty with glass walls like a greenhouse, the water stretching so far it created its own horizon. The glass was fogged by the heat and tinged yellow. It was an empty weekday morning, only one older woman slicing back and forth along the surface. My dad gave me a copper key that unlocked a private changing room at the far end of the pool, then quickly fell asleep in a pool chair by the entrance.

We unlocked our room, running barefoot along the benches, all of it ours. A door along the back wall led to a small shower room. The shower door closed behind us and we began pumping shampoo, gelling our hair into pointed peaks. My sister wanted to return to the pool, but couldn't open the door. Sure she wasn't doing it right, I went over and jiggled the knob myself until I realized we were stuck. She stood there in a metallic rainbow suit, goggles glued to her forehead, elbows resting on her little belly, hands holding her face, looking at me expectantly. I told her it was a little jammed so we just had to wait for dad to come. We sat in silence under the shower, I was putting shampoo back on my head, but it was not as fun anymore. Soon the water ran cold. I didn't know how to say "help" in Chinese. *On the count of three, just yell HELLO, okay?* I said. Before I got to three, she was screaming like I'd never heard her scream before. What scared me more was the silence that followed, no padding of feet, no jostling of the door handle.

Whenever my sister is crying, I am thinking. I crawled up on the sink ledge to peer out. There was nothing but highway. I imagined our naked limbs running down the road along a river of semi trucks. Then I noticed ventilation slats at the bottom of the wooden door. I pushed the meat of my palms against the first plank of wood until it snapped like a breaking bone. I cracked the second. I cracked the third, the splintered pieces lying defeated around my knees. Hands sore, I turned around to see if my sister could help, but she stood covering her eyes. I rested a moment, then worked through all six planks until there was only a wooden frame with nails sticking out on each side like teeth. I bent each nail, curving them away from me. I sucked in my stomach, gingerly placed my arms and my head through the opening. The nail tips grazed the skin on my ribs. I freed myself, but the lock remained broken. I craned my neck to peer up at her through the square, and said, *Stay here and count to one hundred and by the time you are done I'll be back.* I ran the length of the pool, shook my dad awake. As soon as he opened his eyes, I began sobbing, crying my sister's name.

My dad got a guy to come fix the doorknob, while my sister wailed alone on the other side. The guy said it got stuck sometimes. I was furious, can you see that my sister is trapped? As the door swung open and she ran to my dad, I looked at the little pile of broken wood and thought, *I got us out. I will always find a way.*

I was standing in the tiled hallway in my black coat, staring through the thin vertical window of the courtroom door. I could see her sitting there, all the way up at the front of the room, her head pea size in front of the microphone, mouth moving. I wanted to reach my hand in from above, like a claw in a machine, and pluck her gently out of there, to take her by my side, for us to leave this all behind. My eyes burned as I watched her, stuck on the other side of the door.

I met Athena at a bakery to pass the hours until Tiffany would be done, eating apricot hamantaschen in the rain. As it neared 5:00 P.M., we walked back to the courthouse, expecting her to emerge any second. A lone reporter stood outside. The press was not allowed to talk to me, but her gaze latched on and followed us. The way she was tilting her phone made me paranoid that she was taking pictures. It unnerved me, so we stepped inside through security just as the elevator doors parted and Brock appeared, hands in pockets, followed by his whole family and his attorney. I expected them to stop, retreat, an invisible boundary they were not allowed to cross. But they glanced at me and kept coming, and I did not have time to move, simply stood with my back turned as they passed me like I was nobody. When I looked at myself through their eyes, I shrunk one hundred sizes smaller, nothing more than a vacant-headed victim, the rotten stain on his life. Suddenly my advocate appeared. She said Tiffany was already waiting in the car.

We sat in the parked car as the windows blurred. She said we'd go when the rain lessened. I knew what she meant, that she needed to sit mindless for a moment. I learned she had run out of time, would have to return in the morning. I wanted to ask her how it went, to tell me everything, but was paranoid we'd be accused of sharing information. Even in a locked car sealed in by the roar of the rain, the fear of being watched, of doing something wrong, always snuffed the conversation out.

That night we put on a movie with Tom Hanks to take our minds off everything. Her phone rang, interrupting the stillness. It was my DA, my sister slipping away down the hall. When she returned her eyes were wet. She sat on the couch staring at the screen. *I messed everything up,* she said. *That's impossible,* I said. *I did,* she said. My comforting was useless, as she insisted I didn't understand, I wasn't there. I hated that I wasn't permitted to know what was happening. Later I would discover my sister had testified that when she left me briefly that night she thought I'd be fine. The defense was using this to argue that when Brock found me he had every reason to think I was fine too. If they could prove Brock genuinely believed I was coherent enough to consent, they could walk away with the case. *I meant I thought you'd be fine*, she said. I knew what she meant; she meant she didn't think that her older sister would've been raped. Alaleh had called to tell her she needed to clarify and hold her ground, because the defense would nail her on this tomorrow.

I was ready to grab my keys, walk straight out the door. I wanted to pull up to the defense attorney's house, run up the carpeted stairs, and rustle him awake in his stupid pajamas, his glasses on the bedside table. I would throw the quilted blankets off him, revealing his hairy white legs, his tube socks. I'd ask him if he knew how he was disturbing my little sister, couldn't he figure out a goddamn way to do this decently, to keep it between me and Brock, to look at the evidence scrawled across the board, my BAC level, the voice mail, what more do you want, do you want to destroy my sister in the process, because I will end you. Somehow it had become all of our faults, except his.

As I sat there witnessing her crumbling before me, her agony in trying to carry this all, I finally understood. He knew there was a part in us that was self-conscious, the lingering voices that told us we were in the wrong. *Wasn't it you, who left? Who said she was fine?* He found it, hooked into it, injected it, grew it until the guilt was all-consuming. Until we became so inundated by self-blame, so blinded by the pain, we lost the ability to see.

It was happening to her and it was happening to me, the two of us fed distorted realities, our words twisted until we became uncertain, discredited, writing ourselves off as flawed and broken. We willingly rammed our heads against the walls, confused, apologizing, unsure of what right we had to speak. I had unlocked the secret of the game; this was not a quest for justice but a test of endurance. His mistake was that he was going after someone I would go to the ends of the earth for. See, if it had just been me in there, being attacked, I might've backed down, retreating to my places of self-doubt. But her? I had been asked, earlier in the day, what I meant when I'd said I was more of a mother to her than a sister. I wanted to say, I don't know, you tell me. What happens when a person gets in between a mother bear and her cub, have you read about the maulings, faces ripped clean.

I took my meticulously typed guidelines and encouragements, threw them in a drawer, gave myself a new mantra: *fuck the fried rice.* Fuck what you sipped, how you sipped, when you sipped with whom, fuck if I danced on the table, fuck if I danced on the chair. You want the truth, the whole truth, and nothing but the truth? Your whole answer was sitting with his shoulders low, head down, his neatly cut hair. You want to know why my whole goddamn family was hurting, why I lost my job, why I had four digits in my bank account, why my sister was missing school? It was because on a cool January evening, I went out, while that guy, that guy there, had *decided* that yes or no, moving or motionless, he wanted to fuck someone, *intended* to fuck someone, and it happened to be me.

This did not make me deficient. This did not make me inadequate. But it did make me angry. My sister allowed me to see what I needed to see. Pain, when examined closely, became clarity. I knew now what the attorney had come here to do, and I would not let it happen. He believed he could break us, but from this day forward, I would begin to build.

8.

THE TRIAL WOULD continue for the rest of the week, though I wasn't allowed inside the courtroom. I lived inside my strange parallel universe; all day I'd putter around aimlessly and at night I'd check coverage on the local news. On Tuesday, Tiffany finished her testimony and I asked my DA who was next. *A blackout expert,* she said. I waited a beat for her to tell me she was kidding. I wanted to say, *I'm the real blackout expert am I right.* The expert, Dr. Fromme, had been paid ten thousand dollars by Brock's side to testify. She claimed I could have been ready, willing, and able to consent even if I could not remember it.

On Wednesday, the day Brock testified, I laced up my running shoes. He'd be taking out the curated version of me, pulling her like a dusty mannequin out of a box, dragging her out onto the stage, grinding her hips in a strange dance, peeling her lips into smiles, garnishing her with kisses, feeding her words he had written. I found the whole thing sick, suffocating, my body stuck in his hands in that small, square building. I ran for miles, winding through thin trails, past hills with barrel-bellied horses.

The news appeared that night, the article glowing in the rectangular screen. I blurred and refocused my eyes, debating whether I should read what he'd said. I decided to scan, one quick scroll, and then stopped when I saw a tiny new word, yes. I counted how many he had given me; he said I'd said yes to dancing, yes to going to his dorm, yes to fingering.

In a film literature class I once took, Mr. Hernandez showed us the scene in *Jaws* where Martin, the lead, is about to get on the boat and is saying good-bye to his wife, Ellen. Ellen is worried about losing him, but instead of saying, *Please be careful, I love you!* She says, *I put an extra pair of glasses in your—black socks and, and there's the stuff, your nose, the zinc oxide, the Blistex is in the kit.* And in response, instead of saying, *Don't worry, I'll come back for you!* He says, *Don't use the fireplace in the den because I haven't fixed the flue yet.* She nods and says, *What am I going to tell the kids?* He says, *Tell them I'm going fishing.*

Love is implied, love is the black socks she packed, the promise he'll return to fix the flue, the desire to protect the kids, the detailed attention to each other's lives, the urgency of comforting one another amidst the gravity of what's about to happen. The most important messages are felt, never stated explicitly. That is real dialogue.

Then we had Brock's testimony.

I asked her if she wanted me to finger her.

Did she reply to you?

Yes.

What did she say?

She said yeah.

He admitted he had tried to kiss Tiffany.

DA: Did she say anything to you about it?

No. She just left.

He said he had removed my underwear, pulled them down my legs, over each boot. He said I orgasmed. *And I fingered her for a minute, and I thought she had an orgasm and then—well, during that time, I asked her if she liked it, and she said uh-huh.* When I learned this, I went from a seated position, to crawling on the floor, to lying down. He said the dry humping made his stomach upset. Said he'd decided to leave when *I realized there was a guy standing right next to me*. Said he was scared because they were speaking in *some foreign language*. He said they had broken his wrist. When he was handcuffed, he'd never mentioned wrist pain. Now he explained to the jury how he'd had to get a cast. How he'd suffered from bruises and scratches. When Brock explained he only ran because he was scared the guys would hurt him, Alaleh asked, *You weren't concerned that they might try to hurt Chanel?* He said, *I didn't look back at her*. In second grade, we had this currency called fuzzies, tiny colorful pom-poms. If you were well behaved, turned in your homework on time, you'd be awarded fuzzies. Brock's fuzzie count started off awful low. But on the day of his testimony, he'd come in with a truckload; they poured across the floor, flooded the room up to his knees, and suddenly he was rich enough to win the prize. I wondered if the jury would see that his fuzzies were fake.

DA: And as you sit here today, you admit that you ran?
Brock: Yes.
DA: So what you told Detective Kim was a lie, wasn't it?
Brock: Yes.

Victims are often, automatically, accused of lying. But when a perpetrator is exposed for lying, the stigma doesn't stick. Why is it that we're wary of victims making false accusations, but rarely consider how many men have blatantly lied about, downplayed, or manipulated others to cover their own actions?

He'd made it sound too easy. If I'd really granted him consent, he would've told the officer upon his arrest. The latest script he had crafted was too blatant to be real, too convenient to believe. His reconstruction was just poor writing, almost comical. It was insulting to be on the other end of this dim-witted dialogue.

I called Lucas, laughing. *He said I wanted it! This material is gold!*

This is good for us, right? He's done, it's over. I mean is anyone eating this up? Way stupid. But Lucas went quiet at the other end of the line, said he was going to be sick, and excused himself for a few minutes. As I listened to the silence, I felt the inside of me hardening, anger rising. *You need to play my game. You need to say, Not the sharpest crayon in the box! You need to say, You've got this in the bag!* I didn't get to be sick, be outraged, to choose not to hear it. If I stopped even for a moment to absorb what was happening, I would not make it.

When Lucas went quiet, my illusion faltered, and I got a glimpse of what I was facing, the brutality of it, the oppression. The rules of court would not necessarily protect me; swearing under oath was just a made-up promise. Honesty was for children. Brock would say and do what he needed; unabashedly self-righteous. He had given himself permission to enter me again, this time stuffing words into my mouth. He made me his real-life ventriloquist doll, put his hands inside me and made me speak.

On Thursday, court was closed. My friend Matt and I went to my favorite Indian spot, sat outside scraping orange rice from a metal tin. There was a local newspaper on the table, Brock striding in a suit on the front page. I glanced at it a few times, afraid to show too much interest. Matt scanned the paper. I was biting into a samosa when he said, *Did you hear about the girl who got raped?* I played dumb. *Recently?* I said. *No, it happened like a year ago,* he said. *Oh,* I said. I felt a tide swelling, my head going under, then it drained and I was back. *How'd you hear about it?* I asked. *He's infamous around here, plus it's all over Facebook,* he said. When we left, I kept the newspaper, claiming there was a coupon inside I wanted to use. As Matt drove, I casually flipped through it. *Do you think she's at fault?* I asked. He winced and gave one strong shake of the head. *Hell, no,* he said. It was all I needed to know. We drove to my house, Matt plucking his mandolin on the couch while I tried to play alongside him on the piano, enjoying my freedom before court resumed the next day.

On Friday, the final day, Brock's defense attorney brought in four character witnesses. No one from Stanford testified, which meant only people from Brock's past life were flying in to speak for his present self. The lineup included his best friend from adolescence, an ex-girlfriend, his high school swim coach, and high school French teacher. I took six years of French too, but it never occurred to me to bring Madame Jensen in to let you know I gave an excellent presentation on *Le Petit Prince*. What were they here to say? He never took his penis out in class, never fondled his coach.

If I were to do a performance piece, I'd place Brock on the ground atop a half-naked body, while these four people stood around him in a half circle, peppering the scene with the same things they'd said in court. Take the French teacher: *That would be the farthest type of behavior, the sexually aggressive or assaultive behavior that I would ever, ever, ever associate with Brock Turner.* I would sample the *ever, ever, ever* and put it on loop, Brock thrusting to the tempo of each *ever*. As Brock disrobed the body, *I don't believe that he would do anything that would harm anybody.* And as Brock took off sprinting, the coach would say, *I think that Brock is a very respectful and courteous and, you know, that he knows what right and wrong is.*

Their platitudes did not come as a surprise. What I wondered was, in a trial meant to examine facts, why hours were set aside to shower him in accolades. His history included his childhood, education, summer jobs, sweet relationships. My history was blackouts one through five. My character was just as much on trial as his character; my behavior, my composure, my likability, were also being evaluated. But there was nothing to suggest that I was a person extracted from a full life, surrounded by people who cared about me.

My DA didn't waste any time on the cross-examinations:

Now, you obviously—have you ever been with him where he was drinking to excess?

No.

You haven't seen him when he's intoxicated?

No.

And you weren't with him on the night of the 17th, were you?

No.

So you have no idea what happened that day?

Correct.

Her questioning was brief, swiftly confirming they were useless. She asked his French teacher if she'd ever talked with him about his sexual desires or preferences, to which she said no. When questioning his ex-girlfriend, she'd said,

And you would never get intimate in public, is that true?

I mean, define your . . .

Sure. You never had sex in public?

No.

Okay. That would be out of the ordinary?

Later someone would describe to me the look of shock that came across the ex-girlfriend's face, the way she reared her head back when my DA asked about public intercourse. I wanted to say, yes, it is alarming, sex behind a dumpster. My DA said the only time she saw Brock cry was when his ex-girlfriend had testified.

I was ready to dismiss their insignificant stories, deeming them unworthy of energy or attention, but reading them now I pause. During trial, the jury was forced to pick; is he wholesome or monstrous. But I never questioned that any of what they said about him was true. In fact I need you to know it was all true. The friendly guy who helps you move and assists senior citizens in the pool is the same guy who assaulted me. One person can be capable of both. Society often fails to wrap its head around the fact that these truths often coexist, they are not mutually exclusive. Bad qualities can hide inside a good person. That's the terrifying part.

Brock had a sister my age. The French teacher had three daughters, the swim coach had a daughter and two sons, all close to my age. But it was no help to me that they had girlfriends and sisters and daughters. Somehow I was different, cast outside their range of empathy. In that courtroom, my identity had been reduced to something in the category of "other."

On Saturday, I thought I'd feel relief after all testimonies had been given. Instead I felt paralyzed. Every day I had less control. Proceedings had digressed, strayed away from seminal questions, everything more corrosive and irrelevant than I could've imagined. I read on the news how I'd *sobbed so uncontrollably*, read updates on *the woman's vaginal area*, about the way the *Ohio native made eye contact with the woman, crossed his right leg over his left, tapping his foot*. Online it sometimes seemed I had done nothing more than cry. In real life, my basic functions began to falter: I stopped sleeping, forgot to eat, couldn't even shit properly. By the end of the two weeks, my mind had withdrawn, my body withered.

My mom called. *Can you go see Gong Gong?* She had driven him to the airport for his flight to China. His bags were packed, hair combed, passport updated, Chinese opera downloaded, pots and pans put away, and shoes lined up by the door. On the other side of the world a family member would be waiting to bring him to a dinner with pickled mustard greens, rice noodles, and quail eggs. But when they arrived at the airport kiosk, they discovered a single letter of his Chinese name on his ticket had been mistyped. The airline turned him away, did not let him board, and my mom drove him home. It was the first time she'd seen tears run down his cheek. She asked me to go cheer him up. As I drove to his place, my temper rose.

How could one little letter prevent him from going halfway around the world? I barely greeted him when I arrived. Marching to the phone, I started making calls. My grandpa and his friend looked at me, mouths slightly agape as I screamed at a helpless agent. *He needs to be in fucking China, tell me how that makes sense, well there must be an office that's open.* He'd never seen me act like this. I felt his hand on my back, comforting me, saying I could go home, that they would handle it. But I was incensed. A single letter! Incomprehensible that all his plans collapsed because of one tiny typo. How something so small could ruin everything.

In trial, all evidence had been filed. But what if there was one error, one minuscule oversight, one letter. If a teaspoon of doubt leaked into one of the juror's minds, it would all be over, there would be no trip, we would all turn around and go home, defeated.

I woke up the next morning to a bowl of boiled eggs on the counter, shallow pools of pink and yellow dye. I'd forgotten it was Easter. Only my dad would insist, during a rape trial, that we'd still sift through poppies in the garden to find rainbow eggs. In the gutter, in the birdhouse. Tiffany drove back to school with a massive bag of eggs to begin her final quarter. I slept well, relieved she had fled the sinking ship, was back on track, studying textbooks instead of transcripts. I technically could have left town too, but wanted to see it through the end. I also stayed because I had no routine to resume.

All that was left was the closing statements before jury deliberation began. My DA said she'd never had a victim sit in on the closing statements before. She advised me to sit out the first half of her presentation due to the graphic elements. There'd be a break halfway through where I'd be able to come in. She seemed appreciative that I was willing to come. *The jury will see how much you care.* More points toward the unspoken tally.

My family and friends assembled for the statements on Monday morning. My dad was in court with my mom, Grandma Ann, Anne, and Athena. Finally my bench was almost as full as Brock's. I sat alone on a wooden bench in the hallway to wait. I knew people were seeing things they were keeping from me. But I kept my curiosity on a tight leash, figured they were protecting me for a reason. Reading the transcript of Alaleh's closing now, I get a glimpse of what I missed. *She had no idea these photos were taken.... Look at her dress and how he left her.... But those photos speak for her when she could not speak for herself.*

My dad emerged out of the courtroom doors, shaking his head and muttering to himself. He walked right past me. Stunned, I said, *Dad.* When he looked up at me, the tension on his face cleared. He seemed dazed. *Have you seen that photo, the one of you lying by the ...?* I shook my head. *You looked dead,* he said. *Like someone tried to toss a body into the dumpster and missed. If something doesn't happen soon, I'll sue.*

My dad is not one to sue. He makes hummingbird nectar by the pitcher in the fridge and refills the feeders every weekend. Whenever I said the word *hate* growing up, he said, *Be careful, hate's a powerful word.* He's the one who will clap for the man playing clarinet in the street. Summer afternoons he cooks risotto while singing along to Crosby, Stills, Nash & Young. But I heard a new register of rage in his voice, like he would tear the whole place down if I just said the word.

People began spilling into the hallway for recess. I watched a man approach Alaleh, a neon-orange sticker on his shirt that said JURY and thought it was funny jury members were walking around labeled like Chiquita bananas. *Sorry to bother you,* he said, *but I have a dentist appointment this Thursday—do you think I'll need to cancel it?* I smiled to myself, knew the answer before she said it. A taste of my life, of abandoned plans, unknown endings.

Brock emerged. I should've been in my victim closet. He walked past me, guided by his father's hand on his back. His father glanced down at me, then lifted his eyes back up and kept walking. It was one second, but enough to make my insides seize. These were the things I felt but could never explain. The wordless affronts that went unrecorded. His siblings lingered in the hallway. Reporters mulled about.

One had cornered Tiffany's friends the previous week, tried to slip in a few questions when she was alone. Onlookers arrived every day to take and take. I was tired of existing as an object of observation, powerless as my narrative was written for me.

When recess ended, I joined my family in the courtroom. I enjoyed blending in as an observer. My DA stood to face the jury. *Now, the fact of the matter is, these types of crimes are often [crimes] of opportunity. It doesn't matter whether the victim is beautiful, whether the victim behaves in a certain way or dressed in a certain way. All that matters is, she's incapable of saying no, she's there, and she's vulnerable.* I was nodding along, everything brilliantly plain and clear.

A trial is a search for the truth. Now, the truth doesn't always come in a pretty package with a bow on top. Sometimes, there's deliberate attempts to cloud your ability to see the truth.

She walked us through slides that compared the mismatched facts of Brock's testimonies, exposed the faulty reasoning, the way new information materialized. She explained that the act of running exhibited consciousness of guilt. It was a wonderful thing watching myself being fought for; I envisioned myself speaking through her, using words like *collude* and statements like *I am going to prove to you.* She tugged the thread of his arguments little by little until his facade began unraveling. *And I'm going to ask you to return a just verdict for Chanel that says it's not okay what he did to her, it's not okay the way he did it to her, and it's not okay for anyone to violate a human being like that.*

When she finished, I fought the urge to applaud.

As she took her seat, the defense rose. For a second, I contemplated slipping out. I wanted to end on this high note, this fullness. But I heard *Ladies and gentlemen;* it was too late. The defense began by asking the jury to find Brock not guilty.

Let me explain why, he said. *When I left Kappa Alpha, Chanel appeared to be fine, so I wasn't worried about leaving her there. Who told us that? That was Tiffany, her sister. Who knows her better than Tiffany out of all the people that testified at this trial? Nobody. Tiffany knows her the best.... That was how she described her sister whom she has known her whole life.*

I stood halfway up. But leaving or staying would not matter, he'd go on. So I braced myself. I did not notice I had squeezed my mom's hand to a pulp. She leaned over, whispering into my ear, *Don't listen to him.* These words let me settle back in.

We know from Brock Turner and from the DNA evidence that he put his finger into her vagina. I clenched my knees tightly together. *One can reasonably infer from that that he didn't just put it in and hold it there. He was rubbing it back and forth. That's totally consistent with what the SART nurse found. So she doesn't really add anything about the findings of the case.* Alaleh had pushed us into the light and now we were being dragged back into the dark, logic disfigured. Mom whispered, *Evil, teeny-weeny old man.*

To explain Brock's inconsistencies, he said, *So it's not uncommon for people to not remember details of incidents, especially things that happened so fast and with emotional tension.* Brock was allowed a messy mind. Victims often have inconsistencies due to traumatic blockage, alcoholic gaps. His inconsistencies came from what he said before he had a lawyer versus what he said after he hired one. When Brock was arrested and questioned by the detective, all the supposed dialogue between us that he failed to mention was not due to a lack of memory. It was due to the fact that he did not have an attorney to help him construct a narrative, feed him words, brush the clouds from his mind, and figure out which story might get him off scot-free.

The defense's arguments weakened, slipping through my fingers. He said the reason I sounded slurred in the voice mail was my *silly way* of speaking to my boyfriend. Said that when I said I'd reward Lucas *he knew darn well what was intended . . . I think it gives us very good insight, at 12:18, into Chanel's thinking. . . . She's saying that twice, and she's saying it for a reason.*

He put his finger in the vagina of Chanel. . . . And he did it when she was consenting, conscious, and there was no way he could have believed from what he saw and heard that she wasn't capable of consenting at that time. He stood there with his notepad like an unenthused student reading off his book report. *I'd ask you to take the burden off his shoulders that's been there for 14 months . . .* Instinctively I looked at Brock's shoulders.

The attorney I'd been so afraid of, had lost sleep over for months, was standing before me, stern faced and shrunken, having delivered an unconvincing monologue. How could this be the closing statement of a year's worth of investigating? If you're going to fight me, fight me. But this was it? All these people had been summoned, endured weeks of debate after fourteen months of waiting. All this damage and energy wasted for this underwhelming finale, puttering on about *her vagina, or whatever.* When my DA was presenting, you felt the room mold around her, eyes watching her pace back and forth. She spoke with fire and urgency and wit, her words laid before us, layering the room with reason and truth. I felt real change was happening, the whole room expanding. She was piercing without being vicious; made it clear we're not after you, we're after what you did, and now we are here to hold you accountable.

But when the defense finished, his words did not fall and settle, only floated almost weightless, with nowhere to land, eliciting nothing. The air in the room became still, like sails emptied of wind, all of us left sitting on a flat sea. It bothered me the way the ends of his sentences had lifted, as if he himself had been questioning his own arguments, knowing they had been constructed on a feeble foundation.

My DA stood up for rebuttal. I imagined the defense loose toothed and swaying—all she had to do was deliver the final punch and the bell would ring. *I'm not going to rebut everything, because some of the arguments I frankly don't think are—warrant anything . . . the fact the defendant latches on to that to say Tiffany said Chanel was fine does not absolve the defendant . . . the obligation is on him before he inserts his finger in someone's vagina to make sure they're capable of consenting, not that their sister thinks that they're fine.* She swung the spotlight back to him, where it belonged. She pointed out that all he had to do to complete the rape was unzip his pants. I'd never put this together; the only thing between my open legs and his erection were the tiny golden teeth of a zipper.

No woman, no woman wants to have debris in their vagina when they met a guy five minutes before. No woman. Not just Chanel. No woman. Her, me, every woman in that room. It was as if she were tossing my shoes out into the audience urging everyone to try them on.

You're not a bad person or a good person, but what you did on that night is not acceptable, it's not okay, and it violates the law. Once you stripped everything of complex terms and formalities, the truth was solid and pure. It's not okay, never okay, for someone to hurt you. There are no asterisks, no exceptions, to this statement.

Don't forget that there's a victim in this case that he violated. And when you do that, you'll see that there's only one reasonable verdict and that's one of guilt on all counts. . . . The burden that he has in this case is the burden of guilt. I looked at Brock's shoulders again. That, that I could see.

Alaleh found us and told us to go home and wait. The jury would deliberate every day from nine to five, and the verdict could take anywhere from a couple of days to weeks. As soon as a verdict was reached, she would send me a text and I would have fifteen minutes to get to the courtroom. Which meant I was on call, unable to stray farther than a few miles from the courthouse.

Tuesday morning I made a list of everyone I'd have to notify as soon as the verdict was announced. I got dressed in my black flats and a blouse I was careful not to wrinkle. I reapplied deodorant every hour. I put my hair up in a tight bun, watched it gradually droop. In the afternoon, my mom taught me how to make my favorite shrimp dish. Together we removed the shells, chopped garlic, sprinkled chili flakes. When their watery gray crescents of flesh hit the hot oil, it spurted out, flecking my blouse. I rushed to wash it. They'd be calling me at any minute.

I looked online, saw an article by the *Mercury News,* saw they'd written *Chanel Doe.* I began shaking, my cover blown, anticipating the wave of notifications. The reporter had sat in the room with me; it felt like betrayal that she'd outed me so carelessly. My DA fixed the small leak, but the damage had been done. I trusted no one, could not escape the pervasive sense of invasion. Grandma Ann told me a reporter had leaned over to her in court, whispering, *How are you affiliated?* My grandma silenced her with one wave of the hand. I called to check in on her. Because she was hard of hearing, she'd missed most of what was said in the courtroom (a tiny blessing). Instead she had primarily paid attention to body language. She felt confident from my DA's posture, expressions. She told me to take a hot shower and put on pajamas. She said, *I am crossing all ten of my fingers and all ten of my toes.*

The sun sank and I'd received no word from Alaleh. I slipped off my flats, curled into bed. It's okay. They just need a little more time. But the feeling in my chest made it difficult to breathe. Didn't they hear what had been said?

I knew I was not going to sleep, so I tucked myself under my covers and watched *Mister Rogers.* When I was little I was entranced by the choreography in the opening scene: He comes in, removes his suit jacket, hangs it in the closet, exchanges it for a sweater, takes off his work shoes, slips on soft Keds, ties the laces. This ritual promised control and safety for the next half hour. Lying in bed, locked in the glow of my phone, I dragged the dot backward along the video's timeline, rewinding the segment to view it again. Watching the sweater zip and unzip, peel off and on and off and on, lace and unlace. When the sun appeared outside, I stepped out from beneath my blankets, stepped into my black flats, pulled up my hair, sat on the bed again.

How long can humans live in suspended states? I felt like a lone cow, a rope around my neck, staring into a metal building, where I could see the huge pink cocoons lined with white ribs dangling from chains. Behind me was a meadow, the scent of grass in the wind. One of two things would happen; I'd be led by my rope up the metal walkway to be churned to red mush, or I'd be set free in a sun-filled pasture. Until then, I just stood, feeling the itch of rope on my skin.

The sun peaked in the sky then rolled downward. It was four o'clock. If the jury did not decide in the next hour, Wednesday would come to a close. Thursday was an off day. Friday a holiday. Saturday. Sunday. Which meant I'd have to wait at least another four days. If the jury found him innocent, I had to tell myself these cases were extremely hard to win. That it did not make me a failure. I tried to ready myself, but knew that if I lost, I was scared for what I might do.

When Lucas called, I let the phone rest on my face as tears trickled out. He kept telling me to go outside, get fresh air. I only scratched my head, grease shiny on my fingers. The neckline of my knitted sweater was loose, my black pants had collected stray hairs. My phone buzzed against my cheek as he spoke, a text. *It's time,* I said, and hung up before he could reply.

I am on my feet walking toward the bathroom. The verdict will be read in fifteen minutes. It's an eight-minute drive to the courtroom, twelve minutes with traffic, which means I have three minutes to get ready. I can't figure out the order of what I'm supposed to be doing, if I should wash my face or call somebody or put on shoes or change my sweater. I splash water on my eyes but stop midway, realizing I should notify everyone first. I turn to get my phone, chin dripping and thumbs wet, coating my phone screen in water. I don't know what to type. I set down my phone, hastily combing fingers through my hair. I must take a shower, no time. I stand frozen at the sink, faucet running. The list. I am calling my grandma, the long rings excruciating, *It's time.* I hang up. I type out each text with shaking hands. My car keys are missing. I can't find my phone. It is on the sink. I walk out to the living room. My mom is sitting at the table with a friend having tea. I tell her *this is it* and when she looks up at me her face changes and she's immediately out of her seat. She takes me by my hand back into the bathroom, pulls lip gloss from the wooden drawer. She paints it on and I watch my lips become pink and shiny and flecked with glitter. I rip off a piece of toilet paper and wipe it off, I need to be taken seriously. *It brightens you,* she says. I see her standing there, lip gloss hovering in one hand, desperate to revive me. I turn to see myself in the mirror through her eyes, this limp-haired, thin-limbed person with tired eyes, someone who has forgotten to care for herself. I turn to face my mom, letting her coat my lips again and then I am out the door unable to wait, telling her she can meet me there.

My mind is already inside the courthouse, while some part of me attends to the reds and greens of the lights. I ride as a passenger inside my own body, looking out the window as if on a ride, the car smooth and gliding as if on a track, making all the right turns. I worry I'll be the only one there, had the texts gone through, will they come? I do not remember parking or arriving, only know that I am seated in the front row, it is 4:24, Athena on my left, my grandma on my right, Anne, they have come.

I can hear my heart thudding unevenly like a tennis ball in a drying machine. I wonder if I'm going to have a heart attack. Is that possible for people this young? I need to puncture a hole in my chest to release the pressure. The judge is speaking, but I can't hear him over the thumping. The thought of having a breakdown here, of having to leave, is unbearable, I try to orient myself. I stare at the gray, square back of Alaleh's suit. I see my Grandma's hand clasped around my shaking knee. I am pushing air out of my mouth, pressing a flat hand to my chest, envision myself deflating. In my head I make my lungs disappear, my heart disappear, and I am a simple, empty shell. I am surrounded by infinite amounts of air. I take the air in slowly and then I let it out, in and then out.

I hear the judge talking, going over questions that had been raised by the jury during deliberation. *And then finally, we received jury question No. 5 which states or asks, "Is contact with the inner lining of labia majora or any portion of labia minora considered penetration?"* I see this labia like a piece of sashimi, turned over in their hands, existing on its own independently from me. Finally, the judge asks, *Juror No. 5, has the jury reached a verdict?*

A man from the jury box rises, *Yes, Your Honor.* The judge says, *If you could please hand the verdict forms to the deputy.* I hadn't expected the answer to be on a piece of paper. I watch the jury member lean over the ledge of the box to give the paper to a deputy. The deputy walks casually as if carrying a cabbage to his grocery cart, *go fucking go*, across the room and passes it to the court clerk. I want to leap up and rip it out of her hands.

The clerk stands up, her tufty blond hair glowing under the skylight, glasses reflected so that I cannot see her pupils, a dark pink shirt, the paper in front of her. I've never seen her before. It turns out she had been there the entire trial, had been the one who stood two feet in front of me administering the oath as I was sworn in before testimony, but this is the first time she registers in my mind. She has no microphone, no microphone! speaking so softly! I can't believe it. *LOUDER.* I lean forward, squinting, as if this will help my hearing, staring as her lips shape the words.

The People of the State of California, Plaintiff, versus Brock Allen Turner, Defendant, Information No. B1577162 . . . she reads out each number. I am going to pass out . . . *verdict of the jury: Verdict. Count 1, Penal Code section 220 (a) (1), felony* . . . I am only looking for the hard sound of the "g" . . . *We, the jury, find the defendant, Brock Allen Turner, guilty of a felony, a violation of California Penal Code section 220 (a) (1), assault with intent to commit a rape of an intoxicated or unconscious person. Dated March 30th, 2016, by foreperson, Juror No. 5.*

The air is broken by the wail of someone being stabbed. My head snaps to the right and I watch Brock's mother's pointed feet extend straight up into the air and come slamming back into the ground. She stomps, yelling into this room stricken by silence. His father has thrown his body over her as if shielding her from a showering of arrows. Suddenly, I feel vulnerable, my face open and unprotected. What do I look like, should I be reacting? Her wailing tries to insert itself into me, but I need to drown out the sound, to focus. I turn back to the front of the room, muting the cries. There are two more counts.

The woman's words remain soft as she continues, there are too many numbers. But I hear the smack of Athena kissing me on the cheek. That must mean we have won two counts, we're at two. I feel the emotional tides of the room swelling on each side. There is grief and suffocated celebration, muffled cries, the air brimming with indistinguishable sound. I stare at this woman at the front of the room, her blond hair and glassed-in eyes and realize she is an angel. I hear *guilty* one final time and that's when I know. We have done it.

The clerk asks each juror to state their individual vote. She reads the first count. *Is this your personal verdict?* Juror number one replies, *Yes.* She goes on to juror number two. *Yes.* Three. *Yes.* Four. *Yes.* Five. *Yes.* I watch a man subtly smile as he states his vote, like this is his victory too. I see nods as they deliver this syllable. This jury, a cluster of people in my mind, begins separating into individuals. For the first time I allow myself to see them. I take in each face, want to commit them to memory, tracing the outlines of their profiles, the specks of hair on their cheeks, the width of their glasses, hairlines, eyelashes, dimples, sideburns. She moves on to count number two, and again they go around, *yes, yes, yes, yes, yes, yes, yes, yes, yes, yes, yes, yes.* She reads count number three, is this your personal verdict,

yes,

yes,

yes,

yes,

yes,

yes,

yes,

yes,

yes,

yes,

yes.

It is a pure and constant rhythm, beating into me. A recitation of truth. The yesses go on unbroken, like steps taking us somewhere. As my eyes follow them one by one, I feel anger draining out of me, making space for something else.

I thought I would look at the defense attorney's pitiful face, see Brock's head hung low, and call for confetti, feeling triumphant. But I do not think to do or feel any of that. As I watch the jury members, all other sounds fall away.

It was like looking back at a sandy shore from the water and realizing how far I had drifted. How far I had let myself go. Who was this person sitting here, so hungry to be told the answer was yes? I thought of Emily that morning, standing in the shower, struggling to stand up straight, surrounded by steam. Somewhere along the way I'd become the voices that told her she was a humiliation, should learn to think realistically. I told her she deserved the damage, questioning her instincts. How badly I'd wanted to abandon her. How little I'd thought of her life.

I sit in sadness, inhaling wet air, my eyes closed, my chest shaking. I tune out of the courtroom, the agony too big, my head lowered in apology. I'm so sorry. You were not crazy. For so long I believed I needed permission to return to my life, waiting for validation. I promised myself I would never question whether I deserved better. The answer would always be *yes* and *yes* and *yes*.

The conversation has turned, the judge is scheduling the sentencing, when he'd decide how much time Brock would serve. He points to a calendar on the wall; *sentencing occurs on the nonhighlighted Thursdays in our calendar rotations*. I glance at the small empty rows of boxes, some squares bright yellow. I pay little attention, the sentencing an afterthought.

My DA requests that Brock be remanded. But the handcuffs never touch him, his attorney arguing he should remain out on bail. He will fly home with his family, free for two months until the sentencing sometime in June. We are released.

I sidestep out of the row, eager to get out of the room. I am feet away from the mass entanglement of the arms of his family. There's a heated energy coming off them threatening to consume everything in their grief. Some red-eyed family members glare at me like I am the enemy. I stare back through my own red eyes, unyieldingly. *You are looking at the wrong person.*

My grandma and Athena are supporting my elbows and I realize I'm being carted along. We exit the courtroom like a parade, the media amassed behind us with their bags and small recorders. I am hunched, tucking my head down into my shoulders, feet hurriedly shuffling, worried if we slow down we'll be engulfed by the mass behind us. I need to get through the door to the DA's office, to be sealed off from the public.

As I push through the door, everyone milling around the office begins backing along the walls, ducking into cubicles. I remember the first day I'd come here, my mom massaging my hand as I timidly answered questions. Now I turn to see Alaleh rushing toward me, arms open. Finally, I rest my face on her shoulder, the two of us standing in the middle of the room, holding each other, crying.

My little group stepped into a small conference room. There is no celebration, we are shaken, finally releasing the pent-up fear we carried knowing how close we'd come to an alternate outcome. *I thought my body wasn't worth anything. I thought I didn't matter, but I do.* Strangely I am nodding my head, as if hearing this for the first time. My DA's eyes are large and glistening and she is nodding too. If you had asked me about Brock in that moment, I would've said, *Who?* Thoughts of him had evaporated.

My DA's boss Mr. Rosen says he is proud of everyone, all our hard work. Things will be better because of us. He and my DA step out to address the cameras and reporters that await them like gnats on the front steps of the building. Before she leaves she hands me two envelopes, the tops frayed, already opened to make sure they're safe for me to read. I wonder who they are from, how anyone had even known how to find me.

I tell everyone to go to my house, I will meet them there. A deputy escorts me through the back doors of the building. Outside, I turn around one last time and see the security guards standing along the window, their faces twisted in asking. I give them the thumbs-up and they break into smiles, waving, clapping and pumping their fists behind the glass. Then I am ducking behind the cars, weaving through the parking lot. I need to call Tiffany.

I reach her as she is walking to teach a freshman seminar. *We did it,* I said, *all three.* Her words come back at me sputtered, neither of us finding words. It is the first time I feel joy, because I can finally give her something good, and relief blooms deep inside me. Later she said when she stood at the head of her classroom, she began sobbing. Her sobbing turned into laughter, and the class, unsure of what to make of this, began laughing too. *I'm sorry,* she said, *I'm just having a really good day.*

I call Lucas and I can hear him hollering, tears in his voice. I drive home down the same streets, but I feel entirely new. Something has been peeled off, I am glowing. I see the parking lot that used to be the pumpkin patch. The creek where I caught water bugs. The Taco Bell where we used to go after school dances. I am back, my past selves parading behind me. I have given us a happier ending. Finally, I am home.

I can see my grandma, mom, and Athena through the kitchen window in the courtyard. I walk into their hugs and forehead kisses. My grandma pours a glass of cold grape juice and breaks the slabs of dark chocolate into pieces on the counter. I stuff the chocolate into my cheeks, let it melt on my teeth, chugging the sweet juice. I can feel myself reviving, my mom's soft hands smoothing over my hair, gently massaging my neck.

My grandma says she'd rehearsed a speech just in case it hadn't gone the way we wanted, and I learned that everyone had been preparing to take care of me had it not gone as planned. Athena says she feels grateful to have been there, that something had lifted in her, like she had finally received justice for her own assault. My dad calls from work, *Sweetie, how are you feeling, you did it, is Mom there, are you doing okay, how did Tiffy react?*

Evening arrives, coloring the kitchen a soft lavender as they set off for home. I book the first flight to Philly in the morning, eager to be Chanel again. I throw all of my sweaty court clothes in the hamper and pack my suitcase. My parents peek their heads in. *Are you sure you want to go in the morning, I cut up some strawberries, you can stay here as long as you need, pack a warm coat for the plane.*

I write a list of everyone I'd encountered on this journey. People who came into my life and helped me, asking nothing in return. I do not know how to thank them, except to live out the life they gave back to me. I grab my notebook and draw twelve small faces, summoning them from memory. Those who were willing to bear witness. I remember the cards in my purse and pull them out.

The first card has a monkey that says *hang in there*, from Washington, D.C. The second envelope is light blue, from Ohio, a state I had come to irrationally fear. It is sent to me from a woman named Nadia. The card inside has a black-and-white photograph on the front; a small girl, wearing a flowered coat, frilly socks peeking above her sneakers, holding up a mossy stone three times her size. I open the card and take in the scribbly blue letters,

So many of us have read about you.

When I saw this card in the store, I knew I had to get it for you because this little girl reminds me of your strength.

I'm sending this card to let you know you are not alone.

I can't imagine the hell you've been through.

We are in awe of your courage and resilience and badassery.

Know that you have a huge army of soldiers behind you.

This *you* sounds heroic, mythical. For the past year I had been raking through comments looking for signs of support. I dug through opinion pieces in local newspapers searching for someone to stand up for me. I locked myself in my car in parking lots crying into hotlines, convinced I was losing my mind. All year the loneliness had followed me, in the stairwell at work, in Philly, in the wooden witness stand, where I looked out at a near-empty audience.

Yet all along there had been eyes watching me, rooting for me, from their own bedrooms, cars, stairwells, and apartments, all of us shielded inside our pain, our fear, our anonymity. I was surrounded by survivors, I was part of a *we*. They had never been tricked into seeing me as a minor character, a mute body; I was the leader on the front line fighting, with an entire infantry behind me. They had been waiting for me to find justice. This victory would be celebrated quietly in rooms in towns in states I had never even been to.

For so long, I'd imagined myself wandering across a dry, empty plain. This card was the puddle. The realization that just below the surface, more water led to streams to rivers to oceans. That this was only the beginning. I was not alone. They had found me.

9.

I WAS HALF walking, half running to therapy down the crowded side-walk, past the iHop, through revolving doors, to announce to my thera-pist it was a clean sweep. I wanted an emotional medal. Only seven months earlier I had sat on the couch, immobilized by the thought of going to court. Now there was nothing left to prepare for, we would be nothing more than two people having a chat, like the last day of class before summer break.

Have you heard the good news? I sat down, clasped my hands together, *All three.* She congratulated me. I paused, could feel my face changing. In the time I'd been gone so much had happened. Something inside me uncapped and I began spilling sentences, using up all the air in the room, *and then and then and then,* and the hour was up. The intensity lingered, the air in the room polluted with everything I'd unloaded. Instead of pleased, I was pissed. She had hardly spoken.

I walked back with my hands in my pockets, frustrated. The verdict was supposed to wipe clean the mess that had preceded it. What more could I want? I was angry to still be angry. But I shouldn't have been surprised. I had seen an article in *The Washington Post* announcing the verdict: *critics argued that the jury was harsh on Turner and treated an ambiguous and alcohol-fueled moment with black-and-white certainty.* It said, *With sentencing June 2 and an appeal possible, Turner's once-promising future remains uncertain. But his extraordinary yet brief swim career is now tarnished, like a rusting trophy.* His was still the notable loss.

The sentencing would take place on June 2 and it was recommended, but not required, that I come. Brock's three felonies added up to a maximum of fourteen years in prison. My DA recommended six years. She asked me to write a victim impact statement, two to three pages about how this experience affected me. If I wanted to read it aloud they'd buy me a ticket home. If I didn't want to read it, my advocate could read it for me. I had to submit it by the end of May so the judge had ample time to look it over beforehand. Tiffany and Lucas could also write statements. It was all optional, we had time to think about it. I said I would, put down the phone, and pushed it out of my mind. I had eight weeks, for seven of which I planned to do nothing but live a normal life.

Within five days of returning, I had written a new comedy set, auditioned, and made the cut for the spring show. In comedy I could be unruly and outrageous in ways that weren't questioned. At one meeting, our president, Vince, was writing our introductions. For me he said, *Please give her a warm round of applause as this is the only thing she has going on in her life.* It played to the stereotype of partners. *Is it too mean?* he asked. I was the one who laughed the loudest. *If only you knew.*

Two weeks after the trial, I stepped onto the Helium Comedy Club stage again, my presence met with whooping and hollering. I was engulfed in praise and love. Our group made so much money from ticket sales we treated ourselves to the Barclay Prime steakhouse in Philly. I'd never been to a restaurant so upscale, the waiter walking around with a velvet box of knives asking us each to choose one. As I cut into my soft filet mignon, I wished I could exchange the slab of meat for cash that I could pocket. The meal cost more than I had in my bank account.

I was too ashamed to tell Lucas or my family that my bank account was nearly empty. In one month Lucas would graduate, move to San Francisco, job opportunities lined up before him. I would be unemployed, unable to go out to dinner, pay rent. I had no prospects ahead save for a final court date. I planned to live with my parents again, save again. I was grateful to have my old bedroom as an option, but it was distressing to be back at square one.

Something else was happening that I kept to myself: in between dinners and graduation parties, I shut myself in the bathroom, my shoulders quivered, and tears ran down my face. During trial I had shut down to make it through. Now came the release, my body helpless against the anguish passing through in waves. Each time it would rise in me like the need to vomit, and I'd lock myself in and hyperventilate, my eyes stinging. I was scared of the way my body kept dictating these episodes. I'd grip the sink, turning on the faucet to drown out the sounds. *Why are you sad,* I kept thinking, *you won.* I did not want Lucas to hear me, to realize that I was still broken, not ready to let all of this go.

In my in-box, a message surfaced from Michele Dauber, a Stanford professor and activist who demanded Stanford do more to stop campus sexual assault. She was also an old family friend whom I hadn't seen since my teens. In middle school, her daughter and I had been a part of the same group of friends, biking to Blockbuster to rent *Carrie,* eating Cheetos, tucked inside sleeping bags in the little guesthouse.

When my story first broke, I watched from my bed as news cameras interviewed Michele in the doorway of her home, the same door I'd walked through in middle school with muddy Skechers. I wanted her wisdom, but I knew if I spoke to her, I'd be accused of having an agenda. Even *The Washington Post* article had quoted a critic who said, *The prosecutor was playing to the demands of Stanford female activists.* I watched as Michele gave statements about the case, unaware I was Emily, fascinated by how closely we coexisted. So many times I'd wanted to say, *It's me.*

She had put it together after following the string of articles that repeated my sister's name, my high school, my university. She said she asked her daughter and then my closest childhood friend, Nicole, if it was true. I would have told Nicole, but she'd been studying Urdu in India all year. Both Michele and Nicole sent me outpourings of apology, *If I'd known I would have helped.* Nicole bought a flight home for the sentencing. Michele asked Stanford student leaders if they'd be interested in gathering signatures of support from students. The leaders wrote letters asking for a two-year minimum, citing the need to set a precedent and deter sexual violence on campus. She said a group of them could come to the sentencing wearing ribbons in solidarity, but I was too nervous, quietly nixed this idea, keeping my world small, protected, carefully selected. I called my friend Mel, my best friend in college, who immediately bought a flight from LA for the sentencing. I called Miranda, who would take me to hot springs to relax. I told Cayla, who would skip work and drive in from San Francisco. It moved me how quickly they'd made plans to be there. I could now count the number of friends involved on two hands.

April passed, the end of May approaching. I still had not begun my statement, kept telling myself, *soon.* My DA messaged me, could I send her something in the next two weeks?

For the past seventeen months, every time I had a thought related to the case I would jot it in the Notes section of my phone and label it with Brock's initials. Finally I sat down and searched "B.T." Dozens of notes appeared that I had not read since writing them. I copied and pasted all of the text into a Word document. I had dozens of pages of haphazard notes. I sat and read everything in one sitting. Then I walked out of the room and did not return to my desk for three days.

Through all my years of writing classes, teachers told us that if a topic felt too raw you put it aside for a later time. Create distance. But this deadline had been created for me. I had also never encountered an assignment like this, to write up a list of emotional damages. The prompt was depressing. Why should I document the ways I might be irreversibly ruined? I had a "Making a Victim Impact Statement" brochure that suggested questions: *How do you feel when you wake up in the morning? How often do you cry? How much of each day do you feel sad? Have you thought about suicide?*

One afternoon I received a call from an unknown number. I let it go to voice mail. In the message, a woman identified herself as an officer from the Probation Department. I had learned to be wary. I called my DA, asking if I was allowed to talk to this woman. My DA said the officer wanted my input about the upcoming sentencing and I should call her and tell her I was writing a statement I could share.

I was surprised the officer called me. I was used to being voiceless, my opinion rarely requested. I assumed there were minimum sentences for each felony. I imagined this would be her nice way of letting me contribute my two cents and I expected my words to literally be worth pennies, wishful coins thrown into a fountain.

I told the probation officer I was writing a statement. But she began asking me questions. I responded by telling her I was hurt, and what hurt me most was watching my family suffer. I kept a palm to my forehead and closed my eyes, trying to focus, to stay with her questions, always more questions. I told her I had survived a school shooting carried out by a man who never got the help he needed. I didn't want Brock to slip off the rails and punish more women, needed to be sure he was in therapy, taking classes in jail. *So you want no more than a year,* she said. I was confused, I had never said that. She explained that I had said "jail" and county jail has a one-year maximum. Prison has no maximum. *Oh,* I said. *Well, do they offer classes in prison?* I wondered why no one had explained this to me.

Most importantly I wanted Brock to own up to what he had done. I asked if she had spoken to him and she said no, but she would be meeting with him the following week. I said it was hard for me to fully answer her without hearing what he had to say. *You want him to get it,* she said. She said she understood. The conversation had been brief. I told her I was working on a statement and I'd be more comfortable emailing it to her when I was done. But she said my oral statement had been fine, she'd jotted down a few notes, and that wouldn't be necessary. *You did great,* she said. We both hung up.

I felt a lingering discomfort. I wished somebody else had been there for the conversation. I told myself I was being paranoid, she would take care of things.

Days later I received a call from my DA, her voice fraught. *Can you tell me what you said to her?* Throughout the year I had always been nervous about messing things up simply because I didn't know enough; mixing time frames up on the stand, wearing the wrong thing to court, speaking with an improper tone. She explained the probation officer had offered a lenient sentence, had said I only cared about treatment, not incarceration, suggesting Brock didn't belong in prison. I wondered how I had finally been given a voice, but it had not been the one I wanted. *Laws exist,* I thought. *How is it possible for me to blow it at this point?*

I told her I'd call the probation officer back, but my DA said it was too late, the report had been filed. She would send me the probation officer's recommendation along with Brock's statement so I could respond to them in my own statement. Distraught, I opened the report.

The probation officer had given my input a single paragraph. She had taken my words but constructed her own sentences, shaving all context away. *I just want him to get better,* it said. She gave me a voice of forgiveness and submission, the agony neatly paved over. She'd reduced my suffering to the line, *I don't experience joy from this.* She'd drawn her own conclusion: *He doesn't need to be behind bars.* This woman, who had been absent for the entire battle, had arrived to take the victory away. For months I had been climbing out of this hole, my hands finally gripping the edge. Now I watched the dirt turn to mud beneath my fingers as I slipped down again.

The officer noted she had been *struck by the victim's ability to objectively digest the gravity and ramifications of the defendant's behavior.* That word, *digest.* She had mistaken my strength for digestion. Perhaps she'd expected a hysterical victim, the weeping and scathing kind. She could not hear how my muscles had tensed, did not know the way Lucas found me lying mute on the couch after the call, exhausted from the resurgence of memories.

As a woman, I'd tried asserting my opinion without coming off as self-serving or overcontrolling. So I repressed pissed-off victim. Now I wondered if I had handled it too gracefully, my composure a signal that what he'd done was of little consequence. When I'd advocated for him to take classes and be in therapy, she mistook it as a nurturing passivity, gentle absolution. What I meant was take note of his mental health, because in my experience, when men were upset, lonely, or neglected, we were killed.

A moderate county jail sentence, formal probation, and sexual offender treatment is respectfully recommended. It sunk me. *Moderate* suggested his crime was of low quality, low intensity, tolerable. It was diminishing: *This case, when compared to other crimes of similar nature, may be considered less serious due to the defendant's level of intoxication.*

She had interviewed Brock, reported, *the defendant expressed sincere remorse and empathy for the victim.* I wondered if her suggestion had been light because Brock had finally taken responsibility. I opened that PDF:

I swear I never would have done any of this if [she] wasn't willing . . . we were just in the heat of the moment. If at any time I thought she was not responding, I would have stopped immediately. . . . I never meant to treat her like anything else than an exceptional person. . . . During the trial I didn't want to victimize her at all. That was just my attorney and his way of approaching the case. . . . I have to sacrifice everything . . . things can go from fun to ruined in just one evening. He explained he'd been working on a program where he *speaks out against the college campus drinking culture and the sexual promiscuity that goes along with that.*

I didn't read anymore, didn't need to. As I scrolled, I realized at the bottom of the report were nearly forty letters written and signed by guidance counselors, teachers, coaches in Ohio. I skimmed, then paused at a letter submitted by his grandparents: *Brock is the only person being held accountable for the actions of other irresponsible adults.*

There was another form filled out by the officer I had spoken to. Under victim's race, she had checked *White.* Never in my life have I checked only *White.* You cannot note my whiteness without acknowledging I am equal parts Chinese. This single check mark was a testament to how little time she'd taken to know me, making the assumption I was white over the phone without bothering to ask.

I discarded what my DA said and called the probation officer. Digest my ass, digest, I would pull the needle from the grenade, give her the victim she'd expected. I listened to the long brittle rings, arguments mounting in my head, but a recording politely asked me to leave a message, a beep, then silence. I hung up the phone, laid my palms flat on the desk. I stared at the cup of pencils, the photo of a beach on the wall. Everything was so calm. Nothing matched what I was feeling, my rage had nowhere to go. I smacked the cup of pencils, the thin stems spilling to the floor. *I'M CHINESE.* I screamed, slamming the table with my fists, throwing back my chair. *I'M CHINESE.*

I walked into the living room, Lucas rose out of his seat, resting his hands on my shoulders, talking me down. *It's okay, it's okay, what's going on.* He was speaking in a level tone, trying to get me to match it. I pushed his hands off. I told him, *You need to be angry. When you read this I want you to be angry.* I wanted him to be so mad his body could not help but be anything else, to know what that felt like. I wanted him boiling, wanted him to break things.

Sexual violence labeled *moderate,* why shouldn't we be enraged. Maybe it is not calm they wanted all along, but suppressed, quiet, contained. My statement would no longer be a sad journal entry about my feelings. My DA had asked me to address the judge directly, but I would speak directly to Brock. I called my DA again, *Is there a limit to how long my statement can be?* Technically no, she said.

I typed furiously until my fingers curled. I'd push away from the table, walking a few circles before I could sit back down. Rage activates, but too much of it cripples. *Now. I have to do this now.* But I kept stopping, wiping my cheeks with the backs of my hands. I physically could not handle it, could not funnel my anger into a petty tap-tap of keys, could not worry about syntax when my body was breaking down.

I called my friend Mel, overcome. She said, *Tell me what's wrong.* I explained the never-ending series of hurdles, the hollow apologies. When I finally stopped, she said, *I just typed up everything you said. I will now email it back to you. Use it.*

That night, Margaret Cho was performing at the same Helium Comedy Club. In 2015, she released a music video called *I Wanna Kill My Rapist.* I looked up to her for being unapologetic, honest, and one of the few Asian American role models in mainstream culture when I was growing up. I sat on the perimeter of the audience, watching her step out of the same door I had used to arrive onstage. She wore red heels, yellow *Kill Bill* pants, and a black T-shirt that said OUI. After the show, as the audience trickled away, I walked straight to the greenroom door and knocked. Immediately two bodyguards stepped in, blocking me. *But I performed here,* I said. A woman who worked there told me to leave. I always do as I am told, but my feet remained planted. Two more employees swatted me away with a dish towel, telling me to go. Suddenly, I saw Margaret's head emerge between the shoulders of the bodyguards. I called her name. I said, *I'm a comedian too.* We talked through the men's shoulders, and she looked me right in the eye, smiling. I said,

I just wanted to say I enjoyed your music video. She thanked me and asked me my name. *Chanel,* I said. She nodded, *Nice to meet you, Chanel.* We touched hands above the men's shoulders, and then she was hustled away.

As I turned, something gave. I sat down in a wooden chair with my head in my hands in the empty club and began sobbing. I could not stop. As we walked home I cried openly. I tried to smile while I cried to avoid alarming anyone on the street. My rage had been punctured, had released the despair. She understood how it felt when someone wanted you broken. Kicking and screaming is not a sign you have lost your mind. It's a sign that you have stepped onto your own side. You are learning, finally, how to fight back. Rage had arrived to burn the timidness away.

But how to make them listen? I did not want to be written off as a ranting victim. I remembered learning that anger was a secondary emotion, the primary emotion was closer to pain. I'd make them hear the hurt beneath the fury. To calm down, I taped up the blank poster boards Lucas had bought for me after our first date. I drew a huge road, one loop, creatures cycling around it in wagons and unicycles; a slug wearing a scarf blowing in the wind, flamingos with their necks twisted in knots, an antelope riding a scooter. Drawing until my mind was at peace again.

The next day I called my friend Matt, who was still unaware that I was Emily. Everyone around me had been trained to expect little from Brock and this broken system. I wanted someone's shock to be fresh, to hear the initial incomprehension, *how could that possibly be.* I felt crazy, I was crazy, I just needed someone to say *this makes me crazy too.* When I told him, his sorrow and frustration soothed me. He is Christian and asked if he could pray for me, and he did, right there on the phone. He did not ask God for strength, rather informed God that he knew I was strong enough to make it through this.

I had told my story many times; but with loved ones I told censored versions. In court I could only speak through questions others asked me. I took out my worn copy of Anne Lamott's *Bird by Bird*, which had guided me through college. She wrote, "Remember that you own what happened to you. . . . You cannot write out of someone else's dark place; you can only write out of your own." For the first time I would be telling my version of the story. A letter, from me, to Brock.

That night, I told myself, you are going to sit down and you are going to feel all of it. Dark, nasty things are going to crawl out of you. Images will reappear. The feeling of uncertainty and isolation you had at each stage will be felt again. You will feel sick, you will feel sad. This will not be fun, this will feel impossible, but it will be done. It must be done. The present version of myself would walk through a long, dark tunnel to meet the girl who woke up on the gurney, join hands, and begin the walk back through the timeline of horrible memories, as she slowly learned the truth. As I typed, my face scrunched up, often I spoke out loud, sometimes the skin on my neck tightened, I whispered, I yelled, my eyes blurred with tears, I seethed, I stood up, I slumped in my seat, I walked in circles, but the two selves in my head continued to walk and walk, my present self constantly reminding my past self not to stop and curl up, just to walk through. I wrote all the way up to the present, and then I stopped. Past self and present self hugged, and past self disappeared. It was 7:00 A.M. and in nine hours I had written twenty-eight incoherent pages, my first draft. I looked out my window, the sun rising. I looked over at Lucas, sleeping peacefully. I ate some Lucky Charms cereal in my pajamas, listening to my spoon clinking against the bowl in the silence, the diluted yellow sun coating the buildings. I could see a bus down below, a small rectangle pulling up to its stop, people crossing the street. Another day was beginning. I was okay. The story had not swallowed me.

For the next few days, I'd wake up and roll into my chair without brushing my teeth. I ate only when Lucas forced a plate in front of me. The long showers I usually relished became quick rinses. I didn't have time to waste. I yelled the statement out loud from beginning to end to get the words right. I worried neighbors would call the police, as I screamed YOU HAVE BEEN CONVICTED OF VIOLATING ME, INTENTIONALLY, FORCIBLY, SEXUALLY WITH MALICIOUS INTENT. I wanted to tape a little paper to the front door: Just practicing.

I kept pushing off my deadline, asking for a day or two more. When I had run out of time, I sent it off. The judge would have one week to read it before the sentencing.

Almost immediately I became sick. I completely lost my voice. It was not husky, but gone, shavings of sound in between breath. I went to Rite Aid to buy a bag of lemon mint cough drops and my card was denied. I quickly slid them back over the counter, apologizing with a nod, and left. When I checked my bank account online, I had two dollars and eighty-three cents. This was the account I had proudly opened a year earlier when I'd landed my first job. I sifted through the room, looking for things I had bought that I could return. I spotted a book I had purchased, the receipt still tucked inside the pages. It was Charles Bukowski's You Get So Alone at Times That It Just Makes Sense. I had been drawn to the title. I walked to the bookstore and got my sixteen dollars back.

On the day of Lucas's graduation, I walked to the ceremony alone, voiceless in his large black coat. His parents flew in to celebrate. They took us to Fogo de Chão, a Brazilian steakhouse, where we were each given a coaster; one side red, one side green. If you placed the green side face up on the table, waiters swarmed to you with racks of meat they'd slice straight onto your plate. Red side meant I am content for the moment, please leave me be. I loved the control, the way a flip of the coaster could send waiters into motion around me, the way the red made everything stop.

Lucas's parents still did not know about the case. They had planned a family trip to Lake Tahoe on June 2, the day of the sentencing, but Lucas told them he had to stay in Palo Alto to "help a friend" and would drive up the next day to meet up with them. I trusted them and always felt warmly welcomed, that was never the issue. Being sexually assaulted was not something I imagined I would share with most people. The public nature of the case had put me in a strange position. I felt awful they'd watched the story unfold in the news, unaware their son was involved, but I was torn; do I have a right to privacy or do they have a right to know? I also wanted the chance for them to get to know me better as Chanel before they knew me as Emily.

We spent our final days in Philly packing my books on the windowsill into boxes, wrapping the pots and pans I had accumulated over the year. I left a card by the hot cocoa machine for Anthony, hoping he'd find it during his morning rounds. I hugged the women at the desk good-bye, gave them markers and books for their daughters, who I'd gotten to know through photos and stories. Lucas and I sat in the barren apartment, eating cold canned soup. I asked if I could read his statement, and he hesitated, worried it would hurt me. I assured him I'd be fine.

Chanel has hated talking about the night that she was violated. . . . He'd written about the way I became verbally hostile, upset, abrasive, whenever the case was brought up. I remembered the shattered phone, the screaming matches. I remembered halfway through a movie, a rape unfolding on screen, yelling to *turn it off, turn it off, where's the damn remote,* getting up to leave, slamming the door. He wrote about my inability to sleep by myself, the physical insecurity, keeping the lights on. He noticed times I left the apartment to wander aimlessly around the city, needing to be alone. How the process had been more invasive, public, and longer than we anticipated. *Chanel has allowed me, in confidence and only due to our closeness, occasional glimpses of the pain that comes with this public violation of her body. . . . Please do not confuse that strength with the deep, negative, and permanent impact that comes with a man publicly sexually assaulting a woman while unconscious, and the year-long, media-ridden trial that has followed.* I ached from the way this ugly event had reared its head in our relationship as we struggled to incorporate it into our lives.

. . . Chanel habitually hides in our apartment bathroom and locks the door . . . for hours at a time, unprompted. I can hear her crying through the bathroom door, when I am nearby. I felt my cheeks growing hot, suddenly self-conscious. I was embarrassed by my behavior, my failure to conceal my pain. *Chanel is a courageous woman and should be commended for her emotional fortitude.*

I'm sorry, he said. *I thought this was the assignment. You know how strong you are, right?* I nodded, tears emerging. I was a little mortified, but mostly I was touched. When asked to write a letter about how he'd noticed me changing, he did not say, *Well I don't know, I wasn't there.* He could've kept my pain at arm's length, a safe distance away, or removed himself entirely. Instead he had been on the other side of the bathroom door, listening, trying to figure out how to care for the new me.

When Tiffany sent her statement to my mom, my mom sent back a few words: *Sorry my Tiffy, Mama can't read, cry too hard.* I braced myself to read it. It was as painful as I had imagined, but there was another tone in it too.

Those moments that you assaulted her were just the beginning; you took her down with you because you failed. You saw a drunk girl alone, incapacitated—why would you not try to find her friends? I was trying to find her. You nearly destroyed her spirit, but you did not succeed. You cannot undo the harm you have caused her, the darkness you have put us through, but you can now finally leave us alone to heal. The only sorrow I feel for you is that you never got to know my sister before you assaulted her. She's the most wonderful person in the world.

I'd never heard this defiant note in my sister. *You failed. Leave us alone.* I was stunned by her strength. Maybe my little sister was not as little as I thought. Maybe I'd gone with her back to Cal Poly after the hearing because I'd been the one scared to be alone. Because I wanted her to take care of me, to sleep in her bed as she came and went from classes. This whole time I'd tried to preserve this illusion I could be unwaveringly competent, never dependent. But they had seen through it.

Julia also provided a statement, but her letter was almost entirely about changes she had seen in Tiffany. It was stunning, the effects rippling out wider than I could ever have imagined. I thought of my pain like my personal rain cloud; reading these letters was like watching the whole sky turn an inky black. When all damages were typed up and laid out it was staggering. Everyone had become a victim of this crime. Everyone had their story, had doors they secretly suffered behind. I needed to find a way to clear the skies.

The probation officer's report had been a bump in the road, but with my twelve-page statement, a few letters from loved ones, and over two hundred Stanford student signatures, we had a chance. I was informed I'd have limited time and would need to read an abridged version of my statement. I would focus on what I wanted to say to Brock. I predicted he'd be going away for at least two years, this would be his send-off. My DA said that we may want to leave the courtroom after I read; if Brock was handcuffed and taken away, emotions would run high in his family. I remembered the stomping, the wailing, did not forget the anguish and chaos that accompanied these victories. No matter how angry I was, it never caused me joy to see others in pain.

On the plane ride back, I pulled out my computer to make some edits, elbows tucked in, typing with two fingers. Suddenly, a woman in the row to my left yelled, *He's not okay, somebody help.* I watched the man beside her shake, his neck bent back like putty, his mouth wide open. He had a picture of his family printed on his T-shirt. His young son stared up at him. His teenage daughter was sitting next to me. Two men materialized stating they were doctors. As the mom remained frantic, *do something*, I watched the sister quietly gesture to her brother to come sit on her lap. I watched her wrap her arms around him, then calmly explain her father's medical history of seizures to the doctors. I watched her stare down the people craning their necks into the aisle. *I wish they would give us some privacy,* she said. I understood the feeling of wanting to pull a blanket over your suffering while the public treated it like a spectacle. Her mom was exasperated, her brother gaped, but she had not even blinked. *Digest.*

Tiffany drove home from school the night before the sentencing. She had come for one night, would have to go back to take her final exams. She laid on my bed, scrolling through the letters of support for him from people in Ohio. I could see it bothering her. I was sitting at my desk, making final touches to my statement. I told her to stop reading, not to worry. I've got something better.

I slept well that night, my anxiety hushed. I reminded myself I was only here to seal the deal. That morning I put on my oatmeal-colored sweater. This would be the third and last time I'd be wearing it in court. I put a Pop-Tart in my purse. Tiffany left early to meet her friends at the courthouse. I walked out of the house with my printed statement in hand, forgetting my keys, locking myself out and unable to start my car. Tiffany had to come back and get me. I sat in the passenger's seat re-writing lines as she drove, distracted, talking to myself. As we sat in the victim closet, I read new lines to Lucas, *does that make sense, is this line okay.*

I knew a few friends were coming but I didn't know what it'd feel like to see so many familiar faces materialize on my side of the court-room. Mel, Cayla, Athena, Nicole, Michele and her daughter, Grandma Ann, Anne, Julia, Myers, Tiffany's friends, my mom and dad. All of them had stepped out of their lives without a second thought to be there. This dreary world I had only known as my own, a miserable realm, now looked like a regular room. I told myself, *Do you understand now, your loved ones want to go to bat for you, you only had to let them.*

I smiled at Detective Mike Kim, I felt invincible, excited even. But a couple of things threw me. I thought I would be behind the witness stand, the same way I'd testified, facing the audience to deliver my statement. Instead I would be standing with my back to everyone in the courtroom, facing the judge directly. I understood now why my DA had wanted me to write my statement addressing the judge. Brock and his attorney would be sitting at a table with their backs to me.

It also hit me that the jury would not be there, their box empty. I felt sad they wouldn't be there to watch me reclaim my identity, to rewrite the only version of me they'd seen. To my right, my DA's boss, Mr. Rosen, sat with two pieces of paper on his lap. One speech for if it went well, one speech for if it went poorly. He kept flipping between them.

As we sat there waiting, I realized that my case was one in a line, that the rows were packed with strangers. My whole family watched as a man received his sentence for a DUI. Next a young Chinese woman in a red blouse stood up, holding a thin stack of papers. Her voice was shaking, English was not her first language. She spoke about her ex-fiancé, his physical abuse. She asked the judge if she could show pictures of her face after she'd been beaten. The judge gave a strained smile, said, *Why don't you just show them to me.* She held up a series of large photos. The lower half of her face looked crusted with ketchup. There was an audible intake of breath. It slowly registered that the man standing only a few feet to her right, hands loosely clasped behind his back, had done this to her. She said she was wearing the same shirt she had bled in. As she spoke, the judge's hand went up, asking how long she had left. I was in shock. I did not know he was free to stop you. She said she was almost done, started again, struggling in English to pick up speed. My eyes went back and forth between the judge and her, growing nervous she would not be able to finish. I could see the page she was holding; we were down to the last paragraph, we were almost there. The judge interrupted again, reminding her we needed to wrap things up. He was already organizing papers. She assured him she had only a few more lines. She stood, a few feet from her attacker, fighting for her life in a foreign language in a foreign country, but was indirectly told, your problems are taking up too much time. The man, charged with battery causing serious bodily harm, had asked for a light punishment. She said, *When I get beaten, can I ask for a better offer?*

I had forgotten, temporarily, where I was. The man would be sentenced to seventy-two days of weekend jail, so he could maintain his job during the week. I did not know weekend jail even existed. Incarcerated on Saturdays and Sundays, back in the office every Monday. I felt hollowed by the images of her blood-caked face while the judge swept at her feet, hurry, hurry.

Someone was nudging me, *are you ready*. I looked down at my packet, panicking. No, I'm not. I hadn't shortened it enough, needed to cross out more paragraphs, where's my pen. I was called to the front. I stood up mechanically and wedged my way sideways down the row, bumping into people's knees as I told myself to focus. My DA stood next to me. I tried to smooth out my bent papers on the podium. Just look at the words, just read. As I began, I could hear my voice trembling, like I was wobbling across a string bridge. Come on, find your way, you didn't come this far to get cut before you finished page 1. Don't cry, you've done enough crying.

Then I felt my DA's hand, pressed flat against the center of my back, holding me steady. The gentle weight of her palm centered me, told me, *I'm right here*. Soon I heard people sniffling, they were crying. *It's working, they're listening*, I thought. My delivery smoothed out, my power returning. I realized how loudly I was speaking, my yelling amplified by the microphone. I did not adjust. I looked straight at the judge, meeting his eyes repeatedly, reminding him I was not done. This time I carved his face in my memory. I pointed at the back of the defense attorney's cotton-haired head. He never turned to face me. I bore into the side of Brock's unmoving face, his stoic profile. I was rooted, pointing at him. I wanted everyone consumed by my voice, in my control.

Silence followed my final words. As I sat down I was received back into everyone's arms as if descending from the sky, all of them catching me. People were distraught, crying. They leaned over to whisper, squeeze my arm, rub my back. I was shaking, coming back into myself inside their touches. Settled in between Lucas and Tiffany, I felt my stomach softening. I had done it. I left it all on the floor. That was it, it was over.

To my surprise Brock's father stood up. I appreciated this, thinking he was going to apologize on behalf of his son. But as he stood, he did not look at me. He went straight to the podium, adjusting his belt, locking eyes with the judge. *Brock would do anything to turn back the hands of time and have that night to do over again.*

Soon we were inside a story of Brock in elementary school, weekly spelling tests, baseball, Cub Scouts. I blinked a few times wondering what was happening. If a victim speaks but no one acknowledges her, does she make a sound? He explained Brock was accepted academically before he was considered athletically, he had large amounts of interest from Division I coaches. At one point his father paused, choked up, while the judge waited patiently. Brock had the highest GPA of all freshmen on the swim team. Awarded a 60 percent swimming scholarship. Stanford had a 4 percent acceptance rate.

He explained: *[Brock had been] struggling to fit in socially. In hindsight, it's clear that Brock was desperately trying to fit in at Stanford and fell into a culture of alcohol consumption and partying. This—this culture was modeled by many of the upperclassmen on the swim team and clearly played a role in the events of January 17 and 18, 2015. Looking back at Brock's brief experience at Stanford, I honestly don't believe it was the best fit for him.* Homesickness had never occurred to me a defense. He said Brock's life had been *deeply altered . . . He will never again be his happy-go-lucky self, with that easygoing personality and welcoming smile.*

We had come to Brock's funeral. *I was always excited to buy him a big rib-eye steak to grill or to get his favorite snack for him. . . . Now he eats only to exist.* I could hear my family stirring.

These verdicts have broken and shattered him and our family in so many ways. He spoke of the verdicts as if they were a disease that had befallen them. Verdict of what? Guilt. Guilt for what? Assault. Assault committed by whom? Brock. Your son has broken and shattered your family. But he could never say that.

That is a steep price to pay for twenty minutes of action out of his twenty-plus years of life. I was still. I just wanted him to be finished.

He has no prior criminal history and has never been violent to anyone, including his actions on the night of January 17. This one felt like a direct hit, a message just for me. I looked straight ahead at the blank wall. I felt the tension rising in every row, like a fight was about to erupt. Brock's stance suddenly made a lot more sense. He had lived shielded under a roof where the verdict was never accepted, where he would never be held accountable.

Next came Brock. I had never heard his voice. For over a year he'd been a silent face in the courtroom. Now he stood hunched, holding a single sheet of paper folded in half. The light that shone through the paper showed only a few typed lines. I stared at the weightlessness of it; I could blow from where I was sitting and it'd slip out of his hands. I looked down at the thick, stapled packet of my statement on my lap, marked up in edits. His voice came out slowly, each word pulled like a heavy bucket out of a well, unnervingly monotone. *I'm so sorry for every moment and span of time. . . . My mind, my heart, and my body agonize over the suffering and pain I have caused on Chanel, Tiffany . . .*

I wanted to scrape our names out of his mouth. The statement he read was ten sentences long, generic apologies and plans to educate students *about the dangers of alcohol,* over in less than a minute. He had dragged us around in one small circle. I sat in disbelief. Here we were so far down the line, on the other side of a verdict, and yet again nothing seemed to have changed.

The judge ordered a brief recess. Everyone was brimming with irritation, a storm brewing. *Holy shit, what was that.* I was disturbed, but I told myself it didn't matter, it was their last desperate attempt before being kicked to the curb. The judge heard me.

When we resumed the judge opened by quoting some of my lines. He said he'd read them out loud because they were relevant to the sentencing decision. This made me hopeful. But the judge was speaking quietly, like we were in a library and he didn't want to disrupt anybody. His eyes were cast down on his papers, flipping back and forth. He went over some penal codes and at some point he said the words *six months.* I sat patiently, waiting for him to announce the final sentence. But soon he began explaining his reasoning. He said that *this is a case where probation is prohibited,* and I thought, yes, good, *except in unusual cases . . .* I had not known my case was unusual.

Some weight should be given to the fact that a defendant who is, albeit voluntarily, intoxicated versus a defendant who commits an assault with intent to commit rape, a completely sober defendant, there is less moral culpability attached to the defendant who is legally intoxicated. I had heard this sentiment echoed in the probation officer's statement. Alcohol freed Brock of moral culpability.

The judge laid out reason after reason: he was youthful, had no prior criminal offenses, no weapons, and *the degree of monetary loss to the victim is not really applicable.* He said the crime didn't demonstrate criminal sophistication, Brock did not take advantage of a position of trust or confidence to commit the crime, and registering as a sex offender was already a consequence. *Obviously, a prison sentence would have a severe impact on him.* I was struggling to comprehend, wanted to lean forward and tap my DA, *What's happening?*

He addressed the *adverse collateral consequences on the defendant's life resulting from the felony conviction. And those are severe.* He said the character letters showed huge collateral consequences. If we punished him, we'd hurt his community too. *With respect to the media attention that's been given to the case, it has not only impacted the victim in this case, but also Mr. Turner. Where, in certain cases, there is no publicity, then the collateral consequence on those on the defendant's life can be minimized.* He suffered from media attention, had not been able to keep what he'd done under wraps. I turned his phrases over in my head, examining them, but failed to understand. Then he made it clear.

Number seven is whether the defendant is remorseful. And that's maybe one of the most conflicted and difficult issues in this case. Because Mr. Turner came before us today and said he was genuinely sorry for all the pain that he has caused to Chanel and her family. And I think that is a genuine feeling of remorse. Chanel has stated that he hasn't really taken responsibility for his conduct. And I think at one point she basically wrote or said that "He—he just doesn't get it." And so you have Mr. Turner expressing remorse, which I think, subjectively, is genuine, and Chanel not seeing that as a genuine expression of remorse because he never says, "I did this. I knew how drunk you were. I knew how out of it you were, and I did it anyway." And that—I don't think that bridge will, probably, ever be crossed.

"Chanel not seeing that." It's me, the problem is me. My failure to see something the judge did. I had been deluded into thinking that's why we had all come here today, to cross the bridge. I could see the judge snipping it in midair, the bridge falling, leaving me on my side and Brock to be coddled on his. Everyone around him had succeeded in preserving him inside his illusion. I had tried to pull him out. The judge believed him. I finally felt the ground tilting, everything sliding to his side.

I mean, I take him at his word that, subjectively, that's his version of events. The jury, obviously, found it to be not the sequence of events. . . . Once a jury renders a verdict, everybody is bound by that verdict. Everybody must accept the verdict, including Mr. Turner. But I'm not convinced that his lack of complete acquiescence to the verdict should count against him with respect to an expression of remorse because I do find that his remorse is genuine. Is an apology valid without change? If he says he's sorry, but maintains he's not guilty, doesn't that resemble manipulation more than reconciliation? I was watching him release the fish back into the water, swim away, into the depths. All along I thought the judge was the head, the jury the body. They were one. But the jury had come and gone, and now only the head was speaking.

I think that he will not be a danger to others. . . . The character letters suggest that up to this point he complied with social and legal norms sort of above and beyond what normal law-abiding people do. If there's anything we had learned in all of this, it was that Brock was actually above and beyond the average person. Four percent acceptance rate. This was not a time for condemnation, but praise.

And, finally, I find another factor reasonably related to the sentencing decision is the character evidence—provided both at trial and in connection with this sentencing hearing—the character evidence with respect to Mr. Turner's past up until the point of the incident.

The incident. The unfortunate result. Twenty minutes of action. In swimming, one one-hundredth of a second is the difference between victory and loss. Yet they wanted to write off twenty minutes as insignificant. Twenty minutes was just the beginning: Who counts the six-hour flights we took back and forth across the country? Who counts the doctor visits, the hours spent wringing my hands in therapy, the nights spent lying awake? Who counts the trips to Kohl's, wondering *is this blouse too tight?* Who counts the days devoid of writing or reading or creating, instead wondering why I should wake up in the morning? Who counts it?

The judge opened up the floor for objections. My DA stood up, rapid-fired everything that was wrong. I was surprised she could string so many points together at a moment's notice. She pointed out that a six-month county jail sentence would only mean three months: every day of good behavior meant a day off his sentence. June, July, August. Brock would be home by the end of the summer, well before Thanksgiving. She said, *At minimum, it should warrant a year in county jail—at minimum.* How did we find ourselves in the position of begging for one year? When did the power shift?

I looked at the people on my side, my DA struggling to gain momentum, everyone in ruins. I turned my head to look at their side, chins lifted, hands folded, collected. No collapsing into grief and wails— instead there was a light air, calm composure. Had they known all along? The defense attorney pushed back his chair as he stood, praised the judge's accuracy, echoing that unusual circumstances called for a probationary sentence, and six months in county jail would do fine.

My final hope was the Probation Department. A woman I had never seen before stood up. She said, *After hearing what the victim had to say today and reviewing the papers that were submitted by the parties . . . the Probation Department did make a fair and complete recommendation.* I felt my chest concaving, but remained perfectly still. It was all for this. *You're ordered to serve six months in the county jail. You have one actual day credit.* He had one extra day off this sentence, since he'd spent a night in jail when he'd been arrested. It wasn't even a full day, I thought. A touch of salt.

If you wish to appeal, you must file a written Notice of Appeal with the clerk of this court within 60 days from today. The defense attorney spoke up; *I believe there's an attorney present in court who's going to be representing Mr. Turner on appeal, and may he speak to the court briefly?* I turned to my right as a white-bearded man stood up, broad chested, holding a briefcase, wearing a fitted suit. He looked like a slightly crisper version of Brock's old attorney. Is this who I'd have to fight next? I turned back to face the front. I thought I had slayed a dragon, but here was the bigger dragon. I was too tired to fight it, wanted it to be over, to curl up in its mouth. He announced he'd already prepared the Notice of Appeal, asked where he could file it. Brock may have been *genuinely remorseful,* but he had hired an even higher-powered attorney to repaint me as a liar, drunk, willing.

The judge said thank you and we were dismissed.

I imagined this was a play, we were on set, that any minute the props would be rolled away, good work everyone. That was all we needed from you, thanks for coming. *Is that it?* my sister said. I burned inside, couldn't speak. I was humiliated, wished no one had come. This is why you don't let people in, why it's better to do things alone. I felt a visceral anger toward myself for presenting this dramatic outpouring, this batshit touchy-feely monologue. I had failed to read the room. It was too much, it was too much and also not enough.

In elementary school we had to write in our yellow journals daily. One day we were doing silent reading while the teacher graded our yellow journals in the back. I heard my name, turned to see her lifting my journal up into the air, pages loosely flapping, *Chanel, there is no such thing as January 42!* I had written beyond January 31, to January 32, January 33, all the way up to January 42. The whole class was laughing, and I grew hot with shame. There were obvious rules in the world I had missed. What other things didn't I know? Now the judge was dangling my statement in the air, everyone laughing, my face burning. January has thirty-one days, rapists get three months; everyone in the world knew this, except me.

I'll be right back. I excused myself quickly out of the courtroom, my purse, I need to retrieve it from the victim closet. I walked down the hallway, tried the knob, but it was locked. As I turned around to see if someone could get me a key, I saw everyone's eyes fixed on me. Everyone I love was looking at me in worry, in need of some hope, *what now,* and even worse the feeling that I had nothing to give them. That I was so sorry, because that was all I had, and I thought I could save us, but I'd failed. My words were worth nothing.

I saw Julia pacing on the periphery. Her arms were pumping up and down, she was crying with her voice constricted, saying, *I hate him, I hate him.* She embodied what we felt, expressing it for us all, while we stood, disquieted and stricken, unable to feel it yet.

My DA showed up with the key. I had only ever seen her strong, it was always *we got this,* but now she looked pale, speechless.

We gathered in a conference room in the back. I could hear the anger in my dad's voice, telling Mr. Rosen, *His father didn't even look at her, how could he not have looked at her.* I was invisible again, someone who needed parents to fight for me, pathetic and powerless. Mr. Rosen said I did great, but I also knew which speech he held in his hand. His colleague said it was the most amazing statement he'd heard in twenty years. He told me I had said what so many victims feel but could not articulate. I nodded, knowing this must be what he said to every victim, this was a spiel. The detective reminded me they could never have come this far without me, my advocate assured me this was true. The compliments poured like water off me. I just looked at them, too familiar with that soft-shouldered posture, the gentle arm extensions, delicate tones. I didn't want it, the sympathy, the consolation.

I had failed to see this was a case in a long line of many, wedged into a schedule. The man who beat the woman was sentenced to seventy-two days, which I now realized meant thirty-six, halved by the same rule. In my eyes this had been a big deal, but the judge probably saw cases like these all the time, I was just one in passing. I suddenly found myself questioning what I'd been doing all year, what I'd even been grieving. I couldn't remember why I'd left my job, why I'd been living on the East Coast. I bent my statement into smaller and smaller squares, hiding it inside my purse.

Mr. Rosen and Alaleh were asking if they could release it. I said sure, if you think it'd be helpful. I imagined it on a community forum or on the local newspaper's website. Michele said we would keep fighting, which was supposed to register as a comfort. I nodded, but I was done. Alaleh and Mr. Rosen went out to the front steps to address the hungry cameras. He said, *The punishment does not fit the crime. The sentence does not factor in the true seriousness of this sexual assault, or the victim's ongoing trauma. Campus rape is no different than off-campus rape. Rape is rape.*

My family and I made our way down the back stairwell. For once, I did not rush. I no longer felt the urgency to protect myself, all my armor already gone. The day was sunny and quiet. Cars rolled by on their way to California Avenue for lunch. For most people it was just a regular afternoon. I tried to comfort myself by saying, you get to be a normal person again. But this was not how freedom should feel. I could see his family and the defense attorney about a hundred feet away in the parking lot, standing in a circle. I had a vision of myself strolling over, now that the barriers had dissolved, confronting them. How do you still not see me? My family kept saying, *Let's go home, what are we still doing here.* I just stood on the curb, silently convinced that if we just waited a minute longer, they'd call us back in, say they'd made a mistake. People left one by one and still I stayed.

My friends took me out to get frozen yogurt. We sat around the table Googling the difference between jail and prison, trying to understand. County jail is usually for misdemeanors; you can get six months for digging a bonfire pit at the beach, flying a drone, tampering with a fire extinguisher, trespassing on a construction site. We said maybe I should go dig a hole in the sand and get sent to jail to deal with him myself. We talked about his father's mention of steak, Brock's spelling proficiency. I said once I'd been eliminated from the spelling bee for misspelling *zucchini*. We realized half of us still didn't know how to spell it. We went around and shared stories of assault, harassment, virginities stolen not lost, unwanted touches, in a tent, at the dance, times we wished we had asked more for ourselves. We all had a story, many stories. I had come the furthest out of all of them in terms of getting justice. I suppose this is what justice looked like, sitting exhausted with a melted cup of dripping yogurt.

As the afternoon faded, Lucas drove to Lake Tahoe to join his family. Tiffany rushed back to school for final exams. My friends returned to their offices. At home my parents settled back into their corners of the house. By nighttime I was completely alone again. I had been looking forward to this moment since I could remember. At least I was done. I saw an email from Michele, who had been in touch with Amy Ziering, the producer of the documentary *The Hunting Ground*. Amy's daughter had suggested the statement be published on BuzzFeed, by a trusted journalist named Katie J.M. Baker. I thought this would be fine. I scrolled through Craigslist looking at gigs and summer jobs. I wanted to teach art at a summer camp. I wanted to sit outside on a picnic bench and glue feathers to sticks, for stakes to be low, eating peanut butter sandwiches out of brown paper bags. I did not mind if I was paid eight dollars an hour, living in my high school bedroom. Whatever I did next, I'd get to choose. I jotted a few notes of camp names. This will be great. Tears started coming out of my eyes. I closed all the tabs.

They tell you that if you're assaulted, there's a kingdom, a courthouse, high up on a mountain where justice can be found. Most victims are turned away at the base of the mountain, told they don't have enough evidence to make the journey. Some victims sacrifice everything to make the climb, but are slain along the way, the burden of proof impossibly high. I set off, accompanied by a strong team, who helped carry the weight, until I made it, the summit, the place few victims reached, the promised land. We'd gotten an arrest, a guilty verdict, the small percentage that gets the conviction. It was time to see what justice looked like. We threw open the doors, and there was nothing. It took the breath out of me. Even worse was looking back down to the bottom of the mountain, where I imagined expectant victims looking up, waving, cheering, expectantly. *What do you see? What does it feel like? What happens when you arrive?* What could I tell them? A system does not exist for you. The pain of this process couldn't be worth it. These crimes are not crimes but inconveniences. You can fight and fight and for what? When you are assaulted, run and never look back. This was not one bad sentence. This was the best we could hope for.

At the very start of the sentencing, the judge said that the question he had to ask himself was, *Is incarceration in state prison the right answer for the poisoning of Chanel's life?* I thought it had been strange the way he'd phrased it. To him, my lost job, my damaged hometown, my small savings account, my stolen pleasures, had all amounted to ninety days in county jail.

I wondered if, in their eyes, the victim remained stagnant, living forever in that twenty-minute time frame. She remained frozen, while Brock grew more and more multifaceted, his stories unfolding, a spectrum of life and memories opening up around him. He got to be a person. Where was her redemption story? Nobody talked about the things she might go on to do. I had laid my suffering bare, but I lacked a key element. The judge had given Brock something that would never be extended to me: empathy. My pain was never more valuable than his potential.

There would be no transformation. Behind bars or not, the judge had set him free, let him return to the recesses of his mind where he could do no wrong. So what was the meaning of all this? What's the objective, the end game? Not once was he forced to imagine the life of the human on the receiving end of his actions. If anything, the fight had cemented Brock inside his distortions, fortified his need to hold his ground.

I wondered if I was waking up to a truth that I had been the last one to realize; you are worth three months. A smarter part of me knew this was not right, but I could not pretend to know better. At that moment there was nothing to do but give in. I accepted that this would be one of the most painful nights of my life.

I let myself be broken. Cries rippled through me. I had two arms locked around my pillow, my chin dug in, staring straight ahead. Hold on, I said. I felt my teeth against my pillow, suffocating my cries, careful not to wake my parents. My poisoned life, three months.

But I also knew this feeling would not be infinite. As soon as the sun came up, the worst would be behind me. When the sun rose, I'd be inside a new life. One where I would never set foot in that courtroom again. Where is the sun right now, I thought. I kept looking outside, the world endlessly black, waiting for colors to shift. The blackness stayed immovable for hours and I wanted to run east, where the sun would pass over me sooner. Alone in my bedroom, eyes closed, I imagined it moving, this glowing power inching its way toward me, the earth turning heavy and slow. If you get through this night, you are promised to survive all the days ahead.

I opened up my notebook. I stared at the empty page. Then I wrote, *You are worth more than three months.* Again. *You are worth more than three months.* My face crumpled, twisted, my hand trying to outrun my mind. Listen to what your body is trying to tell you. *You are worth more than three months.* A voice in my head said, What do you like? I said, I like drawing. What are you going to do? I will draw, I will speak. *You are worth more than three months.* I am not a burden. I am not limited, I am ever expanding. Your suffering means something. *You are worth more than three months*. They could never truly have rejected me since they had never fully known me. *You are worth more than three months*. The assault was never all of me. I could feel myself fighting, driving the pen into the page. *You are worth more than three months*. My hand tensed, struggling, then softening. The light in my room was gray, I parted my blinds to peek through, outlines of trees and cars emerging. I put down my pen. Sleep.

10.

IN THE MORNING my eyes were sore, it was bright outside, a fresh day. I wanted to relish being released from the clenched jaws of the case. I would fill my Friday with slowness and sun. I was going to ride Tofu down to the salt marshes to see the white herons. I would buy a milkshake from the creamery. I would go for a swim. At that moment in time, that was the entirety of my life's plans.

But my phone was cluttered with missed calls and messages. An email from Amy: Katie J.M. Baker was waiting for my permission to release the statement on BuzzFeed. None of the coverage of my case had given me reason to think a reporter would have my best interests at heart. But Katie had handled these kinds of cases before, and I felt so worn out, and the statement seemed of such little consequence, that I didn't care much where it ended up, as long as my name wasn't on it. I sat in bed saying *hellooooo* to clear my morning voice away, then called her. She sounded excited, effusive and kind. I told her they were free to cut whatever they wanted. She said the editors weren't going to touch it. This struck me as strange; I knew there were too many pages, run-on sentences, misplaced commas. Instead, she asked if there was anything I'd like to add. I told her, *I want the judge to know that he ignited a tiny fire.*

The statement went up at 4:00 P.M. that afternoon. At the top of the article was a red rectangle calling out sentences from the statement in white lettering. Powerful formatting. But looking at it was like standing in an empty auditorium decorated with crepe streamers, worried nobody would show up. I couldn't stand it. I shut my computer, went to the kitchen. I took the plastic ice-cube trays out of the freezer, popped ice cubes out into my cup. I wished for a silver refrigerator with dispensers from which ice effortlessly tumbled out. Those were the mundane things I wanted to go the rest of my life thinking about.

I returned to the article; in the upper-left corner, there was a counter. In twenty minutes, there'd been fifteen thousand views. Katie had begun forwarding me emails from readers to me.

I am crying at my desk. I can't say much because I am at work but I will say that . . .

I wept for your pain and wept for your triumphs. I do not easily weep . . .

While I feel sick to my stomach after reading your article, I . . .

It was hard to read, I had to stop and come back to it multiple times. I barely made it through, but I am glad I did . . .

I may or may not have almost thrown up at work given my ability to relate to a lot of it, but it was comforting to have—for a moment . . .

Almost every message I received opened with someone telling me the location of where they were crying. They were enraged and then devastated, and then they said thank you, said everyone must read it. It was a reaction too complex to categorize, but it sounded like, by the end of reading, they'd emerged in a clearer space. I was taken aback by this collective murmuring, a little worried I'd made them cry.

I watched the numbers rise. A few hours later, when it hit eight hundred thousand views, I called my dad, telling him to go online. *Buzz bee? How can I find—can you send me the link?* Lucas was on a bike trip through the forest. When he texted me a picture of him in a helmet, I replied, *Something is happening.* Tiffany was studying for her final exams. I didn't want this to distract her, *Keep studying, get offline!*

At one million, I texted my mom, who was at the grocery store. *My story went viral.* She responded, *Mama bought 4 different kinds of ice cream for you!* Three firework emojis. I don't think any of us had grasped what it meant. The emails were steadily streaming in. I was nervous to look at the comment section of the article, expecting the same minimization I'd heard from the judge. But when I looked, I found heartening words. *She looked straight into the sun and laid it all out for us. You mean something to this world. PREACH IT.* Detective Kim texted me, *You are a superstar.* A text from Tiffany: *All it took for any ambiguous or mean or victim-blaming comments to disappear was your voice.*

When my dad got home, he began printing out some of the comments; he liked to underline them and sit with them. I, too, was fascinated by the words people were using. *Eloquent. Searing. Gut-wrenching. Visceral. Courageous. Cogent. A newly minted hero.* Emily was a hero. Courageous and clearheaded, defiant and unapologetic, a figure of truth and power. In this person, I did not yet see myself.

I think if I read this years ago, I would have felt less guilty, less stupid, more empowered, more validated, and simply worth more as a human being.

As Friday came to a close, I stared at my glowing screen. My dad came in to say goodnight, smiling, *Maybe the White House will call next!* This was the very thing a dad would say, reaching for the moon. Saturday morning, the count kept climbing. My household was tingling and sweet, ripening with affirmation. Katie was forwarding me emails by the hundreds. My mom came in with a bowl of rice congee. She told me to stop leaning so close to the computer screen, *bad for your eyes.* But I was addicted to the unending streams of messages, felt the need to fill up on them before the moment passed. In the last year and a half, every time my case came up in the news, I'd watch it give way to bigger news.

By Sunday evening, I assumed my celebration would be ending. The new week would begin, the world would redirect its attention. When I fell asleep, I wrote down the count:

Sunday June 5 11:00 P.M. 4,432,947

Soon, the statement was published in *The Guardian*, *The Washington Post*, the *Los Angeles Times*, *The New York Times*. It was trending on Twitter, columns of red rectangles in my feed. Michele told me Ashleigh Banfield would be reading my letter on CNN. My first instinct was to tell her she didn't have to read the whole thing. But she filled the entire segment. The statement was shoving its way through the world, clearing its own path. I began texting myself numbers as if I'd be able to map the trajectory.

Monday June 6 8:50 P.M. 6,845,577

Tuesday June 7 8:40 P.M. 10,163,254

Wednesday June 8 5:04 P.M. 12,253,134

Thursday June 9 11:30 P.M. 14,523,874

Friday June 10 12:40 P.M. 15,250,000

Video compilations emerged of people reading the entire statement aloud. Rape hotlines were ringing, calls and volunteers increasing. New York mayor Bill de Blasio hosted a reading with his wife, Chirlane McCray. California congresswoman Jackie Speier led a one-hour reading on the House floor. Congressman Ted Poe of Texas said, *She wrote the Bible on what happens to sexual assault victims*. The cast of *Girls* dedicated a video, *She Is Someone*. *My Favorite Murder* podcast covered it. *Glamour* would later honor Emily Doe as one of the 2016 Women of the Year. The statement was translated into French, German, Portuguese, Spanish, and Japanese. An undergraduate in Korea, named Youngki Kim, asked for permission to translate it into Korean. The statement was performed in sign language, in a video produced by Crystine, who was unaware we went to high school together. A feminist group in China posted photos of women holding signs: *Nobody earns the right to rape. It is still rape when he is a good swimmer.* I received emails from around the world. *Though very much across the Pacific, I am so very near to her and her pain and so very grateful for all those who did come to her aid.* Another note: *You have reached out to someone in a sleepy town here in India with your agony, your perseverance your will.* A man from Australia told me he was weeping on his porch at three in the morning. For days I was sitting in my room with my laptop next to a crusty bowl of conjee, in tears. Every message was pushing me closer to a space in which I was beginning to see myself more clearly.

One of Brock's former high school classmates, AJ, wrote a post: *Finally, I just want to make a statement for myself. Before all of this, I knew I'd never forget you. Over 8 years ago, you called me a fag and formulated opinions about me before knowing who I was. Look where we are now. The "fag" I am knows how to treat humans, wherever they may fall on the gender spectrum, with dignity and respect, and you are the face of sexual assault in the United States of America.*

I drove to meet Alaleh at the courthouse. She had a sign taped to her door: #BeTheSwede. This tiny courthouse had been flooded with colorful rectangular envelopes, clogging the mail slots. She handed me a heavy bag that I cradled with both arms. We were both still in shock, didn't know what to make of this new ending we'd been given. As I carried my loot to my car, it rattled, full of small treasures: a Ganesha necklace to offer me protection. Dangling bicycle earrings. Letters from a teacher in New Zealand, a softball team in Arizona. A woman had taken stunning photographs of pine trees to replace the triggering memory with beauty. A watercolor painting of a lighthouse. Two purple chocolate bars from a woman in Ireland, to replenish the supply that Grandma Ann had given me.

If you had told me that morning on the gurney that in a year and a half, a woman would be licking a stamp in Ireland to send me a package full of candy, I would have laughed. My mom was right: *You have to wait and see how your life unfolds.*

One day I heard from the White House. Joe Biden wrote me a letter. I was in disbelief. I still had blockades up to protect me internally, scared to fully open up to all that was happening. I told myself to move my internal obstructions aside for a moment, to truly listen.

In his letter, he wrote, *I see you.* What did it mean that the vice president of the United States of America had stopped every important thing he was doing, to write *I see you.*

Assault buries the self. We lose sight of how and when we are allowed to occupy space. We are made to doubt our abilities, disparaged when we speak. My statement had blazed, erupted, was indomitable. But I was holding a secret fear, that there must be a cap, an end to this road, where they'd say, you have achieved enough, exit this way. I was waiting to be knocked back down to size, to the small place I imagined I belonged. I had grown up in the margins; in the media Asian Americans were assigned side roles, submissive, soft-spoken secondary characters. I had grown used to being unseen, to never being fully known. It did not feel possible that I could be the protagonist. The more recognition I gained, the more I felt I was not supposed to be on the receiving end of so much generosity. Yet people kept pulling me up and up, until I heard from the highest house in our nation. The vice president was not lowering down to my level, he was lifting me up to bow with gratitude.

What did it mean that he stopped to read my statement? That millions of people had paused what they were doing to take it in? *I see the limitless potential of an incredibly talented young woman—full of possibility. I see the shoulders on which our dreams for the future rest.* For the first time, I was beginning to understand what my dad meant when he said he was proud of me. I believe, out of the millions who knew I was brave and important, I was the last to know it.

Biden said, *You have given them the strength they need to fight. And so, I believe, you will save lives.* I thought of the man in the thick black jacket, sitting by the tracks in the foldout chair, hired to save lives. I realized, since I was seventeen, that was the job I wanted. The only difference was that I sat on a chair at home, writing the words that would get you to stay here, to see the value of you, the beauty of your life. So if you come on the worst day of your life, my hope is to catch you, to gently guide you back.

Even when 99 percent was positive, the 1 percent still invoked my worst fears. When my house phone rang, the illusion of safety was broken. It was a news anchor from a major morning talk show. She said, *I'm half Asian too so we can be friends.* This is like me saying, *You look pretty when you're sleeping.* How could she see me? Lucas's phone wouldn't stop ringing, Tiffany's LinkedIn views were up by the hundreds. A reporter had contacted Julia's grandparents, to get to Julia, to get to me. The media offering to blur my face and warp my voice, *to protect me,* they said. Disturbing letters from strangers started showing up at my house. I submitted them to the lab for fingerprinting. Reporters came knocking, my dad saying, *I don't know who you're talking about,* shutting the door while I hid under the covers.

The statement would be read eighteen million times on BuzzFeed alone. You can find virtually anything online, but I remained unknown. I see this as a testament to the world's grace; they did not push me into the glaring light, to a microphone, saying we want more. They did not ask for credentials, did not say, *Well, who are you really.*

One woman signed her letter *Sincerely, Past Emily Doe.* Many wrote to me saying they had been in my position before, wanted to show me who survivors become, told me about their careers, their kids, caring partners. This is what your life can look like in ten, twenty years. They gave me one thousand futures to grow into. In my anonymity, I tried on their lives and watched as they tried on mine. They became young again, finally declaring what they deserved, reclaiming all that had been taken. Healing was possible in that empty space.

The statement had created a room, a place for survivors to step into and speak aloud their heaviest truths, to revisit the untouched parts of their past. If I had come out with my identity the room would have collapsed, its roof weighted by distractions; my history, ethnicity, family. The few that had discovered my identity had taken screenshots of my old spoken word videos, leaked with the caption, *Brock Turner has yellow fever. Wouldn't put my nuts in her chink chute. Crazy gook. Asian women can't handle their alcohol. Asian glow, red faced, lightweight, slut.*

Instead, I became the lady with blue hair, the one with the nose ring, I was sixty-two, I was Latina, I was a man with a beard. How do you come after me, when it is all of us? One of the greatest dangers of victimhood is the singling out; all of your attributes and anecdotes assigned blame. In court they'll try to make you believe you are unlike the others, you are different, an exception. You are dirtier, more stupid, more promiscuous. But it's a trick. The assault is never personal, the blaming is.

Since no photos of me were published, I was curious about what photos would accompany the articles; a silhouette of a girl looking out a window, a teardrop on a cheek, duct tape over her mouth. All of this was accurate, in terms of the solitude, the silencing. But the incredible thing is that a victim is also the smiling girl in a green apron making your coffee, she just handed you your change. She just taught a class of first-graders. She has her headphones in, tapping her foot on the subway. Victims are all around you.

Looking back on this summer, I remember it in scenes, given to me through thousands of letters in grocery bags, handed over from my DA. A woman who said she was sitting on the couch with her daughter, surrounded by boxes, preparing to flee her abusive ex-husband, telling me she knew they were no longer alone. A mother who plucked the holiday card of her toddler from the inside of her cubicle, scribbling on the back, *This is who you're saving.* A wife who woke up her husband, turning on the side light, to tell him her story. I received an email from a sixteen-year-old who said that for the first time in two years she could finally get out of bed in the morning. That's the image I am left with, the now-empty bed.

Can I tell you, throughout the year before the trial, I spent nights secretly peeling back a curtain that concealed a life parallel to the one I was living, a life in which none of this ever happened. I imagined what I would be doing, who I would be; my nine-to-five, sunny days, a healthy body, holiday parties. Then I'd close the curtain, sitting back in my reality. Now, I see her vacant bed, and I understand why I went on this journey: It was the only way to get to her. Finally, I accepted what happened, aware of what it led to. I never touched the curtain again, knowing that one morning, a sixteen-year-old swung her legs out of bed and gently stepped back into her life.

My twenty-fourth birthday coincided with Stanford's graduation ceremony. Some students in black caps held up signs, sunlight shining through the paper covered in bold, red-painted letters: STANFORD PROTECTS RAPISTS. BROCK TURNER IS NOT AN EXCEPTION. YOU ARE A WARRIOR. Their courage felt like a birthday gift. I could imagine a mother holding a camera with one hand, making swatting motions with the other, *Jason put the sign down for one minute, just smile,* and Jason saying, *Mom! This is important!* It meant something to me that they had brought hard truths to a cheery celebration. I hoped Stanford would soon find you can only sweep so many humans under the rug, before your rug becomes mountainous and lumpy. Commencement speaker and documentary filmmaker Ken Burns said, *If someone tells you they have been sexually assaulted, take it effing seriously and listen to them. Maybe someday we'll make the survivor's eloquent statement as important as Dr. [Martin Luther] King's letter from the Birmingham jail.* A generous comparison.

Mr. Rosen proposed a new mandatory prison sentence for those convicted of sexually assaulting an unconscious or intoxicated person and expanded California's definition of rape. Two bills were signed into law by California Governor Jerry Brown. Alaleh mailed me a copy of the signed document, like a certificate that granted me the right to sleep peacefully, knowing this botched sentencing would not be repeated. I began to believe again in justice.

Michele Dauber launched a campaign to recall Judge Persky. This was unheard of—no judge had been recalled in California since 1932. Michele wanted to include the recall on the ballot for the next election, which would be held in two years. Nicole became one of the cochairs and the codirector of field operations; she galvanized volunteers, spending hours writing newsletters, keeping spirits lifted. She explained they'd need to collect at least 58,634 signatures in Santa Clara County to get Persky's name on the June ballot. Once on the ballot, they needed at least 50 percent of the vote for him to be recalled.

It was common to have people forward me the statement saying, *You have to read this.* I wanted to respond, *I wrote it.* Once a friend said, *I heard it's someone we know.* I froze, searching her face to see if she was testing me, but there was nothing. I feigned indifference, shrugged, *I haven't heard anything.* When my sister met a guy in her neighborhood with a dog named Broccoli, the owner explained, *Well at first his name was Brock, but have you heard of the Brock Turner stuff?* My sister nodded. *It hurt my dog's brand, so I changed it.* I found a new therapist in San Francisco, but it took me months and multiple sessions before I told her I was Emily Doe. All I said was that I'd been sexually assaulted, and in response she said, *Have you read the Stanford victim statement?* She'd recommended me my own story, said something about thoughtfulness and power, turning the tables. I nodded, and moved on to another topic. I wanted to be known as Chanel, in all my fumblings, my confusion, managing everyday life, before being seen as Emily, who was defiant and courageous, who seemed to have all the answers.

I began to see the world through a softer filter. If somebody honked at me in traffic, I looked in my rearview mirror and thought, *Maybe you have cried for me.* In crowded lines at the grocery store, I wondered if the woman in front of me had written a letter, if she'd shared with me her hidden grief.

When I left the courtroom that June day, after reading my statement, courage had been the furthest thing from my mind. Now I understood that in this life I've been given, I had done something good, created power from pain, provided solace while remaining honest about the hardships victims face. In turn, they showed me who I was. Now it was just a matter of figuring out how to say thank you.

Novelist Anne Lamott was connected to me through Katie. I asked her for guidance. She replied:

I believe you will get a tug on your sleeve, and something from deep deep inside will get back to you on what might make sense for you to pursue or try. . . . You know how you can dive under a wave that is going to crash on top of you? Writing can help me do that—to pull way back from turmoil and impending overwhelm, and find a bit of sanctuary in the process, the action of scribbling down memories, visions, musings . . .

After struggling for so long to move away from this case, it felt counterintuitive to immerse myself again. But I also understood that moving through was a way of moving on, that I needed to go backward before I could go forward again. I now had my instructions. The statement was the wave. It was time to submerge even deeper, return to the beginning.

11.

THAT SUMMER, I told myself the worst was over, normal life could resume. But what was normal now? At night my bad dreams intensified. The relief and elation felt temporary. I felt sure that if I was being blamed for Brock's pain, someone would want to torment me to even out the score. These were the rules of Elliot Rodger's universe: *I desired girls, but girls never desired me back. . . . It is an injustice that cannot go unpunished.* I kept a bag of letters by my bed, working through them slowly to preserve them for as long as I could. Every night I read two to three. They helped put me to sleep, a warm thought from a mother in Wisconsin, tucking me in.

Lucas and I walked heavy footed up hills in San Francisco, looking at apartments, losing out on the first few we applied to. Next to my credit score, place of employment, and reference from prior landlord, it was blank and blank and blank. I wanted to write *good emotional intelligence, proficient at self-examination, been through a lot of shit that I cannot explain.* Finally we found a tiny, square home we called the *tissue box.* We planted jade succulents out back, scattered birdseed on the railing, put basil on the kitchen windowsill that yellowed in a day. I bought what domesticated adults buy: checkered hand towels, a salad spinner. I was careful not to put my new address on anything, my home a hideout. Here I planned to rebuild my life, begin writing.

You commute to the South Bay? a friend asked. *What?* I said. I forgot the old office where I'd worked was thirty minutes south, forgot they still believed I worked there. *Oh, it's fine. Bad sometimes, but it's fine. Podcasts.* I wanted to say my commute was twelve seconds, from my bed to my desk, occasionally breaking from this trajectory to boil coffee in my pajamas.

Freshly graduated, Lucas was negotiating his next job; before business school he'd been a consultant, flying away four days a week, and was given a glowing offer to return. But the idea of him being gone made me panic. I did not want my inhibitions to become his. I wanted to say, *Be free, I am an independent woman!* But it felt impossible.

If you asked me, *Could you sleep alone?* the short answer was yes. The long answer was I put a metal coatrack against our front gate around four in the afternoon. As the sun dipped down, I flipped on every light. I made sure my furnace was lit downstairs, which would save me from going down once it was dark out. Tiffany used to build traps for Santa, surrounding the chimney with chairs laced with bells and plastic bags. I stacked chairs in front of the door. I marked a dot of Sharpie on the nozzle of my pepper spray to ensure I'd spray in the right direction. I slept with large scissors, because knives can slip, whereas scissors have grip and can still poke a hole in his jugular. Then I'd lie down on the couch, never the bedroom, watching darkness engulf my house, the world shutting down, leaving me to fend for myself.

What exactly were you afraid of, one might wonder. *You weren't raped in a house, there was no invasion or break-in.* But it's the sleeping itself that got me, the unconscious, vulnerable state in which anything can happen. The night of my assault, I'd missed the chance to fight back. I tried to outsmart the system, sleeping with one eye open, one eye closed, drifting in and out. Times I have accidentally dozed off, I've woken up with alarms blaring in my chest, *what did I miss.* At five o'clock in the morning, when light became a promise, I'd drift off to the sound of newspapers being thrown, the first bus rattling, birds.

I was always groggy the next day, behind the regular rotation of the world. When the postman rang the doorbell I'd perform the droopy-lidded ritual of removing my contraptions, yelling for him to hold on as I unstacked the chairs. In the daytime, these protections felt silly, the blockades and pepper spray, evidence of the strange and imagined realities in my head, private battles I'm fighting. In the past few years, I have not slept alone for longer than three days.

My ability to doze off used to be a point of pride. When I'd studied abroad in China in college, everyone complained about how the maintenance men had woken them up to fix the air-conditioning units above the beds. I said, *They didn't fix mine.* But my roommate said there'd been men in mint-green jumpsuits, boots balanced on my bedside table, while I snored below. It was funny at the time, but now this terrifies me.

When I find out female friends live in studio apartments I'm in shock. *But who's your witness? Who's going to protect you from all the any-things that can happen? Don't you understand that alone they'll never believe you?* I try to imagine that sort of life, coming home alone, cooking pasta with a glass of Riesling, watching TV, yawning, brushing my teeth, and calling it a day. I envy those who live unguarded.

I remember skinny-dipping in college. My greatest fear at the time was that the water was going to be too cold. Five or six of us, boys and girls, would escape the cliffside apartment parties to trot down the wooden stairs to the lumpy sand, bath towels slung over our shoulders. We'd pluck our heads out of our shirts, weaving arms out of sleeves, returning to the way we were when we were born. We threw our clothes on mossy boulders as we sprinted toward the glassy water. Mel and I threw our heads back shrieking and laughing. Seaweed lassoed and slimed around our ankles and we picked it up and draped it across each other's shoulders like glossy scarves. We paddled out to where the water was calm and deep, our heads bobbing on the surface, which shimmered in moonlight as if littered with tinfoil.

When skinny-dipping, there was only the expanse of sky, open sea, and a circle of pure, white moon. The lighting was soft, the landscape limitless. The penises nothing more than noodle shapes, breasts like mounds of silly putty. We all looked funny and natural and free.

These were the greatest nights; taking turns standing beneath the hot shower, sand piling around the drain. Making quesadillas, wearing old T-shirts, wrapped in worn blankets, huddled three to a bed like bears in a den. We'd fall asleep at four in the morning, our clothes crusted with salt, sand caked in the curves of our ears, wet hair soaking into pillows. I remember all of it warmly, but don't know how to do it again.

One night, Lucas and I were driving home from Southern California, passing through Santa Barbara. I asked him to pull off the highway, an exit I hadn't taken in three years. We parked and I led him down the wooden stairs to stand at the edge of the water. It was just as beautiful as I'd remembered, but it wasn't mine anymore. I looked left and right at the long stretches of dark shore I couldn't see into, and wondered how I could've been so loud and naked, drawing attention to myself. The vulnerability of bare skin. It would've been too easy to hurt me, there wouldn't have been any time to resist. No clothes to pull. If something had happened, no one would've ever believed me. *Well weren't you naked to begin with? Drunk on the beach at night? What did you think would happen?* It wouldn't have been enough to say, *I just wanted it to be me, some friends, and the sea.*

There is a certain carefree feeling that was stripped from me the night of the assault. How to distinguish spontaneity from recklessness? How to prove nudity is not synonymous with promiscuity? Where's the line between caution and paranoia? This is what I'm mourning, this is what I do not know how to get back. Still I keep those memories close and remember it is possible to be naked, amongst men, and not be asking for it. The girl running arms wide into the ocean is gone. In her place is a woman wrapped in two coats, staring at the black water, mistaking lumps of seaweed for dormant bodies, the stones for crouching men. Lucas takes my hand and asks if I'd like to walk and I shake my head, trotting back up the wooden stairs.

I found a list while sifting through the transcripts that I was not meant to see. Three pages, descriptions of photographs that had been submitted for evidence. *Photograph of the left side of Ms. Doe's head with vegetation in her hair. Photograph of abrasions below right clavicle. Photograph of abrasions at the base of neck and upper back. Photograph of close-up buttocks with multiple abrasions. Photograph of ruler to show measurements of abrasions of skin next to hospital gown. Photograph of female genitalia. Photograph of female genitalia with debris inside labia minora.*

My body divided into squares, put up on the large projector. My butt, my chest, my vagina, were shown on a screen, a four-foot-tall labia, for the judge and Brock and his brother and his father and every reporter and stranger in that room to see. And while this was happening, I must have been down the hall, smoothing out my blouse in the bathroom mirror, tamping down my hair with water, trying to look presentable. The humiliation I feel now, for walking in oblivious and smiling.

Knowing this makes me want to swallow a match, lighting my insides on fire, my stomach a red, dripping cave, smoke pouring out my ears and nose and eyes, until I become crusty and hollow. A black, empty shell.

Sex goes to court to die. I watched the defense attorney's mouth, the old tongue and old breath, lips the color of old hummus, *Chanel's vagina. Rubbing it back and forth.* It was enough to make me sick, to want to snip his tongue out of his throat. *I just don't need it, sex,* I thought, *I could go my whole life without it.*

Sex was absent of caring. Sex meant inserting A into B, parts labeled separately, my *left buttock cheek* labeled *exhibit 43.* Sex meant digital or penile penetration, how deeply it went in or stayed out of me. His what touched her what where. Sex is hard gravel dug into your palms. Sex is being punctured, your air emptied. Even after the bruises healed, after the hours of couch sitting in therapy, I was still unsure how to inhabit my body. If sex was something that hurt me, how could it provide pleasure or safety? I wanted to spackle up my holes, lock the whole place down, the machines in me shutting off, gears growing rusty and quiet.

Technically, it is illegal to bring up a victim's sexual history in court. But even if never explicitly stated, it was alluded to. *Do you have a boyfriend. Were you exclusive. Are you sexually active.* I felt that if I continued to engage in my body, if I openly desired sex again, I'd be proving the defense right. He spoke of my sexual life as if it was something I was hiding, as if exposing this knowledge gave Brock the right to do what he wanted. I was the victim whose sexual choices were too indiscriminate to be respected.

During sex, my body began asking my mind, *What's happening? Where are you? Who are you with?* I'd reassure myself with familiar signs; the color of my sheets, texture of Lucas's hair. Relax. But something inside me kept yanking out the connecting cords, rewiring, plugging them into the wrong fixtures. My body kept asking permission, *is this okay, will we be blamed?* I needed a face, needed light, needed no surprise, needed step-by-step, *I'm in my own home and I'm allowed to enjoy this.* It was inhibiting, did not allow for stallion-riding, flower-blooming, rooster-crowing, paper-shuffling, passionate lovemaking. Instead I had a small finicky secretary I was reporting to: *What's happening? Where are you? Who are you with?*

The phrase, sexual assault, is a little misleading, for it seemed to be less about sex, more about taking. Sexual assault is stealing. One-sided wants, the feeling of overriding the other. Real sex was meant to be exchange, the power shifting back and forth, responsive and fluid and playful. The pleasure of paying attention, actively engaging with your partner.

DA: So the answer to my question is, you didn't think about her?

Brock: I think it was impossible for me to think about her.

The pivotal question throughout the trial was whether or not consent was issued. Yes or no. We act as if there is a single traffic light, red or green. But sex is a road lined with intersections, which way to go, when to slow down, to yield, to stop, to speed up.

Verbal consent is often mocked for killing the mood. But think of how much organic communication we do in life. A sampling table at the grocery store; you pick up a cracker, make eye contact with the vendor, *May I?* and they nod, *Enjoy.* Subtle and swift.

What I never say out loud is that rape makes you want to turn into wood, hard and impenetrable. The opposite of a body that is meant to be tender, porous, soft. Sometimes I'm too angry, seething after reading a rape story, *I need to slice a dick off.* Sometimes my desire fluctuates, dips to depletion. I wouldn't notice if I didn't have a partner, but once you shrug off affection for the sixth time something's amiss. Sometimes he'll gesture for me to rest my head on his chest, he just needs touch, simple touch, to know we're still connected.

This distancing from my body did not begin with the assault. But in a world where self-confidence is already doled out sparingly to young women, my supply quickly diminished in court. I spent my adolescence soaking in oatmeal baths for my eczema. A boy called me a cheetah, so I used Sally Hansen spray tans to paint over my spotted, discolored skin. I wore peach-colored pantyhose in high school, a purchased epidermis. College was the first time I started wearing dresses. Still my relationship with my body remained halfhearted.

I wonder if there is a time in every woman's life when she feels like swallowing stones. Perhaps she wonders why her period is late or wakes up in an unfamiliar bed, or comes across a list of her body parts divided neatly into numbers. Does it make her want to swallow stones? Large, smooth ones, gulping them down. I imagine them settling into my stomach, a pile, then walking into a pond, not to die, but to sink the body, while only my spirit emerges from the water. Much cleaner, I could start over, unencumbered.

In a tiny bookshop by a lake, I came across a passage by Deepak Chopra: *The body needs reinventing. To have a meaningful life, you have to use your body—you can't experience anything without one—and so your body should be meaningful, too.* I saw pigeons at the park, puffing out their chests and mounting each other. Even pigeons were having sex, understood that it was natural, not a shameful act. You're in your midtwenties. How do you not celebrate your smooth forehead, nice collarbones, and your ripe, red heart. I have a loving man, every day, beside me. I should be celebrating him too, when he emerges steaming from the shower, rejoice! Sex should not only be tolerated, but joyous.

It was roller-skating, of all things, when I realized what I was missing. Lucas and I were scooting and shuffling around a vacant church spotted in disco lights. I retired on a pew that had been pushed against the wall. I watched girls with their arms loose, hips swinging, glimpses of belly button. The ease with which they moved, so in their element, so present, all this grace and muscle and fluidity, I craved it. What does that feel like? To present my body without fear of harm or scrutiny, fully unbound and graceful.

I used to believe yoga was for people who have skin care routines and good posture. I started off clumsy and self-conscious, glancing around to check myself, until an instructor said, *If you mess up, no one gives a shit, like what's gonna happen.* I liked the hour and a half on the mat, my apricot-colored rectangle sealed to the floor, a small border fending off external distractions. Slowly I learned to turn my attention inward, to elongate from my Achilles tendon to the tips of my fingers. I imagined the clenched cells inside me unfurling.

At the front desk there is a box of white tokens. You can place one on your mat to say, *Do not touch*. I like the way it communicates a subtle need, wished I could tape it to my forehead in public. I used to pluck one from the box. Now I do not, and sometimes the instructor will lay a hand on my back, and that gravity, that firm pressure, makes me tear up. It's not crying. It's the tenderness of a palm, my pulse alive beneath a touch, connecting, something bubbles up through me, releases in the form of an eye droplet. Being fully inside my body makes me feel beautiful, powerful, makes me want to be consumed, to share all the small parts of me.

There is no reason to deprive your body of love, beauty, creativity, and inspiration, Chopra said. I wrote out a collection of sensory memories from childhood, recalling how it felt to be nourished and soothed. Rice steaming, rain outside. Standing in a towel heated by the tall furnace, feet dripping on the hardwood floor. The smell of sun on asphalt. Cold water on my face in the morning. Eating a bowl of cereal at midnight. The sound of a page turning as I am being read to. The thud of a peach falling. The dusty smell of sand. The scorch of cocoa, the sticky film of melted marshmallow. Spongy insides of bread sopping up tomatoes and vodka sauce. I am reminded of what I am capable of feeling. The ways I consume, my senses opening to receive, at ease, indulgent.

When I was afraid of the dark during our first year in the city, I tried to reframe the darkness. I told myself to admire the inky lumps of hills, the snoring neighbors with their lemongrass diffusers, the coyotes trotting through the park. With sex I started small, savored the little things; the simplicity of sleeping next to each other. This closeness, this quiet. Sex is this feeling unpeeled. I thought about the language of sex;

I liked the term *lovemaking*, bodies churning and creating sweat and heat, until love is actually made, *bing bing bing*, appears like glistening pink lights that float and drift above the bed as you lie back, skin glimmering.

Still I struggle outside the boundaries of home and familiar hands. I was overdue for a Pap smear, a procedure that sounds like a disease found in penguin shit. I planned to write a note on the sign-in form, *Assaulted, proceed with caution*, but there was no room. Mainly I didn't want to invite an interrogation. I wanted to brave it myself, get in and out like a regular person. I decided I'd barrage the doctor with questions as a way of slowing down the process. But a young ponytailed nurse came in to observe, changing the dynamic. I could see the nurse staring into me, felt myself growing silently and violently angry, *What are you looking at, I'm not a specimen, leave me alone, stop,* my stomach tightened, a wave of nausea. A sailboat appeared on the ceiling. I heard, *All done! I'll give you time to get dressed.*

They left. I don't know how much time has passed. My mind is full of nothing. I can't get my feet in my shoes. I should have brought someone, to tell me to put my arms through sleeves. I train my eyes on the tiny blue stars of my hospital gown. The door opens, the ponytailed nurse pops her head in, *Oh!* She quickly excuses herself, realizing I haven't changed. I cannot think fast enough to verbalize *Don't go*. If I try to stand up I'll pass out. Minutes go by and she comes in again to find me exactly as I was. I ask if she has a snack. She returns with a powdery chocolate drink, I chug it with a shaking hand. *I'm not good at this,* I say, my voice wavering. Something registers. *It's okay,* she says. *Take your time.* She sits with me until I collect myself and leave. I rest my forehead on the steering wheel, exhausted. I wish for a white token.

A teacher once explained we possess an invisible blueprint in the womb to build ourselves. From the mesoderm, one's bones and connective tissues and heart emerged. *We know how to form our being*, she said. *We still have that information, it still informs us.* Even if elements of my physical self had diminished, I believed they could be restored. I trusted that when I gave my body love, soft touch, stretching, sunlight, strength, and sex, what was lost would be regrown in new form.

I think of our backyard pond growing up. Of the goldfish we'd bring home, bobbing in plastic bags on the surface of the water. My dad explained they needed time to adjust to the temperature of the pond before being released. If such a small creature required such care, imagine the complex process a victim must work through in order to integrate back into daily life. There is no right way, there is only listening to what is good and comfortable for your body. Maybe now you are terrified, bobbing inside the clear plastic container around you, thinking, *I am trapped, this is not how it's supposed to be.* Just remember: the temperature is slowly changing, you are adjusting. You will make it into that pond. With a little more time, you'll be free.

———

Lucas accepted a job in the city. I was sleeping peacefully. Still, I wanted a companion at home with me. Wanted a pit bull or a German shepherd, an athletic dog with shoulder blades, sharp eyes, and a wide snout. We drove to the shelter, peeking through chain-link fences. Walking back to the car, we passed a yellow wooden sign propped on the sidewalk: *Muttville Senior Dog Rescue.* We followed yellow arrows up the stairs. Jazz was playing in a large roomful of sunlight and small cushioned beds. Forty tiny dogs were moseying around. A whiteboard on the wall was filled with names; Walnut, Ethel, Eggroll, Tootsie, Cashew, Professor Plum, Bumblebee, Javier. We learned about the foster program; we could take a dog home until he found a permanent owner. A blind Lhasa Apso with a jutting underbite bumped into my ankles, his feet plodding as if his paws were on puppet strings. Long bangs sprouted over his milky eyes. His name was Puffin.

Lucas bought him special green socks that kept him from sliding on our wooden floors. I made him porridge. He spent most of his time sitting with his head cocked, in his green socks, staring at the refrigerator. Since he was deaf and blind, I knew that if I was murdered he'd sit next to my dead body waiting for breakfast. One night, when Lucas was away seeing family, I heard a strange sound, a puttering, like a mini gas-powered boat. I saw his belly rising and falling, and realized I'd provided a place where he felt safe enough to sleep. Healing became the sound of an old dog snoring.

Over the year we fostered six dogs, one at a time. I spent hours wiping urine off the nest of electrical wires, navigating archipelagos of dried poop. If you knew how many paper towels I used I would be arrested. My shag rug carpet was soiled, rolled up, thrown out, bought again, thrown out. There was Butch, who went into our bathroom to pee on the toilet. Remy, who we liked to imagine carrying a metal detector as he waddled incessantly from room to room. Squid the wiener dog, who could sing. Salvador, who loved Korean barbecue. They acted like toddlers, rolling off the bed or slipping in a grate, tumbling down a step if you took your eyes off them. Most had multiple medications, and I sprinkled what looked like pouches of cocaine into their food. I was reminded that having extra needs does not make you too difficult, too time consuming, but worthy of compassion and love.

They took me out walking, often carrying, when back legs were rickety. I ate when they ate, a simple lesson in self-care. My small house became a place of restoration and transition, getting them cleaned up, nails clipped, hair combed, ready for their permanent home. I liked seeing their confidence and personalities emerge, as they grew more comfortable and became themselves.

Tiffany was the one who spotted the dog who stayed. A ten-year-old brown-and-white Pomeranian, an eight-pound loofah with a sprinkling of tiny teeth. She had been found abandoned near Sacramento. A little embodiment of joy, always smiling like someone just told her she was going to Disneyland. Adoption requests were rolling in, but I didn't respond to any of them. I stared at her for a long time.

This wasn't the plan. Fostering was temporary until we got a big, blusterous dog. After an assault, the world tells you to put your guard up, fight back, be careful. The world does not remind you to unclench your fists, to go on a stroll. That you do not have to spend all your time figuring out how to survive. Nobody says, *Adopt the Pomeranian*. I had planned to surround myself with higher gates and sharper teeth, but maybe that was not what I needed. Maybe it was possible to build that security within myself.

We named our dog Mogu (Chinese for *mushroom*). Every day she reminds me of the Muttville slogan: *It's never too late for a new beginning*. It was a promise to her and a promise to myself. Whatever past you came from, you don't have to go back.

Over the course of that year with a rotation of little dogs sleeping on my lap, leaking gases into my room, I wrote. I sat down to look at transcripts for the first time; hundreds of pages of everything that was said during the days I was absent in the courtroom. My commute, it turned out, was long, required traveling back to my past every day. I was stunned that even with the validation of millions, the enraged feelings returned as if untouched. I annotated the transcripts in red pen; *dummy ass nut piece of shit*. For all the clarity and catharsis of that statement, I still struggled. We understand a victim's antagonists to be the perpetrators and lawyers but overlook the enemy who is the victim herself. Old ideas about who I was resurfaced, told me I was damaged, unworthy. Some of the shame had calcified, impervious to praise.

Some days I did nothing, closed the door to my office, as if sealing off the time machine I dared not enter. On the worst days I abandoned it all and jogged to get a banh mi sandwich in my black down jacket, cilantro leaves pasted to my lips, eyes dry and red, and then I'd sit on the carpet in the children's section of the library. I longed for lighter, sweeter worlds. Lucas would see me come in late, windblown with arms full of kids' books about dragons and pancakes, and ask with measured hesitation, *What did you write about today?* It was his way of figuring out what voices were living in my head.

A long time has passed since the last time I was in that courtroom, but I worry I will forever be stuck on the stand. My mind is one step behind where it used to be. I call it the lag. Before I was living in real time. Now I evaluate the moment before I can move into it. I am always asking permission, anticipating having to present myself to an invisible jury, answering questions before a defense. When I reach for a piece of clothing, the first thing I think is, *What will they think if I wear this?* When I go anywhere I think, *Will I be able to explain why I am going?* If I post a photo I think, *If this were submitted as evidence, would I look too silly, my shoulders too bare?* The time I spend questioning what I'm doing, turning things over and talking myself back to normalcy, has become the toll.

One evening I was supposed to pick up gin for a party. But I stood with my cart staring at the blue glass bottle, thinking, *What experience is inside this? Who will drink it, will someone be hurt, will they ask me what brand?* At parties, I measure everything. If there are no shot glasses, I use capfuls, hunched to conceal my obsessive techniques. I see people pouring and I stare. *That's a free pour,* I think, *You can't do that, they'll say how much, how many ounces, one third or half of the cup, what kind of cup?* If someone wanders to the bathroom or leaves with a guy, I grow tense, *What do you mean she's gone, where'd she go, who'd she go with?* I need to know everyone will make it home. I'll text my friend and in the morning I'll get a response, *Ya! Sorry I fell asleep.* They do not know that I spent the night agonizing, my mind spiraling into worst-case scenarios.

When I talked to my therapist about drinking or past sexual experiences, she'd say, *Well, how do you feel about it.* I'd say, *Oh, it doesn't matter how I feel, it's what they think about it.* I stated this like fact. She said, *It is impossible to live under that level of scrutiny.*

Reading Brock's testimony, I noticed how differently our evenings were framed. When questioning Brock, the defense opened with the following questions: *Is [grinding] common at these parties that you noticed? Did people dance on tables? Was that a common thing, too? How about drinking? Was drinking seemingly a major part of these parties? For most everybody that was there? Most everybody that was there was drinking alcohol, is that correct?*

In each line, I found *common, common, a part of, everybody, everybody.* This pattern was not an accident. He was leading Brock back into the herd, where he could blend into the comfort of community. Compare this to when he had questioned me: *You did a lot of partying. You've had blackouts before.* It was *you* and *you,* the lens fixed so close I was stripped of surrounding. For Brock, his goal was to integrate, for me it was to isolate.

I discovered the defense had emailed Dr. Fromme: *I could subpoena records from the ambulance people that transported her to Valley Medical. Query whether they could hurt our case rather than help?* Fromme responded, *It's unclear whether the medical records would be helpful or potentially hurtful . . . it could work against us.*

Throughout testimony, Dr. Fromme used phrases like: *Don't hold my feet to the fire on this. Oh gosh, I'm not totally legally savvy. I'm no Excel wizard. I can tell you that.* I could not stand the whoopsy daisy downplaying as my body was debased.

Dr. Fromme testified incoherent speech didn't infer that I was impaired beyond engaging in voluntary actions. She compared it to being given Novocain at the dentist; *you can't speak very well but you can still think fine. Having slurred speech has never stopped somebody from making a stupid eBay purchase, for example.* This should go without saying: Being raped is not online shopping, and alcohol is not novocaine. If my actions had been voluntary, isn't it possible I could've voluntarily pushed him away? Who's to assume my actions were compliant?

I was always reminded they were just doing their jobs. Now I realize, yeah, maybe this was your job, but it still takes a certain kind of person to do this job. Trial unveiled terrifying and disorienting realities, increased levels of acrimony. I became cynical. The torment makes you crazy, makes you rabid; when people start hacking at my Achilles', I wanted to swing back. I didn't want to be the bigger person, I wanted to make them feel small, to sting.

But I told myself, don't become them. Focus on who you want to be. I fought hard rewriting drafts of this book to dial down the sarcasm, personal attacks. I vowed not to minimize or dehumanize. The goal should never be to insult, it should only be to teach, to expose larger issues so that we may learn something. I want to remain me. So I use my strength not to shove back, but to exercise my voice with control. *Two cyclists.* For every person that wants to hurt me, there are more who want to help. I wish there had been a predatory expert, victim expert, consent expert to better educate the jury. We scrutinized the victim's actions, instead of examining the behavioral patterns of sexual predators. How alcohol works to the predator's advantage, to lower resistance, weaken the limbs.

Brock: She slipped.

Defense: And do you recall how she was dressed that night? What was she wearing?

Brock: She had a dress on.

Defense: Okay. And when she slipped, what happened to her body?

Why was there a pause to detail my clothes? Did my dress explain his behavior? I entered the court system expecting it to be ordered, civil, constructive. Now I was learning whose voices were amplified inside the courtroom, whose were muted. At the sentencing the judge had quoted a letter written by Brock's friend. I will omit her name, trusting she has learned from her mistakes. In her letter, she wrote: *I don't think it's fair to base the fate of the next ten + years of his life on the decision of a girl who doesn't remember anything but the amount she drank to press charges against him. I am not blaming her directly for this because that isn't right. But where do we draw the line and stop worrying about being politically correct every second of the day and see that rape on campuses isn't always because people are rapists. . . . This is completely different from a woman getting kidnapped and raped as she is walking to her car in a parking lot. That is a rapist. These are not rapists. These are idiot boys and girls having too much to drink and not being aware of their surroundings and having clouded judgment.*

When my statement emerged, her letter was uncovered. That summer she was scheduled to tour with her three-woman band, but venues canceled one after the other, announcing they did not tolerate rape culture. The band was dropped from its label, the tour dissolved, and she issued a public apology. Even more disturbing was that out of thirty-nine letters written, this was the single one the judge had quoted at the sentencing. Her misguidance was expected, the judge's was not.

By citing her as a source, he'd endorsed her outdated, distorted definition of rape. We know that acquaintance rape is far more common than stranger rape. When we undercut the severity of acquaintance rape, or drunk rape that happens at parties, healing becomes largely delayed, the recovery process butchered, the predator undeterred.

Brock's mother wrote, *My first thought upon wakening every morning* is *"this isn't real, this can't be real. Why him? Why HIM? WHY? WHY?"* I have never wondered why me. The only thing running through my head when my sister picked me up that morning was, *Thank God me.* Thank God me and not her, not Julia, not an eighteen-year-old who would've had to forgo her schooling. I was privileged enough to have completed my education and to be in stable circumstances. I had a home, not too far from the courthouse, where I could recuperate after proceedings. I had two parents who clicked off my light and covered me in a blanket when I fell asleep. I had money saved. In a strange way I was prepared to go on this journey.

Although millions know my story, I only told two people outside of my family the year of the assault. The next year I told a few more. The year after that I told three. The strange thing is, coming out to someone I don't know is easy. Coming out to someone I know is much harder. Perhaps because they contain pockets of your past; who you were, what they believed you to be. It's hard to watch those ideas dissolve to reconfigure around this new identity. When I tell a loved one, I watch their eyes. They are searching, as if waiting for me to tell them it's not true. When my dad told Grandma Ann that I was the victim, she kept saying, *What? What?* She had been following it in the newspapers for months. She could only say, *It's not true. It can't be Chanel.* No matter how much I heal, the assault itself will always be a sad thing. I have to be okay with this. I have to stop rushing them to the part where the letters flood in. I have to hold a space for grief.

I spend more days curled up than I do exalting, constantly reminded of how much is stacked against victims. But no matter the despair or exhaustion, I believe the wanting of a better world and being here to see it will never go away. The wanting is enough.

My mom's favorite joke is about a spider and a centipede having tea. The centipede gets up and offers to go buy snacks. He goes out the door and hours pass. The spider is so hungry, wondering what happened, and opens the door, only to find the centipede sitting on the doormat, still putting on his shoes. I imagine myself the centipede, struggling to tie each of my hundred tiny shoes, it takes me longer to get going than most. But I will put on shoe after shoe after shoe until I can get up and go again.

12.

ONLY FIVE MONTHS after I read my statement in court, Trump was elected. I was hit by the same feeling I'd had when the judge said *six months*. Blindsided. Disappointed. Wrecked.

When Trump's *Access Hollywood* tape surfaced, the average person acknowledged what he said was vulgar, lewd, foul. Anderson Cooper asked Trump point-blank if he understood he was talking about sexual assault and the nation watched him shrug and say, *locker-room talk*. In the public we grew tired. We heard the tape replayed one thousand times, debated two thousand times, pussy pussy pussy, in print, on air, Democrats and Republicans arguing, *you're inappropriate, no you're inappropriate,* until it dulled on the ears. We grew used to the same patterns of deflect, defend, dilute. *The tape was from 2005, guys talking like guys,* they wanted us to knit our shit and move on.

The language bothered me, but what disturbed me more was the context. *All I can see is the legs. Oh, it looks good.* Trump and Billy Bush were evaluating a woman, not in passing or from memory, but on a bus that was slowly pulling up to her. She was present, visible but excluded. I imagine her standing outside, smiling and waiting patiently. She is the deer while we are made aware of the mountain lions lurking in the bushes, and I am whispering at her to perk up her ears. Run. When the two men descended the bus steps, their crude talk switched off as they turned into their public selves. *How about a little hug for the Donald.* As I watched her greet them warmly, walking in between them with linked arms, I was filled with dread, reminded of all the ways we are unaware.

This was locker-room banter, a private conversation that took place many years ago. Instead of apologizing, he dragged it from the bus to the locker room, another place inaccessible to women. He never said it was supposed to be different, only said it was supposed to be private. He intended to keep us out, we were never meant to hear. He was not sorry for what he said, just sorry he was caught. Trump sounded like someone I knew.

I just start kissing them. Just kiss. I don't even wait. "I kissed her," Brock said. "And you didn't ask her permission before you kissed her, did you," my DA said. "No," Brock said. *I moved on her like a bitch.* "I kissed her cheek and ear," Brock said. "I touched her breasts. I moved her dress down." *Grab 'em by the pussy.* "I took off her underwear . . . and then I fingered her." *I did try and fuck her.* We live in a time where it has become difficult to distinguish between the President's words and that of a nineteen-year-old assailant.

Society gives women the near impossible task of separating harmlessness from danger, the foresight of knowing what some men are capable of. When we call out assault when we hear it, Trump says, I don't think you understand. Just words. You are overreacting, overly offended, hysterical, rude, relax!!! So we dismiss threatening statements and warning signs, apologizing for our paranoia. We go into a party or meeting thinking it's just a party or meeting. But when we are taken advantage of, and come crawling back damaged, they say, *How could you be so naive, you failed to detect danger, let your guard down, what did you think would happen?* Trump made it clear the game is rigged, the rules keep changing. It doesn't matter what you think is assault, because in the end, he decides.

At 1:10 in the *Access Hollywood* recording, you can hear the Tic Tacs sliding in their little box. *I better use some Tic Tacs just in case I start kissing her.* Some will say, *He's just a man! eating a mint! on a bus!* But it triggered me the way, if you hear the click of a lock when a man closes a door behind you, your body tenses. Women have been trained to notice micro-movements, to scan and anticipate all subsequent action, constantly measuring how far threatening words are from realities. We are tasked with defending ourselves in every imaginable scenario, planning escape routes, walking with keys between knuckles, a natural instinct in our day-to-day routines.

On July 6, 2016, a month after my statement was released, Philando Castile, a young black man, was driving home from the grocery store when a police officer pulled him over for a broken taillight and shot him seven times. His fiancée in the passenger seat recorded him slumping over, his white shirt stained red like a Japanese flag, while a four-year-old girl sat in the back. I thought, *Evidence, this is it, the case that gets the verdict*. It's right there, you can't turn away from it, can't reason your way out.

But on June 16, 2017, the jury returned a not guilty verdict. In Oakland, people stormed the highways. Some called it chaos, but I saw reason. My testimony was incomplete because I'd blacked out. Philando couldn't testify because he was dead, couldn't even attend his own trial. I wish the prosecutor had called Philando to the stand, forced the jury to stare at the empty witness box, his name echoing into the silence, proceeded with questions. *What were your nicknames for the little girl? Did your arms get tired when you carried her? Did you know, while getting dressed that morning, those were the clothes you would die in? What kind of cake did you want at your wedding?*

The officer claimed he'd been scared, had reason to believe Philando was reaching for his gun. Show me that scenario. A man seated with a trunk full of melting groceries, wearing a thin layer of cotton, a little girl in the backseat. About to whip out his gun, shoot through the cop's bulletproof vest, to be his own getaway driver? Why would Philando shoot an innocent man within forty seconds of meeting him? Why did the officer?

Let's go back to Mr. Hernandez's film literature class, back to *Jaws*. Mr. Hernandez pointed out that we never actually saw the shark until about eighty minutes into the film. Instead we heard horror stories, glimpsed its sinister fin; primed to be scared, so that when the shark made its grand debut, we saw everything we'd been taught to see, the merciless, blood-seeking Jaws. Before the cop pulled Philando over, he'd reported the man resembled a robbery suspect, commenting on his *wide-set nose*. By the time the cop stepped up to the window, he didn't see Philando, he saw everything he thought he knew about wide noses, blackness, guns, added it all up to *threat* in his head. The problem is not who we are, the problem is what you think we are. The realities you cast on us; that Philando would be violent, that I'd ask for sex behind a dumpster.

Philando's officer had testified, *I thought, I was gonna die, and I thought if he's, if he has the, the guts and the audacity to smoke marijuana in front of the five-year-old girl and risk her lungs and risk her life by giving her secondhand smoke and the front seat passenger doing the same thing, then what, what care does he give about me?* In his testimony, I heard the familiar expectation that a victim be flawless, in order to be worthy of life. *The audacity to smoke marijuana* provided sufficient reason to die. The defense calling me a *party animal* meant I, too, deserved to be raped.

Brock had written in his statement: *Coming from a small town in Ohio, I had never really experienced celebrating or partying that involved alcohol.* A search warrant was obtained for Brock's phone, uncovering texts the summer before college, photos of him drinking liquor, smoking from a pipe, a bong: *Do you think I could buy some wax so we could do some dabs?*

Dabs being a highly concentrated form of cannabis. *Oh dude I did acid with Kristian last week.* Texts from friends, *I've got a hankerin for a good acid trip. I'm down for sure.* Texts about *candyflippin,* a combination of LSD and MDMA. *I gotta fucking try that. I heard it's awesome.*

I did not mind, this is not proof that he is bad, I am not here to judge his drug consumption. Rip that bong, boy. You can eat mushrooms for breakfast, lunch, and dinner. You can dab your heart out whatever the literal hell that means. You know why? Because it's your life, and you are free to consume as you please. But what you cannot do, is come into my courtroom with the statement, *I was an inexperienced drinker and party-goer, so I just accepted these things that [the guys on the swim team] showed me as normal... I've been shattered by the party culture and risk taking behavior that I briefly experienced in my four months at school.*

On the day the verdict of my case was read, a *Washington Post* article quoted Brock saying that in ten years he hoped to be in residency to be a surgeon. His sister wrote, *Goodbye to the Olympics. Goodbye to becoming an orthopedic surgeon.* Another letter writer said, *As you may have learned, Brock had gone to college with the intent of studying Biomedical Engineering... his personality was quite consistent with the typical engineering student, respectful, unobtrusive, unassuming...* I found his résumé in the probation officer's report. At the time of the assault, he had worked as a lifeguard for two years and then at a store called Speedy Feet. But I never read this anywhere. He was not forced to acknowledge the facts of his present. He was talked about in terms of his lost potential, what he would never be, rather than what he is. They spoke as if his future was patiently waiting for him to step into it. Most of us understand that your future is not promised to you. It is constructed day by day, through the choices you make. Your future is earned, little by little, through hard work and action. If you don't act accordingly, that dream dissolves.

If punishment is based on potential, privileged people will be given lighter sentences. Brock was shielded inside projections of what people like him grow up to become, or are supposed to become. *Orthopedic surgeon. Biomedical engineer. All-American Athlete. Olympian.* The judge argued he'd already lost so much, given up so many opportunities. What happens to those who start off with little to lose? Instead of a nineteen-year-old Stanford athlete, let's imagine a Hispanic nineteen-year-old working in the kitchen of the fraternity commits the same crime. Does this story end differently? Does *The Washington Post* call him a surgeon?

My point can be summed up in the line Brock wrote: *I just existed in a reality where nothing can go wrong or nobody could think of what I was doing as wrong.* Privilege accompanies the light skinned, helped maintain his belief that consequences did not apply to him. In this system, who is untouchable? Who is disposable? Whose lives are we intent on preserving? Who goes unaccounted for? Who is the true disrupter, the one firing, the one fingering, who created a problem where there never was one? Brock said he'd failed to tell the detective so many crucial details upon his initial arrested because . . . *my mind was going a million miles an hour, and it was impossible for me to think clearly about what happened.* Meanwhile victims are always expected to think clearly, we don't get to use fear as an excuse. Senseless violence continues to play out, while you ask for more and more evidence, telling us it's not enough, try again.

Even when sexual assault claims are brought to police, only a small percentage will be taken up by prosecutors. This is not because prosecutors do not believe the victims, it is because they know the burden of proof is extremely high, as one must prove the assault occurred *beyond a reasonable doubt.* Prosecutors will not put you through the entire process if evidence is scant and chances are low to begin with, which means even if the victim wants to move forward, it is not always up to her.

That leaves filing a lawsuit in civil court, which requires a lower standard of proof, *preponderance of evidence.* Still she has to find, convince, and hire an attorney who will take her case. In a civil lawsuit the victim's name is not protected, and she will likely be accused of suing for money. This process can take two to three years.

When a victim is assaulted on a college campus, often all the victim wants is to be assured she is safe and he will never repeat his offense. Universities have been accused of lacking the sophistication needed to handle these cases, due to ongoing confusion about their varying disciplinary systems, so victims are again advised to report to the police. Serious crimes need to be handled by serious systems, I agree. But she would be sacrificing her education to spend years struggling in the criminal justice system. Schools are not equipped to conduct full trials, but they have the power to create safe environments, and inflict limited punishment by removing the perpetrator from campus. It is absolutely true and undeniable that everyone deserves due process, especially when consequences are severe. If colleges were capable of sending men to prison it would be absurd. But this is not what we're asking. All the school can do is say, you cannot study here anymore, you cannot use our library anymore, or the cafeteria, you have to go find another library and cafeteria. If students can be swiftly expelled for plagiarism or dealing drugs, the same punishment should be inflicted if there's enough evidence to suggest they pose a threat to others. *Oh but his reputation! That's really where he suffers.* My advice is, if he's worried about his reputation, don't rape anyone.

Brock wrote, *Before this happened, I never had any trouble with law enforcement and I plan on maintaining that.* On November 15, 2014, three months before my assault, Deputy Shaw spotted a few young men walking through Stanford campus with beer cans. When apprehended, they ran. One guy was caught and detained, confessed the guy who escaped was Brock. Brock was summoned back. The police noted: *He returned wearing a bright orange tuxedo and Deputy Shaw smelled the odor of alcohol on him. . . . He had a black backpack on with Coors Light beers inside, as well as a beer in his hand. He admitted trying to hide the beer and knew he was not supposed to have it because he was not 21 years old. He stated that when he saw Deputy Shaw approach, he made the decision to run. While running, he heard the verbal commands to stop, but continued evading. He said it was a split-second decision and he regretted making it.* Deputy Shaw would be the one to photograph my body three months after this incident.

Six months after my assault, two young women found Detective Kim and reported they'd encountered Brock at the KA fraternity the weekend before I was assaulted. The police report noted: *He put his hat on her and she took it off. He then started to dance behind her and tried to turn her around to face him. She felt uncomfortable and tried to turn her body away so that he would not be directly "behind" her. He became really "touchy" and put his hands on her waist and stomach. He even put his hands on her upper thighs. She felt more exceedingly uncomfortable and got down off of the table. She said the Defendant "creeped" her out because of his persistence.*

The same location, a week before. I was grateful the girls had taken the time to find my detective, knew it would've been easier to see the news and say, *Woah, that was the same guy at the party*, and carried on. Instead they'd contributed their story, then returned quietly to their lives.

Shortly after the Defendant's arrest in the early morning hours of January 18, 2015, Detectives noticed a text message in the "Group Me" application that appeared on the Defendant's screen. It stated, "Who's tits are those?" The images had been erased by a third party in the group. There was speculation Brock had photographed my breasts and sent it out. If this is true, I do not want to know.

The stories about Brock running from police with a backpack full of Coors, rubbing up on girls, smoking weed, tripping on acid, photographing tits, were all absent from the image his loved ones and the media projected. *The Washington Post* called him *squeaky clean* and *baby-faced*, a rosy-cheeked cherub. The letter writers insisted *he was misconstrued as a criminal*. They called him *an innocent man, fighting for his freedom. Fun loving. Not a malevolent bone in his body. Blushes at the drop of a hat. If I could choose one word it'd be gentle . . . there are some people I equate to Labrador retrievers . . . Gracious, caring, talented. Humble, responsible, trustworthy. Wouldn't hurt a fly.*

Even after the conviction, they believed he remained entitled to impunity. Their support was unwavering, they refused to call it assault, only called it *the horrible mess, this unfortunate situation*. And still they said, *Brock is not one to believe that he is above the law or has any special privilege. . . . As a woman, I have never felt intimidated by him whatsoever.* In his mother's three-and-a-half-page single-spaced statement, I was not mentioned once. Erasure is a form of oppression, the refusal to see.

On January 20, 2017, four months after the release of the *Access Hollywood* tape, the nation watched Trump smile, lift his hand, be sworn in as president of the United States. I was shaking. It was the rattling, the sound of thousands of sliding Tic Tacs. *You can do anything.*

The news found me in the snow. It was December 2, 2017, a year and a half after the sentencing. Lucas and I were visiting a friend's cabin. In my half sleep I heard the *swish swish* of him walking around in his snow pants, pots in the kitchen, the sink running, heat breathing through the vents. I picked up my phone, did my routine squinty-eyed scrolling in bed. I saw missed calls, news had broken, Brock's appeal filed. Accusations of an unfair trial, citing insufficient evidence. The brief was 172 pages long. *The New York Times* noted that around 60 of the pages were about my intoxication. The snowy view faded, the fir trees. I had to return, to figure out what this meant, call my DA, my parents, saying, *yes I heard the news, yes I'll be all right.*

Appeals are incredibly common and everyone has the right to one, but the idea that the case was not closed for good, that there was a chance, no matter how small, there'd be a retrial, knotted my insides. My DA told me there was nothing to be done. The attorney general of the state would take the next few months to write a response. After that was submitted, an oral argument would be given by Brock's appellate attorney, Mr. Multhaup, in front of a panel of three judges, sometime next year, no saying when. The white-haired appeal attorney I'd seen at the sentencing had been replaced by this widow's-peaked man.

A call from Tiffany. She'd stepped out of brunch, leaving a table circled by friends. *What does this mean. Are we okay.* She stood alone outside while I sat in the room in the snow, wishing we were together. Everyone in the cabin was finishing toast, strapping goggles to their heads, engaged in a reality I was no longer a part of. Lucas came back to the room, noticed I was distracted, glued to my phone, not getting dressed, and asked what was wrong. When I told him, he was determined not to let the news steal our day, we were going to go skiing. I shook my head.

He'd seen this happen too many times before. More than being angry at the appeal itself, he was upset seeing what it did to me. He wanted to shake me out of its grip, to swoop me out onto a ski lift where I was meant to be. But I did not want to mobilize or feign happiness for others. Lucas finally said he would give me privacy and take his phone, we could meet whenever I was ready. I heard everyone shuffling out the door until finally the house was still.

One hundred and seventy-two pages. I looked at the table of contents, saw sections devoted to *Ms. Doe's sister, Ms. Doe's boyfriend, Julia.* I saw the people I love being disassembled again, blamed in a new set of arguments more virulent and insulting than before. I wanted to pluck their names off the page, to hold them closer to me, out of the attorney's hands.

I had written the statement to say stop. Stop treading on me, denying my truths, stop pushing back. I have had enough, I have taken too much, I can't take anymore. It ends now. This was their way of saying *no*. Their way of saying, *Here's one hundred and seventy-two pages of no*. They lived in a soundproof box and planned to keep me suffocating inside it with them.

Do you understand, when you ask a victim to report, what you're telling her to walk into? *Why didn't she go to the police?* I had deputies, a detective, paramedics, I had squad cars, an ambulance. I had them handcuffing him, photographing me, recording witness accounts, jotting down every detail of my body from the thin chain wrapped around my neck to the laces of my shoes, my clothes collected, his clothes collected. I pressed charges within twenty-four hours of the assault and here I was three years later reading the appellate attorney's statements about how I was *clearly in front of the dumpster*, not in any way *"behind"* it. How it was *"merely exterior massaging"* of my *"genital opening,"* how we were *enamored young people expressing their sexual urges*. When you say *go to the police* what do you envision? I was grateful for my team. But the police will move on to other cases while the victim is left in the agonizing, protracted judicial process, where she will be made to question, and then forget, who she is. You were just physically attacked? Here's some information on how you can enter a multiyear process of verbal abuse. Often it seems easier to suffer rape alone, than face the dismembering that comes with seeking support.

When a victim does go for help, she is seen as attacking the assailant. These are separate; seeking aid is her primary motive, his fallout is a secondary effect. But we are taught, if you speak, something bad happens to him. You will be blamed for every job he doesn't get, every game he doesn't play. His family, friends, community, team, will unleash hell on you, are you sure you want that? We force her to think hard about what this will mean for his life, even though he never considered what his actions would do to her. Inherently the victim is outnumbered. She is the sole object of his sexual aggression, expected to single-handedly undo all of their staunch beliefs, backed by years of amiable stories. They'll say, *We've never seen him behave that way, so you must be lying.* This sentiment was echoed in Brock's sister's statement: *The evidence presented during his trial and the conclusions that were made about his character were only from one night of his life, from strangers that didn't know him: a fraction of a fraction of his existence.* Victims are not fractions; we are whole.

When society questions a victim's reluctance to report, I will be here to remind you that you ask us to sacrifice our sanity to fight outdated structures that were designed to keep us down. Victims do not have the time for this. Victims are also students, teachers, parents, who can't give up work or education. The average adult can barely find time to renew their license at the DMV. It is not reasonable to casually demand that victims put aside their lives to spend more time pursuing something they never asked for in the first place. This is not about the victims' lack of effort. This is about society's failure to have systems in place in which victims feel there's a probable chance of achieving safety, justice, and restoration rather than being retraumatized, publicly shamed, psychologically tormented, and verbally mauled. The real question we need to be asking is not, *Why didn't she report,* the question is, *Why would you?*

Brock will always be the *swimmer turned rapist.* He was great and then he fell. Anything I do in the future will be by the *victim who wrote a book.* His talent precedes the tragedy. She was supposedly born in it. I did not come into existence when he harmed me. *She found her voice!* I had a voice, he stripped it, left me groping around blind for a bit, but I always had it. I just used it like I never had to use it before. I do not owe him my success, my becoming, he did not create me. The only credit Brock can take is for assaulting me, and he could never even admit to that.

On June 17, 2017, the first Cosby trial ended in a stalemate; six jury members were left scratching their heads, unconvinced, never mind those two pills, yeah but, I'm just, I'm not sure, we need a little more information. You would think Andrea Constand would have worn down, given up after a grueling mistrial. Proof again, *you can do anything*. But on April 26, 2018, the verdict of the second trial was read aloud, Cosby's arms latched behind his back. More than fifty women joined her, declaring, no, Cosby, you can't.

You can't kiss without asking, can't grab a pussy, can't mask what you're doing, can't turn off the mic, can't wave it away, can't make us forget, because we walk to the tempo of this two-word promise. For so long men could, they really could, get away with it. They got away but what they did never went away, even if our minds wanted to forget; it became a physical memory. Our bodies kept it in storage no matter how many times our brains took it to the trash, no matter how many times we were told to move on, take the blame, grow up, no matter how many years passed, if we built families, had kids, our kids had kids, still our bodies remembered. And while our minds attempted to abandon it entirely, late at night, lying awake alone, our bodies protested, *you can't*.

In October 2017, Ashley Judd and Rose McGowan stood at the front lines as Weinstein fell. High-powered men came down one after the other, or rather women came forward, and as a result these men came down. But it was never an eye for an eye, it was an eye for dozens of eyes. These men failed to realize that throughout the years, as they preyed on woman after woman, they'd created multiple witnesses, more than one backer, and thank God, because one, apparently, is never enough. Cosby, 60. Weinstein, 87. Nassar, 169. The news used phrases like *avalanche of accusations, tsunami of stories, sea change*. The metaphors were correct in that they were catastrophic, devastating. But it was wrong to compare them to natural disasters, for they were not natural at all, solely man-made. Call it a tsunami, but do not lose sight of the fact that each life is a single drop, how many drops it took to make a single wave. The loss is incomprehensible, staggering, maddening—we should have caught it when it was no more than a drip. Instead society is flooded with survivors coming forward, dozens for every man, just so that one day, in his old age, he might feel a taste of what it was like for them all along.

The Me Too movement, started by Tarana Burke, made visible the overwhelming number of situations where assault and harassment happen, the way violence is embedded in our day-to-day lives, pointed out countless conversations and gestures we'd been taught to write off as insignificant. *Me Too* is a tail-end phrase, meant to be tacked on, *in addition to*. It is inextricable from a greater mass, immune to isolation. By stating those words, you didn't have to divulge your full story in graphic detail, you just gave a nod, raised your hand. Speaking up didn't force you to step into a spotlight, only helped you contribute to a glowing, innumerable whole. The Me Too movement offered the relief of finally being given a chance to set the story down, to see what it felt like to walk around, breathe, shake your arms out a little, without it.

Some called it a witch hunt, said *she's after him*. I ask, starting when. Mark the day. Trace it back. I can almost guarantee that after the assault she tried to live her life. Ask her what she did the next day and she'd say, well, I went to work. She didn't pick up a pitchfork, hire a lawyer. She made her bed, buttoned up her shirt, took shower after shower. She tried to believe she was unchanged, to move on until her legs gave out. Every woman who spoke out did so because she hit a point where she could no longer live another day in the life she tried to build. So she turned, slowly, back around to face it. Society thinks we live to come after him. When in fact, we live to live. That's it. He upended that life, and we tried to keep going, but couldn't. Each time a survivor resurfaced, people were quick to say what does she want, why did it take her so long, why now, why not then, why not faster. But damage does not stick to deadlines. If she emerges, why don't we ask her how it was possible she lived with that hurt for so long, ask who taught her to never uncover it.

Victims are often accused of seeking revenge, but revenge is a tiny engine. I know better than to think my peace arrives when the gavel hits, when the handcuffs click shut. He may sit in a cell, but he will never know what it's like to be unhomed from his own body. We don't fight for our own happy endings. We fight to say *you can't*. We fight for accountability. We fight to establish precedent. We fight because we pray we'll be the last ones to feel this kind of pain.

When Hillary Clinton's book *What Happened* came out, I learned she'd quoted my final paragraph: *On nights when you feel alone, I am with you . . .* Then she wrote: *Early on the morning of November 9, when it came time to decide on what I'd say in my concession speech, I remembered those words. Inspired by them, I wrote these: "To all the little girls watching this, never doubt that you are valuable and powerful and deserving of every chance and opportunity in the world to pursue and achieve your own dreams." Wherever she is, I hope Emily Doe knows how much her words and her strength meant to so many.*

At a moment of monumental loss, she had consulted the statement for hope. She had returned to my darkest place to light the way forward.

13.

IN JANUARY 2018, over one hundred and sixty young gymnasts traded bare feet on vinyl mats for flats and tile floors, to stand one by one before a podium to read their statements to Larry Nassar, his face covered in stubble as if dipped in soil. When the news appeared, I was chopping carrots and tofu, feeding Mogu, the TV on in the background. As the voices of these young women entered the room, I let everything burn, the steam rising as I sat mesmerized, watching them. Their words were made of steel. Even when their voices quivered, their eyes stayed fixed. I thought, if I, as a survivor, am made up of the same fibers as them, if it is true we are built of similar threads, I am unshakable. Something in my chest seared that day, I felt like I could lift a car, climb a mountain, I was proud to belong to what being a survivor meant. The power they exuded. *Little girls don't stay little forever,* Kyle Stephens said. *They turn into strong women who return to destroy your world.*

Maybe Larry thought time had been on his side, mastering his technique as the years went by untroubled. But all that time they were growing stronger, looking for the right temperature to safely emerge. Still the source of their power was not lost on me; only after withstanding unbearable amounts of torment could that tone be achieved.

But something was different. My focus kept drifting to the mother who stood next to her daughter as she read, a somber shadow, face vacant and wordless in the background. The rows of parents in the audience, sunken and solemn. Rarely do we see the second ring of effect, this sharp contrast between the mighty, forceful daughters, and the sadder echo of their loved ones, insides undone. The scene was haunting. The role reversal, adults stepping back to watch their fifteen-year-olds step up and demand repair, while they were reduced to helpless onlookers. Behind every powerful speech, a second layer of thought seemed to play out in the parents' eyes, a dialogue of guilt, perhaps, dense and heavy. An aching, *you were too young to learn this*, and still a questioning, *what could I have done to prevent this.*

When Grandma Ann asked my mom, *What was it like when Chanel told you?* my mom said four sentences:

I try not to remember.

My knees softened.

I was the one who drove her.

I should've turned around, driven my babies home.

Julia says, *I was the one who invited you to the party.*

Tiffany says, *I was the one who left.*

Lucas says, *I was the one who spoke to you last on the phone.*

How many times I have told them, you are the reasons I am still here, not the reasons I am hurt. I can still see it in my parents, the way, when the case is brought up, their faces become grave, like when clouds briefly pass over the sun.

Watching the gymnasts speak was the first time I permitted myself to see the inside of a courtroom on-screen. For the last few years, I had avoided courtroom scenes on TV, shows, movies, even cartoons involving legal proceedings. I saw a baby dressed as a judge on Halloween, the little black cloth, the gavel, and I hated that baby, and I hated the parents who thought it was funny, and I knew I was crazy.

I had deemed the criminal justice system too brutal, too time con-suming. My faith was dimming. Where were we supposed to go to? Why is it so hard to hear a story where the victim is cared for, justice properly served? Then came Judge Aquilina. I'd never questioned the short time limit I was given to read my statement, until Judge Aquilina made time for one hundred and sixty-nine statements. She made it clear each one was important. She invited restoration and compassion into a space I had associated only with torture. *Leave the guilt here. It doesn't deserve any more of your family's time.* She shooed off the negative forces. *Quit shaming and blaming the parents,* she said. *Trust me, you would not have known. And you would not have done anything differently.* She said to the women, *Leave your pain here and go out and do your mag-nificent things.* I didn't know instructions like this were possible. In court, the judge is the captain of the ship. My captain sunk us. She turned their ship, pointing them toward the horizon. It was my hope that Stanford could be that kind of an institution, willing to be a leader in protecting survivors.

I was born in Stanford hospital and when I was young I believed this automatically made me smart. I've biked through the palm and eucalyp-tus trees, beneath the red-tiled roofs. I still can't name most of the buildings, but I can provide a tour of my memories, can point to any place on campus and say, *This is where . . .* This is where I sat at a foldout table selling Girl Scout cookies. In middle school I was self-conscious about my height, so Grandma Ann took me to the Stanford women's basketball meet and greets to show me what tall women become. I wore my grandpa's binoculars at every game, lassoed little towels when I cheered, loved the dancing tree mascot that looked like a massive toilet paper roll with googly eyes and floppy leaves. Stanford was where I took Chinese classes by the fountain, and a computer class where I learned how to type and edit videos; I created my first video about a fork that had superpowers (the *Fork Master 3000,* it could dig holes and comb your pet's hair). Tiffany and I would find golf balls in the grass by the Stanford golf course, imagining they were special eggs, and take them home to incubate.

Around twenty students from my graduating high school class were admitted. To visit a friend at Stanford was common, attending silent disco parties or playing Apples to Apples over holiday breaks. Stanford was made up of friends, idols, teachers. I may never have been a student, but it was my community before I knew it was a university. It was home.

After I was assaulted, I was left in silence for ten days. A Stanford dean had my name, but nobody contacted me. Nobody said, *How are you doing. Did you make it home okay.* I figured that since I wasn't a student, I wasn't entitled to support. Still I hoped for an extended hand during that crucial period of time. I had not yet learned how to ask for help, but if it had been presented, things might have been different. I may not have spent so much time calling hotlines in my van. What I mean to say is I wish there'd been some display of care, some directing me to resources, some acknowledgment of what happened.

Stanford's absence became a constant presence as I drove around Palo Alto. The assault harmed me physically, but there were bigger things that got broken. Broken trust in institutions. Broken faith in the place I thought would protect me. Their apathy, their lack of apology I could live with, but what troubled me most was their failure to ask the single most important question: *How do we ensure this does not happen again?* They had treated my assault like a singular, isolated incident. After Brock voluntarily withdraw, they called me once, to inform me he was not allowed back on campus. Other than that, little seemed to be set in motion. My assault came and went. But nothing is ever that simple.

Brock was not one bad apple, he just threatened to expose the greater, underlying issues of sexual violence on campus. Stanford should have taken the opportunity to conduct a systemic review of procedures and policies. To make sure that when a victim is harmed, there are services in place to take immediate action. To reevaluate safety on campus. To make survivors feel supported. They should have said, *It mattered, what happened to you.*

A few days after my statement went viral, Stanford came out with a statement of its own: *There has been a significant amount of misinformation circulating about Stanford's role. In this case, Stanford University, its students, its police and its staff members did everything they could.* They said when they'd learned my identity, *the university reached out confidentially to offer her support.* When I read their statement, unapologetic, almost prideful, *Stanford takes the issue of sexual assault extremely seriously and has been a national leader in taking concrete steps . . .* it was lemon wedges in the wound.

Jennifer J. Freyd, a Stanford alum and psychology professor, wrote an open letter to the administration. She condemned their *self-congratulatory and defensive stance.* She discussed a term I'd never heard of, *institutional betrayal,* which can cause victims *harm that occurs above and beyond that caused by the sexual violence itself. The irony is that institutional betrayal is not only bad for those dependent upon the institution, but comes to haunt the institution itself.*

That summer, Michele was on the news pointing out Stanford's lack of apology. She said my assault *wasn't unpredictable, wasn't random, they'd created a condition for it.* She was protected by her tenured position, allowing her to openly criticize their practices. I assumed it was futile.

The news of the statement had swelled and passed, the summer had come and gone. On August 31, 2016, two days before Brock would leave jail, I received a call from Michele, *good news.* A woman in a position of power informed Michele that Stanford wanted to apologize and pay for my therapy. I will call this woman Appleseed. Eating one apple seed is harmless. But eat enough over time and they can be toxic, subtle and corrosive, impossible to break down. Appleseed said she'd email me the document; all I had to do was sign it to receive the money. I said I refused to receive any money until they agreed to meet with me, to talk about how my assault was handled and understand what they could do better in the future. Michele suggested that we accept the offer before Stanford could change its mind.

It angered me, that this call was taking place two days before Brock's release. I questioned their motives, incentivized to clear their name and avoid negative publicity before the media swelled around my case again. I went to Lucas, *what do I do*. He said, *If they're serious about it, the offer will be there in a few days.* He also asked what the catch was. So I asked about the catch. *We need a commitment from you that you would not bring litigation.*

I finally understood I was visible not as a person, but a legal threat, a grave liability.

I wanted to turn my nose up, I don't need Stanford. *Who is Stanford,* Michele said. *You realize Stanford is a multibillion-dollar corporate trust. You can't personify a complex organization.* It was a brand, an experience they sell you. The same way Mickey Mouse is a grown man, getting paid to mutely stand inside a suffocating, rigid shell, coated in black fur with thick, white gloves. At the same time, she said Stanford was not a monolith, it was made up of different people with different motives. *There are people you are allowed to hate, and there are people who are trying to help you. Listen to the ones who are trying to help you.* Michele believed in Appleseed, in potential for reform. Michele had an idea to replace the dumpsters with a garden accompanied by a plaque with a quote of my choosing. I thought this would be nice and agreed.

On September 2, 2016, I opened the news on my phone, watched Brock walk out of the glass doors of county jail in a button-down shirt, lit up with bulb flashes and budding microphones, before he was neatly tucked into an SUV. I knew it was coming. But that summer I felt I'd blinked, and he was out again. Online I found people posting lists of things that were longer than his sentence. *Average life span of a sea monkey. The time the Macarena stayed in the Top 100* (Odyssey). *My leg hair in the winter* (HerCampus). *The amount of time I wait for a text back* (conniethegoat). *Moms conversation when she runs into her friends* (amy).

I clicked on another video of him checking into a hotel with his parents, cameramen swarming him, *Do you have anything to say to the victim?* For a second I held my breath, listening. He stood in front of an elevator, wearing sunglasses, looking down at his feet, his lips a thin line, his parents scoffing. I don't know what I was still expecting.

I had to get out of my house. I jogged to a diner. A man sitting at the counter smiled and said, *Are you from Colorado?* I realized I was wearing my Colorado sweatshirt. *Beautiful state, like you. I'm from a little town north of—* I walked away into the back patio. I ordered blueberry pancakes, six of them. When I came back in and passed the man, I stared at him, grabbed powdered sugar, maple syrup, returned to my table in the corner. I'd learned by now how to tie myself back to reality, filtering my world down to a set number of immovable, tactile facts: *I am eating delicious pancakes. The sun is out. I am warm. I see pink begonias.*

Brock was out and life kept moving and I was entering some kind of negotiation with Stanford. I was tempted to turn down the money entirely, my pride too big. Mostly I feared the guilt and shame and stigma that arrives when any victim receives any sum of money. But if my sister wanted therapy I wanted her to have that option. If I turned down the money and she came to me for help, what would I say? Go to Dad? Make him work longer hours? I wanted to be able to take care of them, to give them something good for once. If I accepted, would I be leaving all the other victims on campus behind?

After a year and a half of court proceedings, I'd never received a penny from the criminal justice system. Now that all was said and done, I was supposed to file for restitution, submit my hospital and therapy bills, which Brock was court ordered to pay. But since he was unemployed they said a payment plan would have to be set up, he'd pay it back little by little over the years. I wanted all ties to him cut. Plus he already viewed himself as the victim, and if he received an invoice in the mail, I worried his appeal attorney would be motivated to antagonize me further.

Michele had introduced me to a lawyer who laid out our options, all of which boiled down to two or three more years in court. As he explained how a deposition works, how my statute of limitations was almost expired, the logistics turned to murky water in my head. I knew I did not have it in me. Stanford was offering $150,000 total, which would cover therapy for my sister and me for a handful of years. Victims receive heat when given any sum. Few acknowledge that healing is costly. That we should be allocating more funds for victims, for therapy, extra security, potential moving costs, getting back on their feet, buying something as simple as court clothes. As Michele pointed out, *Preventing assault is so much cheaper than trying to address it after the fact.*

I requested there be a case manager, someone who exists exclusively to serve the needs of the victim, keeping them informed, ensuring adequate support. The lack of support I'd experienced would not happen again. I needed them to review the policies they had in place around contacting victims after rape. I wanted training for the Department of Public Safety on campus so they could better inform victims of the court process and their options, especially when it came to pressing charges. Also please add lighting to the dark back area of the fraternity.

Michele requested additional well-lit areas and video surveillance in outdoor and high-risk areas. She advocated for even more systemic remedies, *assessing cultures of sexual violence within athletic programs,* reviewing practices in the fraternity system, working on data transparency, making it more inclusive and expansive.

The meeting took place on September 6, 2016, four days after Brock was released from jail. I was aiming for tempered rage, strong conviction. Go in, make demands! I went in, shook hands. How quickly my face crumpled. I said a few lines before forgetting what I'd come in to say. I did not intimidate anyone or assert anything. It was as if my chest had one tiny pocket of air, as I whispered about how I wish someone had helped me. Michele confronted her, lambasting Stanford for failing to reach out in the aftermath of the assault. They had my number and name, they knew how to find me. Appleseed apologized.

Appleseed said that at the time *they did not have a clear practice on how to connect nonstudents to resources.* She said they wanted to respect my *agency and anonymity.* She said they'd tried to help me, had a note that they'd offered me mental health resources, but I never came in.

My mind dug through old memories, when, when did they do this? Was it that late night, sitting in my locked car in the Ikea parking lot? I'd sifted through my workbag, found the number for the Stanford hotline. I told the lady to just sit with me, I needed to know I was not alone. When I finally calmed, the lady on the phone told me she didn't know the policy for nonstudents, but I could come in, could show up at the office the next day, just tell them who you are. When the call ended, the faceless woman was swallowed back into the void and I was left with questions. If I went in, who would I be seeing, would I have to come out to a person at the front desk? Would I be randomly assigned a therapist? I could not call the hotline back, I would have been linked to a new responder. Part of not seeking help was the self-consciousness about where I fit in, the hesitation I heard in the woman's voice, *we don't usually do this, but . . .*

I thought the hotline had been confidential. I was suddenly embarrassed, realizing this whole time it had been my fault, I didn't come in. Plus I was not even a student, there was no protocol, what were they supposed to have done with me? The paper was printed, signed while it was still warm. Appleseed was late for something, and when the door closed I understood that was it, I'd signed away what she needed. Michele was optimistic, this would be an ongoing conversation, but I worried the promises around the money had been fluff.

I returned home that night, turned it over in my mind. The night I'd called I'd already hit a dangerous low and reached out in desperation. She had missed the point; responding to a hotline call is different than taking initiative, extending resources to the victim earlier, stepping in before she unravels. *I tried,* I should have said back. *That was me, not you. I called you.* I should have pushed back. Hadn't I already felt echoes of this in the court system? *Chanel not seeing that.* The subtle gaslighting, the shifting of blame and burden back onto the victim.

I had gone into the meeting seeking an open, personal conversation about making amends, reasonable requests, discussing solutions. I should have realized that from a legal perspective, they were not incentivized to admit to dropping the ball. Appleseed was also under pressure, speaking on behalf of stakeholders and lawyers, acting as a spokesperson for the university.

That night I felt sick, went to sleep early. At two in the morning I woke up vomiting into our new wicker basket, congealed liquid dripping through the cracks of woven wood. I took off my clothes and laid in fetal position on the bathroom mat, crawled between toilet and shower, my cheek pressed to the drain. It felt like someone was cutting up the insides of my stomach. The whole bathroom smelled sour. I laid there for nine hours.

I couldn't believe how I'd gotten food poisoning. It was odd because in China I'd eat meat cooked in unfamiliar oil, ate where men waded barefoot into the water to catch fish, gutting them on wooden stumps, stewing them before me. I wrote a list on a pink Post-it note: *Thursday, pesto pasta. Friday, chicken.* The cramping continued. My parents visited a week later, saw I had stopped eating, and told me to go to the doctor.

What brings you here today? I sat on that crinkly paper and presented my pink Post-it note: *Thursday, pesto pasta. Friday, chicken,* on and on until the doctor stated, *You must have gotten a bug.* The doctor advised me to take Pepto-Bismol. I shook my head. *I already finished all of mine, it just turns my vomit pink.* The doctor said I should try the chewable tablets, not liquid, and wait for the bug to pass. It hit me then. I had created the wrong list. *Thursday, talks with Stanford. Friday, rapist out of jail.* A panic attack, a failed meeting, guilt from money, the politics of negotiating, all repressed in my gut. I didn't know how to say any of this. *I've also been experiencing anxiety.* The doctor asked, *Have you tried therapy?* I nodded. *Okay, well maybe that's something we can explore next time, but anxiety is common, so let's give it a few months and . . .* I stared at the floor.

After my statement was released and the outpouring of support came in, I believed I was in the smooth sailing days. The worst is behind me days. I felt I had power. I'd been so excited, some had said I'd *moved the needle.* If I could move it I could surely redirect it entirely, could change the world overnight. I went into that meeting naive, thinking *I was* going to end sexual violence on campus over the course of an hour.

But Michele understood how long things take. She'd been battling Stanford for over a decade. *Social change is a marathon,* she'd said. *Not a sprint. You do all you can in the time that you have.* By time she meant lifetime, that over the span of our lives we may not see everything we want corrected, but still we fight. I was awakening to the excruciatingly long process of substantive change, how huge and imbedded systems are, how impossible they are to dismantle, how tiny I was.

A week later, I apologized to the lawyer, sorry I had not done enough. I hoped we could still work together to bring change to Stanford. He said, *We both hope this is a really positive step forward for you . . . we admire your tremendous strength. . . . You have a light that shines and that is something that Turner couldn't touch.*

His legal partner said, *I hope anxiety about not doing enough quickly vanishes, you've done so much.* But the shame rang through my head, *stupid, small, selfish,* canceling out their encouraging voices.

A check arrived in the mail. I drove to a new bank, opened an account, and gave my dad the password to use for any family emergencies. I put money into my sister's retirement account.

One night I overheard my parents talking about financial strain and my face filled with heat. I wanted the money to solve everything, everyone should be happy now. No more suffering, no more struggle. I ended our sadness. I did this one thing.

Since the location would soon be converted to a garden, Michele took me to see it in the daylight for the first time since the assault. The stomach cramping returned.

What struck me was how uninspiring, how underwhelming all of it was, this patchwork dirt lawn, saggy-limbed trees, a slope of dead pine needles, shit and beer cans, plastic spoons and broken glass, a ketchup packet and two black dumpsters. This? This is it? This is where my whole life was defined, the place that led to sacrificed relationships, unemployment, loss of identity, everything reduced and stolen by this pathetic shitty fraternity yard. How had the years passed with me still not free of this place, negotiating with Stanford over something as simple as a fucking light. A light! All my life and all my pain, standing there, felt like a joke, I wanted to laugh, to dig my fists into the ground, rip out clumps of the earth, to smash the glass patio doors with the wooden chairs I remember dancing on. Instead I said nothing, stood blinking in the sun, and after a few minutes, turned and walked back to Michele's car.

Half a year passed. Appleseed sent a message, passed through my lawyer to me. *I hope that you are thriving.* There would be a case manager, lighting added. She informed me that information about my assault should have come from my DA's office, it had never been their responsibility. They wouldn't say it, would never say, *We were supposed to protect you, and we failed. We should have followed up, and we did not. We should have come to you sooner, we will next time.*

I attended the art therapy program for survivors of sexual assault and relationship violence on campus. One evening I drove the hour from San Francisco to a small room tucked behind a dining hall. The workshop was led by two women; one who was a confidential support person and one who was not. When I told them I'd be coming, I was paranoid they'd mark that I was there, a note passed on to Appleseed, so if I ever said Stanford should have done more they'd say, *We have a note here that Chanel benefited greatly from the pipe cleaners and markers.* I told myself I would simply observe.

A metal pitcher of water and gummies sat in the corner. It was pouring rain. The workshop did not include discussion, so we worked in silence, shaping clay. There were little cards we could flip over on our desks if we wanted to talk. If you flipped it, the confidential woman would come talk to you in a whisper. Sitting in the company of other survivors brought me peace. There was no pressure to speak or feign cheer. A part of me ached, found myself secretly willing healing into those quietly working around me, and in turn I began directing some of that well-wishing toward myself. I wondered what it meant, that these students, who must have had plenty of homework, still showed up for two hours to make tiny sculptures. What was that longing, what brought them here, what needed nourishing. And where were the perpetrators who put us here? Why were we the ones gathered in silence on a rainy night, touching clay, while they carried on with their lives?

I tried to come back when I could. There was a session called *Unmasking Anger.* We would be making cardboard masks that personified rage; a mask would be a way to identify the presence of the emotion, but create enough distance not to be fully consumed by it. I planned to make a big ass mask. When I showed up I was the only one there, me and the two women and a scattering of empty stools. The confidential lady asked if I wanted to stay and talk and I said yes, so the nonconfidential lady left so I could speak freely. Maybe this was my chance to say what I was never able to say to Appleseed. But again I cried, revisiting the feelings of abandonment, diluted apology, the emotional bruising, the refusal to acknowledge lack of care. How pathetic it was to keep waiting for someone to restore my faith in this place I so valued since childhood.

You belong here, she said. *And anger is allowed to be embodied.* Rage for the perpetrator, bystanders, society, was a healthy and normal response. *Some direct anger inward toward themselves, feeling that this is the only safe way to be angry.* This could result in negative self-talk, blaming ourselves for the trauma, struggling to reconcile prior beliefs about justice, systems of meaning.

The question came back to me, *Who is Stanford?* If she is Stanford, then Stanford is kind and validating. *Who is Stanford?* A boy outside was playing "Feliz Navidad" on the tuba. Is he Stanford? Is Appleseed Stanford? I spent the next two hours cutting out a large, flat cardboard mask, with wiggly horns and a snout. I drove one hour home exhausted, leaned the mask against the wall, watching it slide down to the floor.

When I share with people that Stanford was more intent on self-preservation than caring about one person, people say in the gentlest way possible, *No shit.* But why? Why no shit? Why do we expect so little from universities? Why is it rare to hear the occasional story in which the university responded correctly and worked with the victim to improve campus safety? The few of us in the art therapy room were just a sampling, for there are rooms full of survivors across the country, seeking help in any form they can find.

Often victims are the ones who drop out of school or transfer. She soundlessly exits while the school keeps moving along, undeterred. I am not naive to expect better, I am not delusional to want more. I've learned the ways transparency heals. Accountability heals. Appleseed said, *That such quiet violence could have been perpetrated on our bucolic campus . . . is never far from my mind.* In that line I hear the disbelief, how could such a thing have happened here? She speaks as if this was a dark stain on an otherwise spotless campus. But we know the statistics, all those glaring red bodies, her and her and her. It is commonplace, omnipresent to those who live it.

I returned to art therapy. The woman began by talking about evolution, can we think of anything that evolves? When we were quiet, she suggested a frog, talked us through its stages. I thought for a minute, looking around again at the young students. Are they here because they hope to one day become frogs? By definition, wouldn't I be a frog? I had gone through the legal system, grew my legs, confronted my attacker, stated my truths. But I felt no different from them.

No matter how formidable or self-assured I might become, I will always be a tadpole. I believe that's what being a victim is, living with that little finicky, darting thing inside you. Most people say development is linear, but for survivors it is cyclic. People grow up, victims grow around; we strengthen around that place of hurt, become older and fuller, but the vulnerable core is never gone. More than becoming a frog, I believe surviving means learning to live forever with this trembling tadpole.

Appleseed asked for a quote to be placed on a raised bronze plaque in the garden. I provided the lines from my statement about relearning my worth, which began: *You made me a victim. . . . I had to force myself to relearn my real name, my identity. To relearn that this is not all that I am. . . . I am a human being who has been irreversibly hurt, my life was put on hold for over a year, waiting to figure out if I was worth something.* Appleseed rejected the quote. My lawyer pushed back: *A pretty garden with a softer message that no one notices is actually less useful than the dump-ster that preceded it.* Appleseed succumbed and agreed to have a mock-up made. For months I received numerous updates about the intricate site plans for the garden; *stone veneer seating wall, dark-colored river pebbles, topsoil, wood bench without armrest, stone color: Hillsborough and Willow Creek (50 percent of each color), flagstone mortar joint color to be determined, Swirl Fountain by Stone Forest, exact location of bench to be determined, batter exterior side of wall only, samples to be reviewed by landscape architect.* But there was still no Title IX investigation, no policy review. Still no plaque.

I received an email one evening informing me of their scheduled ceremony; it would open with the provost (five minutes), an announce-ment about support services (five minutes), a speech/letter from Emily Doe (five minutes), closing words, moment of silence in support of sex-ual violence survivors (five minutes). What do you do when you're in-vited to your own rape garden ceremony, that's been scheduled to last twenty minutes? I wanted to give a speech, *Thanks for the stones.* For being so concerned with agency, they had taken it upon themselves to create a public display of support, inviting cameras, a tidy itinerary, the figurative ribbon cut. They gave me three dates I could choose from. I appreciated that the area had been cleaned up, that students may find solace in it, but it was odd the plaque was still missing. I told my lawyer to politely inform them there would be no ceremony.

I thought more about anger, about the art piece I would create. A more fitting tribute: a piece called *Construction;* each victim is given a nail for every day she has lived with what happened to her. There's a haphazard pile of wood in the center of campus. Victims can come as they please, hammering nails into the wood. All day people hear the banging, all the drilling and incessant interruption. This is a lot of what surviving is like, trying to carry on and get work done, while your past pounds into you, distracts you, makes it impossible. At the end there'd be an immense wooden structure, randomly nailed together, large, useless, pointy, and dangerous in the middle of everything, people forced to walk around it, interrupting the pretty view of the trees. This is also what assault feels like, what to do with this, where to put it, what is it.

Or maybe a light installation. I could come in the night and install living-room lamps with extension cords throughout campus, large paper lanterns to dangle from trees, littering the campus with bright bulbs until every dark corner was glowing. I'd called that piece *All I Wanted*.

Or something more disturbing; I'd make mops, attaching dark, long hairs at the end of wooden poles, dragging them through the pine needles and leaves. Mopping all the vegetation and debris, dragging trails throughout campus, a victim custodian. That performance piece would be called *We Wanted to Respect Your Agency, Anonymity*.

One year after our meeting, a month after the garden installation, the plaque was still not there. When my lawyer inquired about it, Appleseed wrote that the space was meant to be *inspirational,* and it was not okay to *target* or *condemn a single individual.* She said they would not be placing it on a plaque because they had to *prioritize the well-being of all of our students.* She proposed the following quote:

I'm right here, I'm okay, everything's okay, I'm right here.

There is a world in which this is funny, the irony and absurdity too clear. These were words I'd used to comfort my sister straight out of the hospital in the moments I was least okay. In a way it summarized my experience, and I almost green-lighted it, but of course, I could not, due to the fact that it was grossly taken out of context. I began to think if they had a garden for every person assaulted at Stanford, wouldn't they have rolling acres of gardens, landscaping businesses booked out for eternity? Dry hillsides, littered with benches, cargo loads of pavers? Each marked with this plaque, with this lie we tell ourselves, *I'm okay, everything's okay.*

The other two quotes Appleseed suggested were from the final paragraph of my statement. *On nights when you feel alone, I am with you.* Those words were written from a place of deep hope, cultivated alone in a high apartment in Philly, when hope was the single thing I had. I wrote those words to survive. How could you abandon me these last two years, to reappear and take those lines. To hide the damage, then present the polished. I wanted to offer students a sentiment of solidarity, but could not give Stanford words of hope when they had not provided me reason to feel any. I could not sell victims a false dream, a tranquil and bright-eyed existence. On nights when you are alone, you are left alone. *Please let us know which of these quotes works.*

I should have backed out then, said enough. Instead I submitted a new quote: *You took away my worth, my privacy, my energy, my time, my safety, my intimacy, my confidence, my own voice, until today.* Appleseed said she'd shared the quote with the Confidential Support Team, and the next sentence started with *while we appreciate,* and that word again, *concerned.*

She explained it could be *triggering and upsetting* instead of healing. They said I could either choose what they'd selected or find a quote that was more *uplifting and affirming.*

As a survivor, I feel a duty to provide a realistic view of the complexity of recovery. I am not here to rebrand the mess he made on campus. It is not my responsibility to alchemize what he did into healing words society can digest. I do not exist to be the eternal flame, the beacon, the flowers that bloom in your garden. I emailed my lawyer: *Whenever you get the chance, please let [Appleseed] know I've decided not to provide a quote.*

I struggle with how I am supposed to live as a survivor, how to present my story and myself to the world, how much or how little to disclose. There have been numerous times I have not brought up my case because I do not want to upset anybody or spoil the mood. Because I want to preserve your comfort. Because I have been told that what I have to say is too dark, too upsetting, too *targeting*, too *triggering*, let's tone it down. You will find society asking you for the happy ending, saying come back when you're better, when what you say can make us feel good, when you have something more *uplifting, affirming*. This ugliness was something I never asked for, it was dropped on me, and for a long time I worried it made me ugly too. It made me into a sad, unwelcome story that nobody wanted to hear.

But when I wrote the ugly and painful parts into a statement, an incredible thing happened. The world did not plug up its ears, it opened itself to me. I do not write to trigger victims. I write to comfort them, and I've found that victims identify more with pain than platitudes. When I write about weakness, about how I am barely getting through this, my hope is that they feel better, because it aligns with the truth they are living. If I were to say I was healed and redeemed, I worry a victim would feel insufficient, as if they have not tried hard enough to cross some nonexistent finish line. I write to stand beside them in their suffering. I write because the most healing words I have been given are *It's okay not to be okay*. It's okay to fall apart, because that's what happens when you are broken, but I want victims to know they will not be left there, that we will be alongside them as they rebuild.

Appleseed did not hear the secret in the quote, which lives in the last two words, *until today*. I can't promise your journey will be good, I actually guarantee that it won't. I can't promise glorious days or shining redemption. I am here to assure the opposite; you will be faced with the hardest days of your life. The agony is incessant, unyielding, but when you get to the point where you feel like everything's gone, there's a little twist, a flame, a small shift. It is subtle, it comes when you least expect it. Wait for it. This is the rule of the universe, this is the one thing in life

I know to be true. No matter how awful and long your journey, I can promise you the turn. One day it will lift.

Victims exist in a society that tells us our purpose is to be an inspiring story. But sometimes the best we can do is tell you we're still here, and that should be enough. Denying darkness does not bring anyone closer to the light. When you hear a story about rape, all the graphic and unsettling details, resist the instinct to turn away; instead look closer, because beneath the gore and the police reports is a whole, beautiful person, looking for ways to be in the world again.

By now Michele and Appleseed were no longer talking, too much betrayal, mistrust, Michele was livid, Appleseed wasn't budging. Over a year had passed since the initial meeting, promises were not upheld, no investigation completed. *The Fountain Hopper,* an anonymous student publication, uncovered the news of the rejected quotes and email blasted the story across campus with the headline: STANFORD'S FINAL "FUCK YOU" TO BROCK TURNER'S VICTIM.

In the words of Appleseed, *I end where I began.* A year after Brock had been released, and I'd received some money, vomited, took a few art classes, received plants and no plaque, a burbling fountain. There was a light installed, which was good, thank you. The dumpsters were moved to the front, cedar walls erected around them. I was hard on myself for a long time, feeling like I did not do enough. But I am learning.

I worry Stanford will see this as a bashing, a reputation tainting, and will now release a statement asking me to stop naming their staff members after poisonous seeds. But before jumping to a position of defense, I hope they listen, because in an odd way, this is a love letter. My unending attempts to reconcile and reconstruct the world I grew up in. I write in hopes that schools will see how much power they have to help or hurt a victim. Listen to survivors when they come to you. Offer help when they don't. Do not write polite emails about how you did the best you can, about how actually that was not your job. Just help them. If I accuse

Stanford of failing to support victims, I hope they prove me wrong by saying they care about victims and then show everyone how they do.

I encourage you to sit in that garden, but when you do, close your eyes, and I'll tell you about the real garden, the sacred place. Ninety feet away from where you sit there is a spot, where Brock's knees hit the dirt, where the Swedes tackled him to the ground, yelling, *What the fuck are you doing? Do you think this is okay?* Put their words on a plaque. Mark that spot, because in my mind I've erected a monument. The place to be remembered is not where I was assaulted, but where he fell, where I was saved, where two men declared stop, no more, not here, not now, not ever.

When they held him down, they freed me. Without them, there would've never been a chance for me to speak my words in the first place, no hearing, no trial, no statement, no book. Because of them, I am here now. They gave me a chance, to grow and fight and come into myself again. It took a long time, it is still a strenuous process, but I would be nothing without that chance.

I often get scared of speaking out, of confronting lawyers and institutions bigger and better equipped than me, but when I'm afraid, all I have to do is think of the two of them. I think of how I want to return the favor; to pull the heaviness off you, to be the one yelling it is not okay, pinning your demons down in the dirt, so you suddenly find yourself free, given the chance to begin your journey, growing on your own, uncovering your voice, finding your way back. I want to stay and fight, while you go.

14.

WRITING IS THE way I process the world. When I was given the opportunity to write this book, whatever God is up there said, *You got your dream*. I said, *Actually I was hoping for a lighter topic*, and God was like, *Ha ha! You thought you got to choose*. This was the topic I was given. If something else had happened to me, I would have written about that too. When I get worked up over what happened, I tell myself, you are a pair of eyes. I'm a civilian who's been randomly selected to receive an all-access pass to the court system. Feelings will include invasion, shame, isolation, cruelty. My job is to observe, feel, document, report. What am I learning and seeing that other people can't see? What doorways does my suffering lead to? People sometimes say, *I can't imagine*. How do I make them imagine? I write to show how victims are treated at this moment in time, to record the temperature of our culture. This is a marker, and I hope that in twenty years this grueling aftermath of victimhood will feel foreign.

During trial, the judge was like this black peak, bolted in at the highest seat in the center of the room. We rose and sat around him, only referring to him as *Your Honor*. I never thought to question if it was possible to move the pieces.

If ever I was distraught or heartbroken, my mom would always say, *Go read history*. Her solution for everything. For so long I believed history was a thick book you carried around in your backpack, not something you could create. It was one hour in an air-conditioned portable classroom after lunch, watching Civil War reenactments. Our teacher making us eat expired crackers called *hardtack* so we could empathize with a soldier's diet in World War II. It'd take me a long time to realize history is happening now, and we are a part of it.

History is where you will find people who have been through what you're experiencing. Not only been there but survived it. Not only survived it but changed it. Whose struggles informed them. History shows you what people have endured before you. The year before I was born, Anita Hill testified before the Senate. In 2018, she sent her support to Michele, thanking her for forcing judges to take rape seriously, signing off, *All my best, Anita*. History shows that if you were in the minority, if no one believed you, it didn't mean you were wrong. Rather, it meant society was slow to catch up to you. And if those in the minority did not buckle, did not give up their truths, the world would shift below their feet.

The *San Francisco Chronicle* reported the judge saying, *There is a caricature of me that has been allowed to flourish*. He protested against the one-dimensional nature of his new identity. I understood, because it was what I had felt like as a victim. All my character traits vanishing, narrowing my identity to a label, the drunk victim.

Signatures were still being collected to put him on the ballot. Nicole told me about the volunteers, the retired couple who drove an hour every weekend to staff a table at the Palo Alto Farmers' Market. I heard about a girl who had been standing with her clipboard collecting signatures, when a man came up and verbally assaulted her, and afterward she sat down in tears, wiped them away, and kept going. So many of the volunteers were survivors, vulnerable to being accosted while petitioning. Yet they still showed up.

There were many times strangers reminded them that *the victim should not have drunk enough to pass out,* and part of Nicole's job was to help them know how to respond. Jim McManis, Persky's lawyer, stated, *This woman was not attacked.* These insults, that were meant to make victims crumble, only fueled them to mobilize.

Every Christmas, my Gong Gong selects something from Walmart for me and Tiffany, and every year I imagine him wandering the aisles thinking, *What does an eight-year-old want? A nine-year-old?* We've been gifted slippers, a striped vase, stuffed unicorn, purple binder, manicure set, hair wrap, mosquito repellant candles. Due to his old age, I drove him for the first time. It was a cloudy Tuesday afternoon, and as we walked through the parking lot, I saw Brock and the judge's flat heads hanging off a table by the front doors. As we came closer I saw an older man behind the table. I quieted as if seeing a deer in the wild. People passed him left and right, the afternoon was windy and chilly, his pages blowing about as he clamped his hands down on one paper after the other. He was spending his afternoon in the blustery shade, in the hopes of collecting a few more signatures. I went up to him and said, *Thank you for being here.* He said, *Well, it's important,* and wished me a nice day. My grandpa asked in Chinese why I'd spoken to him. Since I couldn't say, *A letter I wrote ignited a firestorm and now our community is rallying to recall the man that presided over my legal nightmares,* I said he was my friend's dad. My grandpa nodded. We went in, Gong Gong taking his time to browse. This year we got chocolate oranges and mugs.

I watched signs bloom across lawns in my hometown, couldn't drive a few blocks without seeing Brock's eyes peering out at me. I was playing a game of *they love me, they love me not,* with the houses in my neighborhood. It took me a long time to realize that it was possible for someone to oppose the recall, but still support me. There were many attorneys, judges, law professors, who agreed the sentence had been too lenient, but endorsed Persky, arguing he had remained within the rules of law. Slowly I began to take the opposition less personally.

In January of 2018, nearly ninety-five thousand local signatures were gathered and submitted, piles of pages submitted in stacks of white boxes. I stared at the boxes on the news, wondering how many hours had gone into them, how many people had sat in the shade, and how many passersby had stopped to sign their names, and I suppose this was why I teared up, looking at the pile of boxes.

As the election edged closer, I received disturbing letters. My house was put on alert. A detective from the Special Victims Unit arrived, tall and gray suited. He said the bushes below my window would need to be cut back, they could hide four to five people. I'd always thought of that bush as a lush, flowering bush, not a place you can hide four or five people. My writing desk was up against the window, visible from the street, so I'd need to move it. We needed a video camera installed and a second lock for our back door. My neighbors were put on alert. I was advised to be vigilant and avoid walking alone. My DA's office held meetings over my safety, offered to put me up in a hotel.

I kept writing. Numbers for the SFPD were taped to the refrigerator next to family photos. I kept the blinds in my office closed, ignored the darkness, amplified the artificial lighting, and kept writing. I stopped playing music, suspended myself in silence, one ear always listening, while I kept writing. Every time another unsettling letter arrived, I'd text the new detective, who would come by and add it to his growing folder of evidence. Police cars were on rotation around my house. As threats increased I stopped walking Mogu. My arms ached in the morning from clenching my fists at night. One day I stopped writing.

That day I stood before the round hedge holding shears. I hacked at it, snapping branches, cutting through stems thick as fingers. White secretions slid out of broken stems, splintered wood scraped my calves. I yanked weeds from the scalp of the earth, found wasps bound up in translucent sacs, pincher beetles spilling out of holes in the dirt with their little tonged butts. Dirt stuck to my heated skin, my knees pink and imprinted by the texture of the pavement. The sun lowered and I was peeling off my gloves when I caught sight of the discarded stems on the cement driveway, the little magenta buds, tightly bound. In my fervor, I'd severed them off. Those were supposed to be my flowers, set to bloom beneath my window. So much of surviving was sacrifice, cutting things short, suppressing life to do what's needed to make it to tomorrow. I wanted those bright petals to unfurl. I ran upstairs, my arms full of green stalks, sliding them into water.

The fight for the recall was growing increasingly heated. Signs were stolen off lawns, arguments veered into dark and personal tangents. On June 1, a *Huffington Post* piece by Julia Ioffe stated: *Emily Doe's statement, too, was the subject of fevered speculation among the anti-recall crowd. "I can't prove it, but I think [Michele] Dauber wrote the victim letter," Cordell told me. Babcock echoed her suspicion. "It's so sophisticated for someone who was so young," she said. Persky's lawyer, a fellow Stanford alum named Jim McManis, was also sure that Emily hadn't written the statement. "A person whose identity I am not at liberty to disclose says that it was written by a professional battered women's advocate," McManis explained. "I can't verify it, but the person who told me this, I value her judgment."*

In some ways it was a compliment. I was too "sophisticated" to be believed. I also didn't mind the suggestion of it being an advocate; the advocates I had were thoughtful, assertive, intelligent beings. But I took issue because of the implication that victims are frauds, liars, not to be trusted. Who would I commission to write a twelve-page first-person narrative? How would that conversation even go? *Hey, would you mind writing seven thousand words about the innermost private pains of my life?*

What they were really saying is, victims can't write. Victims aren't smart, capable, or independent. They need external help to articulate their thoughts, needs, and demands. They are too emotional to compose anything coherent. It cannot be the same drunk girl who was found unconscious, the one who the media said *uncontrollably sobbed* throughout testimony. On a deep level, they wanted to take away my writing, which I would not give up so easily. Some history:

When my mom was twenty-six, she appeared in the documentary film *Bumming in Beijing*. It followed a group of counterculture artists, living in poverty, defying conformity inside China's Communist regime. In this group, she was the writer. She said, *When I think about going to America, it's like going back to the womb. It's very dark and you don't know how bright your future will be. When I arrive in America, I think I should get a job first.*

Throughout my childhood, my mom worked at the dry cleaners, as an aerobics instructor, crossing guard, at the flower shop, Frame-O-Rama, local newspaper, as a real estate agent, but every night, I saw her sitting in the dark living room, blanket around her shoulders, in front of the glow of the computer screen, writing. When my dad took us to school every morning, I'd pass her door, see her asleep. Once I found her crying; her Chinese website with her writing had been banned and shut down. I was unaware speech could not be free.

After my twenty-fourth birthday, I took the train to New York to sign a contract for my first book, celebrating with a dessert of grilled peaches. I sent my mom a photo of the sun setting over the tall silver buildings. She responded, *You are mommy's dream.*

My writing is sophisticated because I had a head start, because I am years in the making, because I am my mother and her mother before. When I write, I have the privilege of using a language that she fought her whole life to understand. When I speak in opposition, I am grateful my voice is uncensored. I do not take my freedom of speech, my abundance of books, my access to education, my ease of first language for granted. My mom is a writer. The difference is, she spent the first twenty years of her life surviving. I am a writer, who spent twenty years of my life fed and loved in a home and classroom.

In a sense they were right. I don't deserve credit. It belongs to my mom, who held my hand in line at book signings, to Grandma Ann, who read to me on the corduroy couch, to Mrs. Thomas in second grade, who laminated our covers and bound our books, turning our classroom into a publishing house. I owe it to public school English teachers, Mr. Dunlap, Wilson, Owen, Caroline, Ellen, Teddy, Kip. To my grandmother, Bam. To my grandfather, Lovick, a six-foot-two World War II veteran who read books thick as bricks, but sat in his office with a little handwritten pile of my poems beside him, typing them up one by one, so they would never be lost. There are many people responsible for this statement, everyone who taught me how to see the world, to pay attention, to speak up, because my opinion was worth something, the ones who told me I deserved to be heard and seen.

On June 5, 2018, the judge was recalled. I remembered a quote from him in the *San Francisco Chronicle: Women are frustrated by how they are treated by society, how they are treated by the criminal justice system. That passion is genuine. It needs to be expressed.* Expressed was the wrong word. We the victims are tired of expression, I expressed a lot in his courtroom. The word we need is: acknowledged, taken into account, taken seriously.

The day I'd read my statement, I'd gone home believing I had failed. How many victims have been insulted, made small, because there were no other voices to counter that belief. How many of us have been made to feel humiliated, melodramatic, instead of brilliant, brave. One man could have kept me from awakening millions. Question who your realities are being written by. Reexamine who dictates it. Who decides you are important. The judge was not God. He was one man, wearing a black smock, head of a small domain, ruler of a one-room kingdom on

Grant Avenue. He was not the sole truth speaker, the rule maker, the final word. He was an elected official, voted out by 62 percent.

When he was recalled, there was no formal ceremony. I imagine there was simply a day he woke up knowing he would not zipper up the black smock, left it hanging lifeless in his closet. The *Los Angeles Times* reported that after the sentencing, the judge said, *I expected some negative reaction. But not this.* The judge knew I'd be unhappy with the sentencing, he just didn't know eighteen million people would be indignant, and that two hundred thousand people in the local county would vote for his outing. Whether one agrees with the recall or not, the volunteers taught me something I will know for the rest of my life: the world is not fixed.

On July 25, 2018, Brock's appellate attorney appeared in court before a panel of three judges to present his case that Brock had only intended to have *outercourse.* The *Mercury News* reported Justice Franklin Elia responding, *I absolutely don't understand what you are talking about,* which summed up everything I could say.

On August 8, 2018, my DA texted me, *Judgment affirmed!* The appeal was denied. It was like the sound of a last breath, a beat, the lightness of a bird lifting off a wire. Three years and eight months after that night in January, the case was closed. It brought to mind a Hafiz poem:

> And then, all the *and thens* ceased.
> Nothing remains *to be done* in the
> Order of time, when all is still.

No more calls, no more updates, no more what's next, no more *no way of knowing.* I had forgotten it was possible to exist without him, to have a life not tied to his. That night I celebrated alone by buying Oreos, pouring them in a bowl of milk, letting them sit, scooping out the remains. I did not respond to my DA's text that day, or the next, skeptical it could really be over. I let weeks pass, wary of the good news, wondering if it was true I was finally free.

I am not sure exactly what healing is or looks like, what form it comes in, what it should feel like. I do know that when I was four I could not lift a gallon of milk, could not believe how heavy it was, that white sloshing boulder. I'd pull up a wooden chair to stand over the counter, pouring the milk with two shaking arms, wetting the cereal, spilling. Looking back I don't remember the day I lifted it with ease. All I know is that now I do it without thinking, can do it one-handed, on the phone, in a rush. I believe the same rules apply, that one day I'll be able to tell this story without it shaking my foundation. Each time will not require an entire production, a spilling, a sweating forehead, a mess to clean up, sopping paper towels. It will just be a part of my life, every day lighter to lift.

Ram Dass said, *Allow that you are at this moment not in the wrong place in your life. Consider the possibility that there have been no errors in the game. Just consider it. Consider that there is not an error, and everything that's come down on your plate is the way it is and here we are.* I don't believe it was my fate to be raped. But I do believe that *here we are* is all we have. For a long time, it was too painful to be *here*. My mind preferred to be dissociated. I used to believe the goal was forgetting.

It took me a long time to learn healing is not about advancing, it is about returning repeatedly to forage something. Writing this book allowed me to go back to that place. I learned to stay in the hurt, to resist leaving. If I got stuck inside scenes in the courtroom, I would glance down at Mogu and wonder, if I am really in the past, how did this blinking thing get in my house? I assembled and reassembled letters in ways that would describe what I'd seen and felt. As I revisited that landscape, I grew more in control, could come and go when I needed to. Until one day I found there was nothing left to gather.

The transcripts that once overwhelmed me were now only pieces of paper. I began to belong more to my present than my past. I was no longer trying to get somewhere, only asking myself, *Are you improving?* Sometimes the answer was *not today.* Sometimes I was regressing. But the voice in my head was now gentler. Whatever the answer, I was patient and understanding.

From grief, confidence has grown, remembering what I've endured. From anger, stemmed purpose. To tuck them away would mean to neglect the most valuable tools this experience has given me. If you're wondering if I've forgiven him, I can only say hate is a heavy thing to carry, takes up too much space inside the self. It's true that I'll never stop hoping that he learns. If we don't learn, what is life for? If I have forgiven him, it's not because I'm holy. It's because I need to clear a space inside myself where hard feelings can be put to rest.

Many of us struggle to crawl out from under what we've been given, to build ourselves beyond the small definitions we've been assigned. I feared, at times, that I'd lost my imagination, because I felt boxed in my role as victim. But when I was trapped, I learned I could still move internally. When I felt depressed, I wrote and imagined my future down to the coffee bean, the children's books I will illustrate, the chickens I will have in my yard, the soft cotton linens, the sauce-dipped wooden spoons on the counter. The need for it to come true according to plan was not important. The act of imagining was.

I wrote this book because the world can be harsh and terrible and often unforgiving. I wrote because there were times I did not feel like living. I wrote because the court system is slow as a snail, and victims are forced to spend so much time fighting, rather than spending their days creating, drawing, cooking. I wrote to expose the brutality of entitlement, gender violence, and class privilege in our society. But I would be failing you if you walked away from this book untouched by humanity, without seeing what I saw: those thousands of handwritten letters, the green-lipped fish at the bottom of the ocean, the winking court reporter. All the small miracles that sustained me. We may spend half our time wandering around, wondering what we're even doing here, why it's worth the effort. But living is an incredible thing, just to have been here, to have felt, if only briefly, the volume and depth of others' empathy. I wrote, most of all, to tell you I have seen how good the world could be.

I never could have known that, after college, I'd be assaulted within seven months, live in Providence then Philadelphia, scuba dive and weep during testimony, write twelve pages that would resonate globally, move in with a tall boy and a tiny dog, and spend two and a half years writing. I have created a self inside the suffering. Looking back, the assault is now inextricable from the greater story. It is a fact of my life, the same way I was born in June, and I was raped in January. Awful feelings may remain the same, but my capacity to handle them has grown. I can't tell you what happens next because I have not yet lived it. This book does not have a happy ending. The happy part is there is no ending, because I'll always find a way to keep going.

On September 23, 2018, a candlelight vigil was held for Christine Ford in Palo Alto when it was confirmed she would testify before the Senate Judiciary Committee. It felt strange calling it a vigil. Perhaps it was a collective strengthening before sending her into battle, knowing what she would face. A huge, white moon sat in the sky. I drove out of San Francisco, taking familiar roads. As I drew closer, I saw glowing clusters of people trailing through the streets, lanterns swinging, toward the center, to gather at the intersection of El Camino and Galvez, close to my parents' home. I heard cars honking their support. I pulled over to the side of the road, the lights framed in my rearview mirror, a long rectangle full of glowing dots. I meant to get out, but sat there, door open, feet on the curb, weeping. I listened to the night air full of honking, incessant, blaring horns, the beautiful rage, the support of my hometown, people packing the sidewalks I grew up on, these streets where I'd scootered with Tiffany, eating lemon drops. I heard them chanting, *We are her, she is us.* A younger version of myself had been hungry to see this for a long time.

My mom arrived, slipped me a red bean mooncake she'd been carrying in her pocket, and we walked into the crowd where Grandma Ann was waiting, chanting, *We believe you.* The next day, Mid-Autumn Festival, my mom's mom passed away in China. I thought of the two things she would say every time I visited, *You have pretty dimples! And huge feet!* Her grandma's feet had been bound. Four-inch feet, and now mine, size 9½. Every generation, we get a little more free.

A few days later, Ford testified. I woke up to see Ford's photo, eyes closed, hand raised and flat. I held my breath when I saw it, knew how it felt, that symbol of surrender, about to step into your own wound. All morning I could not focus, went walking through a eucalyptus grove in the city. It had rained that morning and for hours I surrounded myself in the mint and wet mulch and breathed.

I returned to the news to see Kavanaugh testifying. Exasperated, sniffling, snarky, sarcastic, inflamed with glistening eyes. When Senator Amy Klobuchar asked if he'd ever drunk enough not to remember, he said, *You're asking about blackout, I don't know, have you? I'm curious if you have.* I had been asked the exact same question. I had sat with restraint, never raised my voice, never retaliated. I wondered why a man, who was about to sit on the highest court of the land, could not maintain his demeanor, could only spit back, embittered by the unfairness of it all.

I watched Lindsey Graham, beet red, teeth flared, finger-pointing. I used to shrink at harsh tones, used to be afraid. Until I learned it takes nothing to be hostile. Nothing. It is easy to be the one yelling, chucking words that burn like coals, neon red, meant to harm. I have learned I am water. The coals sizzle, extinguishing when they reach me. I see now, those fiery coals are just black stones, sinking to the bottom.

For years, the crime of sexual assault depended on our silence. The fear of knowing what happened if we spoke. Society gave us one thousand reasons; don't speak if you lack evidence, if it happened too long ago, if you were drunk, if the man is powerful, if you'll face blowback, if it threatens your safety. Ford broke all the rules. She had none of the requirements society tells us we need before we dare open our mouths. She had every reason to stay hidden, but stepped straight into the most public, volatile, combative environment imaginable, because she possessed the single thing she needed, the truth.

The barricades that held us down will not work anymore. And when silence and shame are gone, there will be nothing to stop us. We will not stand by as our mouths are covered, bodies entered. We will speak, we will speak, we will speak. There was a line survivors had been taught never to cross. She crossed it, the moment she lifted her hand.

So much of that day was beyond language, was not heard, but felt. Kavanaugh and Graham's words ricocheted around the room, mean and flighty, nervous, erratic. There was spittle and eruptions, faces wrinkled and cracked, diatribes like swarms of flies, of insults and unclarity. Who held the gravity in that room? It was her. Her words rose from the center of her being, resonated throughout the nation. She was the mountain, their words like fleeting winds and harsh rain, while she did not move. When she spoke it was sobering, the sadness filling our insides with sand until everyone had sunk in their seats. The truth holds weight.

Trump mocked her at a rally days later in Mississippi: *How did you get home? I don't remember. How'd you get there? I don't remember. Where is the place? I don't remember. How many years ago was it? I don't know. What neighborhood was it in? I don't know. Where's the house? I don't know. Upstairs, downstairs—where was it? I don't know—but I had one beer. That's the only thing I remember.* The crowd laughed openly, clapping. But all I saw was Trump chucking coals, while we remain water.

I began this story alone as a half-naked body. I remembered nothing.

There was so much I did not know. I was forced to fight, in a legal system I did not understand, the bald judge in the black robe, the defense attorney with narrow glasses. Brock with his lowered chin, his unsmiling father, the appellate attorney. The obstacles became harder, I was up against men more educated, more powerful than me, the game rougher, more graphic, serious. I read comments that laughed at my pain. I remember feeling helpless, terrified, humiliated, I cried like I've never cried before. But I remember the attorney's still shoulders as *guilty* was read. I know Brock slept ninety days in a stiff cot in a jail cell. The judge will never step foot in a courtroom again. The appellate attorney's claims were shut down. One by one, they became powerless, fell away, and when the dust settled, I looked around to see who was left.

Only Emily Doe. I survived because I remained soft, because I listened, because I wrote. Because I huddled close to my truth, protected it like a tiny flame in a terrible storm. Hold up your head when the tears come, when you are mocked, insulted, questioned, threatened, when they tell you you are nothing, when your body is reduced to openings. The journey will be longer than you imagined, trauma will find you again and again. Do not become the ones who hurt you. Stay tender with your power. Never fight to injure, fight to uplift. Fight because you know that in this life, you deserve safety, joy, and freedom. Fight because it is your life. Not anyone else's. I did it, I am here. Looking back, all the ones who doubted or hurt or nearly conquered me faded away, and I am the only one standing. So now, the time has come. I dust myself off, and go on.

ACKNOWLEDGMENTS

Life always needs balance. So let's say you're having a terrible day. Someone comes along and gives you a juicy little loquat and suddenly the day has some good in it, and so becomes balanced. These people are the ones who balanced it out for me, constantly, so I was never left with too much of a bad feeling.

In the hospital, I found good people. In the courtroom, more good people. All my life I've been kept afloat by good people in heavy circumstances. Words cannot adequately thank each one of you. Just know I'm going to keep doing the most I can, because I understand I have you. Thank you.

To Dad, for growing fresh tomatoes, and encouraging me and Tiffy to become whoever we wanted to be. To Mom, I grow in the direction of you. To Tiffany, the little one I will always look up to. To Lucas, for letting me press my cold feet against you when I get in bed late after writing, who helped me face the hardest parts head-on. To Mogu, my eight-pound office manager who never sent a single email, who slept next to my rolling chair. I tried so hard not to roll on you.

Grandma Ann and Newman. LCM. BAM. Gong Gong. Puo Puo. My Miller family. The Zhangs. For your love unending.

Julia, for your big heart and clarity. Anne, who showed up for us every day. Deputy District Attorney Alaleh Kianerci, for your brilliance, I hope girls grow up to be like you. Detective Mike Kim, for your kindness, for creating a nonjudgmental space when I was most vulnerable. YWCA advocates Bree Van Ness and Clare Myers, my companions on the stand, my bathroom buddies, your presence was vital. SART nurses, for your gentle care and levity. Every deputy who tended to me. To Sean, who fended off the media.

Nicole, to the orchard we grew up in. To a bright life for your little one. Claire, may we ride the shit out of these ups and downs. Athena, for always finding a way back to the center. Mel Rosenberg, I am sustained by every stroll, every call, you know me better than me. Cayla, all our nights in San Francisco, bowls of pho, tea sipping. Miranda, with you the saddest things become funny. To TJ, healing over cinnamon buns and coffee. I love Tiffany's friends from Terman and Cal Poly. Lucas's family, for every meal together.

Katie J.M. Baker, who brought my story into the world and shielded me. Michele Dauber, for defining resilience, indomitability. John C., for protecting me. Jon Krakauer, for your encouragement.

I'm sorry to all the math teachers I failed, but I hope my English teachers are happy: Hoover, Terman, Gunn, UCSB. Thank you, Deb, for a safe room in Philly. Thank you to my therapist in the city for seeing me through this book. C&S, my favorite sisters. Afternoons with Bambu. Doorwomen of Walnut Street. The warmth of Saxbys Rittenhouse. Chessy, for your beautiful letter. To every hotline responder. To Bupis.

Muttville. YWCA. Grateful Garments. Victim Assistance Program of Santa Clara County.

To the lives lost in Isla Vista: Weihan "David" Wang. Cheng Yuan "James" Hong. George Chen. Veronika Weiss. Katie Cooper. Christopher Michaels-Martinez. Your names are carried by our collective memory. Thank you, Richard Martinez, for speaking. We follow your lead.

Andrea Schulz, my editor at Viking, thank you for my sanity, for making an impossible thing enjoyable, for being a luminous guide through the roughest terrain. You made me unafraid. Flip Brophy, for the bread pudding, for knowing I could do it before I did. Emily Wunderlich, for getting me to the next layer. Jane Cavolina, my copyeditor, you restored order when my syntax got nutty. Emily Neuberger. Aileen Boyle. Lindsay Prevette. Kate Stark. Mary Stone. Brian Tart. Jason Ramirez. Tess Espinoza and the whole Viking managing editorial and production team. Lara Bergthold. Hillary Gross Moglen. Szilvia Molnar. For the green cake crew at Sterling Lord Literistic.

To the Swedes. You've taught us that we all bear responsibility to speak up, wrestle down, make safe, give hope, take action. We do not have to wait for something wrong to happen to be a Swede. Being the Swede begins with respecting bodily autonomy, the language we choose, the understanding that consent can never be assumed or overridden. We must protect the vulnerable and hold each other accountable. May the world be full of more Carls and Peters.

For all the names I do not know, the ones who carried clipboards for petition signing, who live with tadpoles, and who wrote long letters to me. I kept that box of letters beside my desk while writing; when motivation dipped, I read them. You were teaching me self-compassion, encouraging me to keep going. I hope you understand you are worth fighting for. Your character is not what caused your hurts to happen. You are not a statistic or a stereotype, so when they minimize you, dehumanize you, objectify you, you must push back with your whole weight, with your lifetime of experiences. To the faceless, the ones who remain anonymous. We each have a name. You have taught me to be proud of mine.

EMILY DOE'S
VICTIM IMPACT STATEMENT

PUBLISHED BY KATIE J.M. BAKER
IN BUZZFEED NEWS ON JUNE 3, 2016, AS
*HERE'S THE POWERFUL LETTER THE STANFORD VICTIM
READ TO HER ATTACKER*

Your Honor, if it is all right, for the majority of this statement I would like to address the defendant directly.

You don't know me, but you've been inside me, and that's why we're here today.

On January 17th, 2015, it was a quiet Saturday night at home. My dad made some dinner and I sat at the table with my younger sister who was visiting for the weekend. I was working full time and it was approaching my bed time. I planned to stay at home by myself, watch some TV and read, while she went to a party with her friends. Then, I decided it was my only night with her, I had nothing better to do, so why not, there's a dumb party ten minutes from my house, I would go, dance like a fool, and embarrass my younger sister. On the way there, I joked that undergrad guys would have braces. My sister teased me for wearing a beige cardigan to a frat party like a librarian. I called myself "big mama," because I knew I'd be the oldest one there. I made silly faces, let my guard down, and drank liquor too fast not factoring in that my tolerance had significantly lowered since college.

The next thing I remember I was in a gurney in a hallway. I had dried blood and bandages on the backs of my hands and elbow. I thought maybe I had fallen and was in an admin office on campus. I was very calm and wondering where my sister was. A deputy explained I had been assaulted. I still remained calm, assured he was speaking to the wrong person. I knew no one at this party. When I was finally allowed to use the restroom, I pulled down the hospital pants they had given me, went to pull down my underwear, and felt nothing. I still remember the feeling of my hands touching my skin and grabbing nothing. I looked down and there was nothing. The thin piece of fabric, the only thing between my vagina and anything else, was missing and everything inside me was silenced. I still don't have words for that feeling. In order to keep breathing, I thought maybe the policemen used scissors to cut them off for evidence.

Then, I felt pine needles scratching the back of my neck and started pulling them out my hair. I thought maybe, the pine needles had fallen from a tree onto my head. My brain was talking my gut into not collapsing. Because my gut was saying, help me, help me.

I shuffled from room to room with a blanket wrapped around me, pine needles trailing behind me, I left a little pile in every room I sat in. I was asked to sign papers that said "Rape Victim" and I thought something has really happened. My clothes were confiscated and I stood naked while the nurses held a ruler to various abrasions on my body and photographed them. The three of us worked to comb the pine needles out of my hair, six hands to fill one paper bag. To calm me down, they said it's just the flora and fauna, flora and fauna. I had multiple swabs inserted into my vagina and anus, needles for shots, pills, had a Nikon pointed right into my spread legs. I had long, pointed beaks inside me and had my vagina smeared with cold, blue paint to check for abrasions.

After a few hours of this, they let me shower. I stood there examining my body beneath the stream of water and decided, I don't want my body anymore. I was terrified of it, I didn't know what had been in it, if it had been contaminated, who had touched it. I wanted to take off my body like a jacket and leave it at the hospital with everything else.

On that morning, all that I was told was that I had been found behind a dumpster, potentially penetrated by a stranger, and that I should get retested for HIV because results don't always show up immediately. But for now, I should go home and get back to my normal life. Imagine stepping back into the world with only that information. They gave me huge hugs and I walked out of the hospital into the parking lot wearing the new sweatshirt and sweatpants they provided me, as they had only allowed me to keep my necklace and shoes.

My sister picked me up, face wet from tears and contorted in anguish. Instinctively and immediately, I wanted to take away her pain. I smiled at her, I told her to look at me, I'm right here, I'm okay, everything's okay, I'm right here. My hair is washed and clean, they gave me the strangest shampoo, calm down, and look at me. Look at these funny new sweatpants and sweatshirt, I look like a P.E. teacher, let's go home, let's eat something. She did not know that beneath my sweatsuit, I had scratches and bandages on my skin, my vagina was sore and had become a strange, dark color from all the prodding, my underwear was missing, and I felt too empty to continue to speak. That I was also afraid, that I was also devastated. That day we drove home and for hours in silence my younger sister held me.

My boyfriend did not know what happened, but called that day and said, "I was really worried about you last night, you scared me, did you make it home okay?" I was horrified. That's when I learned I had called him that night in my blackout, left an incomprehensible voicemail, that we had also spoken on the phone, but I was slurring so heavily he was scared for me, that he repeatedly told me to go find my sister. Again, he asked me, "What happened last night? Did you make it home okay?" I said yes, and hung up to cry.

I was not ready to tell my boyfriend or parents that actually, I may have been raped behind a dumpster, but I don't know by who or when or how. If I told them, I would see the fear on their faces, and mine would multiply by tenfold, so instead I pretended the whole thing wasn't real.

I tried to push it out of my mind, but it was so heavy I didn't talk, I didn't eat, I didn't sleep, I didn't interact with anyone. After work, I would drive to a secluded place to scream. I didn't talk, I didn't eat, I didn't sleep, I didn't interact with anyone, and I became isolated from the ones I loved most. For over a week after the incident, I didn't get any calls or updates about that night or what happened to me. The only symbol that proved that it hadn't just been a bad dream, was the sweatshirt from the hospital in my drawer.

One day, I was at work, scrolling through the news on my phone, and came across an article. In it, I read and learned for the first time about how I was found unconscious, with my hair disheveled, long necklace wrapped around my neck, bra pulled out of my dress, dress pulled off over my shoulders and pulled up above my waist, that I was butt naked all the way down to my boots, legs spread apart, and had been penetrated by a foreign object by someone I did not recognize. This was how I learned what happened to me, sitting at my desk reading the news at work. I learned what happened to me the same time everyone else in the world learned what happened to me. That's when the pine needles in my hair made sense, they didn't fall from a tree. He had taken off my underwear, his fingers had been inside of me. I don't even know this person. I still don't know this person. When I read about me like this, I said, this can't be me, this can't be me. I could not digest or accept any of this information. I could not imagine my family having to read about this online. I kept reading. In the next paragraph, I read something that I will never forgive; I read that according to him, I liked it. I liked it. Again, I do not have words for these feelings.

It's like if you were to read an article where a car was hit, and found dented, in a ditch. But maybe the car enjoyed being hit. Maybe the other car didn't mean to hit it, just bump it up a little bit. Cars get in accidents all the time, people aren't always paying attention, can we really say who's at fault.

And then, at the bottom of the article, after I learned about the graphic details of my own sexual assault, the article listed his swimming times. She was found breathing, unresponsive with her underwear six inches away from her bare stomach curled in fetal position. By the way, he's really good at swimming. Throw in my mile time if that's what we're doing. I'm good at cooking, put that in there, I think the end is where you list your extracurriculars to cancel out all the sickening things that've happened.

The night the news came out I sat my parents down and told them that I had been assaulted, to not look at the news because it's upsetting, just know that I'm okay, I'm right here, and I'm okay. But halfway through telling them, my mom had to hold me because I could no longer stand up.

The night after it happened, he said he didn't know my name, said he wouldn't be able to identify my face in a lineup, didn't mention any dialogue between us, no words, only dancing and kissing. Dancing is a cute term; was it snapping fingers and twirling dancing, or just bodies grinding up against each other in a crowded room? I wonder if kissing was just faces sloppily pressed up against each other? When the detective asked if he had planned on taking me back to his dorm, he said no. When the detective asked how we ended up behind the dumpster, he said he didn't know. He admitted to kissing other girls at that party, one of whom was my own sister who pushed him away. He admitted to wanting to hook up with someone. I was the wounded antelope of the herd, completely alone and vulnerable, physically unable to fend for myself, and he chose me. Sometimes I think, if I hadn't gone, then this never would've happened. But then I realized, it would have happened, just to somebody else. You were about to enter four years of access to drunk girls and parties, and if this is the foot you started off on, then it is right you did not continue. The night after it happened, he said he thought I liked it because I rubbed his back. A back rub.

Never mentioned me voicing consent, never mentioned us even speaking, a back rub. One more time, in public news, I learned that my ass and vagina were completely exposed outside, my breasts had been groped, fingers had been jabbed inside me along with pine needles and debris, my bare skin and head had been rubbing against the ground behind a dumpster, while an erect freshman was humping my half naked, unconscious body. But I don't remember, so how do I prove I didn't like it.

I thought there's no way this is going to trial; there were witnesses, there was dirt in my body, he ran but was caught. He's going to settle, formally apologize, and we will both move on. Instead, I was told he hired a powerful attorney, expert witnesses, private investigators who were going to try and find details about my personal life to use against me, find loopholes in my story to invalidate me and my sister, in order to show that this sexual assault was in fact a misunderstanding. That he was going to go to any length to convince the world he had simply been confused.

I was not only told that I was assaulted, I was told that because I couldn't remember, I technically could not prove it was unwanted. And that distorted me, damaged me, almost broke me. It is the saddest type of confusion to be told I was assaulted and nearly raped, blatantly out in the open, but we don't know if it counts as assault yet. I had to fight for an entire year to make it clear that there was something wrong with this situation.

When I was told to be prepared in case we didn't win, I said, I can't prepare for that. He was guilty the minute I woke up. No one can talk me out of the hurt he caused me. Worst of all, I was warned, because he now knows you don't remember, he is going to get to write the script. He can say whatever he wants and no one can contest it. I had no power, I had no voice, I was defenseless. My memory loss would be used against me. My testimony was weak, was incomplete, and I was made to believe that perhaps, I am not enough to win this. His attorney constantly reminded the jury, the only one we can believe is Brock, because she doesn't remember. That helplessness was traumatizing.

Instead of taking time to heal, I was taking time to recall the night in excruciating detail, in order to prepare for the attorney's questions that would be invasive, aggressive, and designed to steer me off course, to contradict myself, my sister, phrased in ways to manipulate my answers. Instead of his attorney saying, Did you notice any abrasions? He said, You didn't notice any abrasions, right? This was a game of strategy, as if I could be tricked out of my own worth. The sexual assault had been so clear, but instead, here I was at the trial, answering questions like:

How old are you? How much do you weigh? What did you eat that day? Well what did you have for dinner? Who made dinner? Did you drink with dinner? No, not even water? When did you drink? How much did you drink? What container did you drink out of? Who gave you the drink? How much do you usually drink? Who dropped you off at this party? At what time? But where exactly? What were you wearing? Why were you going to this party? What'd you do when you got there? Are you sure you did that? But what time did you do that? What does this text mean? Who were you texting? When did you urinate? Where did you urinate? With whom did you urinate outside? Was your phone on silent when your sister called? Do you remember silencing it? Really because on page 53 I'd like to point out that you said it was set to ring. Did you drink in college? You said you were a party animal? How many times did you black out? Did you party at frats? Are you serious with your boyfriend? Are you sexually active with him? When did you start dating? Would you ever cheat? Do you have a history of cheating? What do you mean when you said you wanted to reward him? Do you remember what time you woke up? Were you wearing your cardigan? What color was your cardigan? Do

*you remember any more from that night? No? Okay, well, we'll let
Brock fill it in.*

I was pummeled with narrowed, pointed questions that dissected
my personal life, love life, past life, family life, inane questions,
accumulating trivial details to try and find an excuse for this guy
who had me half naked before even bothering to ask for my
name. After a physical assault, I was assaulted with questions
designed to attack me, to say see, her facts don't line up, she's out
of her mind, she's practically an alcoholic, she probably wanted to
hook up, he's like an athlete right, they were both drunk, whatever, the hospital stuff she remembers is after the fact, why take
it into account, Brock has a lot at stake so he's having a really hard
time right now.

And then it came time for him to testify and I learned what it
meant to be revictimized. I want to remind you, the night after it
happened he said he never planned to take me back to his dorm.
He said he didn't know why we were behind a dumpster. He got
up to leave because he wasn't feeling well when he was suddenly
chased and attacked. Then he learned I could not remember.

So one year later, as predicted, a new dialogue emerged. Brock
had a strange new story, almost sounded like a poorly written
young adult novel with kissing and dancing and hand holding
and lovingly tumbling onto the ground, and most importantly in
this new story, there was suddenly consent. One year after the
incident, he remembered, oh yeah, by the way she actually said
yes, to everything, so.

He said he had asked if I wanted to dance. Apparently I said yes. He'd asked if I wanted to go to his dorm, I said yes. Then he asked if he could finger me and I said yes. Most guys don't ask, can I finger you? Usually there's a natural progression of things, unfolding consensually, not a Q and A. But apparently I granted full permission. He's in the clear. Even in his story, I only said a total of three words, yes yes yes, before he had me half naked on the ground. Future reference, if you are confused about whether a girl can consent, see if she can speak an entire sentence. You couldn't even do that. Just one coherent string of words. If she can't do that, then no. Not maybe, just no. Where was the confusion? This is common sense, human decency.

According to him, the only reason we were on the ground was because I fell down. Note: if a girl falls down help her get back up. If she is too drunk to even walk and falls down, do not mount her, hump her, take off her underwear, and insert your hand inside her vagina. If a girl falls down help her up. If she is wearing a cardigan over her dress don't take it off so that you can touch her breasts. Maybe she is cold, maybe that's why she wore the cardigan.

Next in the story, two Swedes on bicycles approached you and you ran. When they tackled you why didn't you say, "Stop! Everything's okay, go ask her, she's right over there, she'll tell you." I mean you had just asked for my consent, right? I was awake, right? When the policeman arrived and interviewed the evil Swede who tackled you, he was crying so hard he couldn't speak because of what he'd seen.

Your attorney has repeatedly pointed out, well we don't know exactly when she became unconscious. And you're right, maybe I was still fluttering my eyes and wasn't completely limp yet. That was never the point. I was too drunk to speak English, too drunk to consent way before I was on the ground. I should have never been touched in the first place. Brock stated, "At no time did I see that she was not responding. If at any time I thought she was not responding, I would have stopped immediately." Here's the thing; if your plan was to stop only when I became unresponsive, then you still do not understand. You didn't even stop when I was unconscious anyway! Someone else stopped you. Two guys on bikes noticed I wasn't moving in the dark and had to tackle you. How did you not notice while on top of me?

You said, you would have stopped and gotten help. You say that, but I want you to explain how you would've helped me, step by step, walk me through this. I want to know, if those evil Swedes had not found me, how the night would have played out. I am asking you: Would you have pulled my underwear back on over my boots? Untangled the necklace wrapped around my neck? Closed my legs, covered me? Picked the pine needles from my hair? Asked if the abrasions on my neck and bottom hurt? Would you then go find a friend and say, Will you help me get her somewhere warm and soft? I don't sleep when I think about the way it could have gone if the two guys had never come. What would have happened to me? That's what you'll never have a good answer for, that's what you can't explain even after a year.

On top of all this, he claimed that I orgasmed after one minute of digital penetration. The nurse said there had been abrasions, lacerations, and dirt in my genitalia. Was that before or after I came?

To sit under oath and inform all of us, that yes I wanted it, yes I permitted it, and that you are the true victim attacked by Swedes for reasons unknown to you is appalling, is demented, is selfish, is damaging. It is enough to be suffering. It is another thing to have someone ruthlessly working to diminish the gravity of va-lidity of this suffering.

My family had to see pictures of my head strapped to a gurney full of pine needles, of my body in the dirt with my eyes closed, hair messed up, limbs bent, and dress hiked up. And even after that, my family had to listen to your attorney say the pictures were after the fact, we can dismiss them. To say, yes her nurse confirmed there was redness and abrasions inside her, significant trauma to her genitalia, but that's what happens when you finger someone, and he's already admitted to that. To listen to your attorney attempt to paint a picture of me, the face of girls gone wild, as if somehow that would make it so that I had this coming for me. To listen to him say I sounded drunk on the phone because I'm silly and that's my goofy way of speaking. To point out that in the voicemail, I said I would reward my boyfriend and we all know what I was thinking. I assure you my rewards pro-gram is non transferable, especially to any nameless man that approaches me.

He has done irreversible damage to me and my family during the trial and we have sat silently, listening to him shape the evening. But in the end, his unsupported statements and his attorney's twisted logic fooled no one. The truth won, the truth spoke for itself.

You are guilty. Twelve jurors convicted you guilty of three felony counts beyond reasonable doubt, that's twelve votes per count, thirty-six yeses confirming guilt, that's one hundred percent, unanimous guilt. And I thought finally it is over, finally he will own up to what he did, truly apologize, we will both move on and get better. Then I read your statement.

If you are hoping that one of my organs will implode from anger and I will die, I'm almost there. You are very close. This is not a story of another drunk college hookup with poor decision making. Assault is not an accident. Somehow, you still don't get it. Somehow, you still sound confused. I will now read portions of the defendant's statement and respond to them.

You said, Being drunk I just couldn't make the best decisions and neither could she.

Alcohol is not an excuse. Is it a factor? Yes. But alcohol was not the one who stripped me, fingered me, had my head dragging against the ground, with me almost fully naked. Having too much to drink was an amateur mistake that I admit to, but it is not criminal. Everyone in this room has had a night where they have regretted drinking too much, or knows someone close to them who has had a night where they have regretted drinking too much. Regretting drinking is not the same as regretting sexual assault. We were both drunk, the difference is I did not take off your pants and underwear, touch you inappropriately, and run away. That's the difference.

You said, If I wanted to get to know her, I should have asked for her number, rather than asking her to go back to my room.

I'm not mad because you didn't ask for my number. Even if you did know me, I would not want to be in this situation. My own boyfriend knows me, but if he asked to finger me behind a dumpster, I would slap him. No girl wants to be in this situation. Nobody. I don't care if you know their phone number or not.

You said, I stupidly thought it was okay for me to do what everyone around me was doing, which was drinking. I was wrong.

Again, you were not wrong for drinking. Everyone around you was not sexually assaulting me. You were wrong for doing what nobody else was doing, which was pushing your erect dick in your pants against my naked, defenseless body concealed in a dark area, where partygoers could no longer see or protect me, and my own sister could not find me. Sipping fireball is not your crime. Peeling off and discarding my underwear like a candy wrapper to insert your finger into my body, is where you went wrong. Why am I still explaining this.

You said, During the trial I didn't want to victimize her at all. That was just my attorney and his way of approaching the case.

Your attorney is not your scapegoat, he represents you. Did your attorney say some incredulously infuriating, degrading things? Absolutely. He said you had an erection, because it was cold.

You said, you are in the process of establishing a program for high school and college students in which you speak about your experience to "speak out against the college campus drinking culture and the sexual promiscuity that goes along with that."

Campus drinking culture. That's what we're speaking out against? You think that's what I've spent the past year fighting for? Not awareness about campus sexual assault, or rape, or learning to recognize consent. Campus drinking culture. Down with Jack Daniels. Down with Skyy Vodka. If you want to talk to people about drinking go to an AA meeting. You realize, having a drinking problem is different than drinking and then forcefully trying to have sex with someone? Show men how to respect women, not how to drink less.

Drinking culture and the sexual promiscuity that goes along with that. Goes along with that, like a side effect, like fries on the side of your order. Where does promiscuity even come into play? I don't see headlines that read, *Brock Turner, Guilty of drinking too much and the sexual promiscuity that goes along with that*. Campus Sexual Assault. There's your first powerpoint slide. Rest assured, if you fail to fix the topic of your talk, I will follow you to every school you go to and give a follow up presentation.

Lastly you said, I want to show people that one night of drinking can ruin a life.

A life, one life, yours, you forgot about mine. Let me rephrase for you, I want to show people that one night of drinking can ruin two lives. You and me. You are the cause, I am the effect. You have dragged me through this hell with you, dipped me back into that night again and again. You knocked down both our towers, I collapsed at the same time you did. If you think I was spared, came out unscathed, that today I ride off into sunset, while you suffer the greatest blow, you are mistaken. Nobody wins. We have all been devastated, we have all been trying to find some meaning in all of this suffering. Your damage was concrete; stripped of titles, degrees, enrollment. My damage was internal, unseen, I carry it with me. You took away my worth, my privacy, my energy, my time, my safety, my intimacy, my confidence, my own voice, until today.

See one thing we have in common is that we were both unable to get up in the morning. I am no stranger to suffering. You made me a victim. In newspapers my name was "unconscious intoxicated woman," ten syllables, and nothing more than that. For a while, I believed that that was all I was. I had to force myself to relearn my real name, my identity. To relearn that this is not all that I am. That I am not just a drunk victim at a frat party found behind a dumpster, while you are the All-American swimmer at a top university, innocent until proven guilty, with so much at stake. I am a human being who has been irreversibly hurt, my life was put on hold for over a year, waiting to figure out if I was worth something.

My independence, natural joy, gentleness, and steady lifestyle I had been enjoying became distorted beyond recognition. I became closed off, angry, self deprecating, tired, irritable, empty. The isolation at times was unbearable. You cannot give me back the life I had before that night either. While you worry about your shattered reputation, I refrigerated spoons every night so when I woke up, and my eyes were puffy from crying, I would hold the spoons to my eyes to lessen the swelling so that I could see. I showed up an hour late to work every morning, excused myself to cry in the stairwells, I can tell you all the best places in that building to cry where no one can hear you. The pain became so bad that I had to explain the private details to my boss to let her know why I was leaving. I needed time because continuing day to day was not possible. I used my savings to go as far away as I could possibly be. I did not return to work full time as I knew I'd have to take weeks off in the future for the hearing and trial, that were constantly being rescheduled. My life was put on hold for over a year, my structure had collapsed.

I can't sleep alone at night without having a light on, like a five year old, because I have nightmares of being touched where I cannot wake up, I did this thing where I waited until the sun came up and I felt safe enough to sleep. For three months, I went to bed at six o'clock in the morning.

I used to pride myself on my independence, now I am afraid to go on walks in the evening, to attend social events with drinking among friends where I should be comfortable being. I have become a little barnacle always needing to be at someone's side, to have my boyfriend standing next to me, sleeping beside me, protecting me. It is embarrassing how feeble I feel, how timidly I move through life, always guarded, ready to defend myself, ready to be angry.

You have no idea how hard I have worked to rebuild parts of me that are still weak. It took me eight months to even talk about what happened. I could no longer connect with friends, with everyone around me. I would scream at my boyfriend, my own family whenever they brought this up. You never let me forget what happened to me. At the end of the hearing, the trial, I was too tired to speak. I would leave drained, silent. I would go home turn off my phone and for days I would not speak. You bought me a ticket to a planet where I lived by myself. Every time a new article come out, I lived with the paranoia that my entire hometown would find out and know me as the girl who got assaulted. I didn't want anyone's pity and am still learning to accept victim as part of my identity. You made my own hometown an uncomfortable place to be.

You cannot give me back my sleepless nights. The way I have broken down sobbing uncontrollably if I'm watching a movie and a woman is harmed, to say it lightly, this experience has expanded my empathy for other victims. I have lost weight from stress, when people would comment I told them I've been running a lot lately. There are times I did not want to be touched. I have to relearn that I am not fragile, I am capable, I am wholesome, not just livid and weak.

When I see my younger sister hurting, when she is unable to keep up in school, when she is deprived of joy, when she is not sleeping, when she is crying so hard on the phone she is barely breathing, telling me over and over again she is sorry for leaving me alone that night, sorry sorry sorry, when she feels more guilt than you, then I do not forgive you. That night I had called her to try and find her, but you found me first. Your attorney's closing statement began, "[Her sister] said she was fine and who knows her better than her sister." You tried to use my own sister against me? Your points of attack were so weak, so low, it was almost embarrassing. You do not touch her.

You should have never done this to me. Secondly, you should have never made me fight so long to tell you, you should have never done this to me. But here we are. The damage is done, no one can undo it. And now we both have a choice. We can let this destroy us, I can remain angry and hurt and you can be in denial, or we can face it head on, I accept the pain, you accept the punishment, and we move on.

Your life is not over, you have decades of years ahead to rewrite your story. The world is huge, it is so much bigger than Palo Alto and Stanford, and you will make a space for yourself in it where you can be useful and happy. But right now, you do not get to shrug your shoulders and be confused anymore. You do not get to pretend that there were no red flags. You have been convicted of violating me, intentionally, forcibly, sexually, with malicious intent, and all you can admit to is consuming alcohol. Do not talk about the sad way your life was upturned because alcohol made you do bad things. Figure out how to take responsibility for your own conduct.

Now to address the sentencing. When I read the probation officer's report, I was in disbelief, consumed by anger which eventually quieted down to profound sadness. My statements have been slimmed down to distortion and taken out of context. I fought hard during this trial and will not have the outcome minimized by a probation officer who attempted to evaluate my current state and my wishes in a fifteen minute conversation, the majority of which was spent answering questions I had about the legal system. The context is also important. Brock had yet to issue a statement, and I had not read his remarks.

My life has been on hold for over a year, a year of anger, anguish and uncertainty, until a jury of my peers rendered a judgment that validated the injustices I had endured. Had Brock admitted guilt and remorse and offered to settle early on, I would have considered a lighter sentence, respecting his honesty, grateful to be able to move our lives forward. Instead he took the risk of going to trial, added insult to injury and forced me to relive the hurt as details about my personal life and sexual assault were brutally dissected before the public. He pushed me and my family through a year of inexplicable, unnecessary suffering, and should face the consequences of challenging his crime, of putting my pain into question, of making us wait so long for justice.

I told the probation officer I do not want Brock to rot away in prison. I did not say he does not deserve to be behind bars. The probation officer's recommendation of a year or less in county jail is a soft timeout, a mockery of the seriousness of his assaults, an insult to me and all women. It gives the message that a stranger can be inside you without proper consent and he will receive less than what has been defined as the minimum sentence. Probation should be denied. I also told the probation officer that what I truly wanted was for Brock to get it, to understand and admit to his wrongdoing.

Unfortunately, after reading the defendant's report, I am severely disappointed and feel that he has failed to exhibit sincere remorse or responsibility for his conduct. I fully respected his right to a trial, but even after twelve jurors unanimously convicted him guilty of three felonies, all he has admitted to doing is ingesting alcohol. Someone who cannot take full accountability for his actions does not deserve a mitigating sentence. It is deeply offensive that he would try and dilute rape with a suggestion of "promiscuity." By definition rape is not the absence of promiscuity, rape is the absence of consent, and it perturbs me deeply that he can't even see that distinction.

The probation officer factored in that the defendant is youthful and has no prior convictions. In my opinion, he is old enough to know what he did was wrong. When you are eighteen in this country you can go to war. When you are nineteen, you are old enough to pay the consequences for attempting to rape someone. He is young, but he is old enough to know better.

As this is a first offence I can see where leniency would beckon. On the other hand, as a society, we cannot forgive everyone's first sexual assault or digital rape. It doesn't make sense. The seriousness of rape has to be communicated clearly, we should not create a culture that suggests we learn that rape is wrong through trial and error. The consequences of sexual assault needs to be severe enough that people feel enough fear to exercise good judgment even if they are drunk, severe enough to be preventative.

The probation officer weighed the fact that he has surrendered a hard earned swimming scholarship. How fast Brock swims does not lessen the severity of what happened to me, and should not lessen the severity of his punishment. If a first time offender from an underprivileged background was accused of three felonies and displayed no accountability for his actions other than drinking, what would his sentence be? The fact that Brock was an athlete at a private university should not be seen as an entitlement to leniency, but as an opportunity to send a message that sexual assault is against the law regardless of social class.

The Probation Officer has stated that this case, when compared to other crimes of similar nature, may be considered less serious due to the defendant's level of intoxication. It felt serious. That's all I'm going to say.

What has he done to demonstrate that he deserves a break? He has only apologized for drinking and has yet to define what he did to me as sexual assault, he has revictimized me continually, relentlessly. He has been found guilty of three serious felonies and it is time for him to accept the consequences of his actions. He will not be quietly excused.

He is a lifetime sex registrant. That doesn't expire. Just like what he did to me doesn't expire, doesn't just go away after a set number of years. It stays with me, it's part of my identity, it has forever changed the way I carry myself, the way I live the rest of my life.

To conclude, I want to say thank you. To everyone from the intern who made me oatmeal when I woke up at the hospital that morning, to the deputy who waited beside me, to the nurses who calmed me, to the detective who listened to me and never judged me, to my advocates who stood unwaveringly beside me, to my therapist who taught me to find courage in vulnerability, to my boss for being kind and understanding, to my incredible parents who teach me how to turn pain into strength, to my grandma who snuck chocolate into the courtroom throughout this to give to me, my friends who remind me how to be happy, to my boyfriend who is patient and loving, to my unconquerable sister who is the other half of my heart, to Alaleh, my idol, who fought tirelessly and never doubted me. Thank you to everyone involved in the trial for their time and attention. Thank you to girls across the nation that wrote cards to my DA to give to me, so many strangers who cared for me.

Most importantly, thank you to the two men who saved me, who I have yet to meet. I sleep with two bicycles that I drew taped above my bed to remind myself there are heroes in this story. That we are looking out for one another. To have known all of these people, to have felt their protection and love, is something I will never forget.

And finally, to girls everywhere, I am with you. On nights when you feel alone, I am with you. When people doubt you or dismiss you, I am with you. I fought everyday for you. So never stop fighting, I believe you. As the author Anne Lamott once wrote, "Lighthouses don't go running all over an island looking for boats to save; they just stand there shining." Although I can't save every boat, I hope that by speaking today, you absorbed a small amount of light, a small knowing that you can't be silenced, a small satisfaction that justice was served, a small assurance that we are getting somewhere, and a big, big knowing that you are important, unquestionably, you are untouchable, you are beautiful, you are to be valued, respected, undeniably, every minute of every day, you are powerful and nobody can take that away from you. To girls everywhere, I am with you. Thank you.